THE
FIRST SIKH

'In *The First Sikh*, Nikky-Guninder Kaur Singh weaves together the various sources of the story of Guru Nanak with true interdisciplinary finesse—reading the earliest sources with aesthetic, philosophical, historical and textual sensitivity and skill. But important as this work is to the history of Indian spiritual traditions, do not mistake *The First Sikh* for a mere historical reassessment. Its readers will also learn that the teachings of Guru Nanak speak to our social, political, religious and environmental moments as if they were meant to be heard today. In Nikky Singh's hands, Guru Nanak's words still hang in the air, as if they have been only recently sung'

LAURIE PATTON, professor of Indian religions,
and president, Middlebury College

'Today we find Khalsa Aid and Sikhs at the forefront, offering help in every humanitarian crisis. This is not surprising because the First Sikh valued human beings above all religious categories and talked of the "indivisibility of people, the oneness of the Divine embodied in the oneness of humanity". Today, once again, society is in conflict and we sorely need his vision of common humanity, transcending all barriers of religion, caste, creed, race and country. Guru Nanak's pluralism, humanity and teachings find great resonance in the 21st century in Nikky Singh's lucid work. *The First Sikh* is an important book for our troubled times'

RANA SAFVI, historian and writer

'Nikky-Guninder Kaur Singh presents rare insights into Guru Nanak's personality and teachings. Her deep study of the Guru Granth Sahib, its complex musical and poetic structures as well as its pluralistic spiritual inspiration, is truly admirable. Singh's tribute to Guru Nanak's astounding genius on his 550th birth anniversary underlines the global relevance of his message today with its focus on humanism, human rights, the environment and gender equality'

NAVTEJ SARNA, author, *The Book of Nanak*

'*The First Sikh* is a splendid celebration of the 550th birth anniversary of Guru Nanak. It will go a long way in deepening the world's understanding of this unique spiritual master and enlightened being. Nikky-Guninder Kaur Singh has applied her tremendous intellect and academic depth with skill and sympathy to reveal essential aspects of the Master's personality, poetic genius and profound spiritual depth. She is a true successor to her illustrious father and Sikh historian Prof. Harbans Singh'

TARLOCHAN SINGH, former chairman of
the National Commission for Minorities, India

THE
FIRST SIKH

THE LIFE AND LEGACY OF
GURU NANAK

NIKKY-GUNINDER KAUR SINGH

PENGUIN
VIKING

An imprint of Penguin Random House

VIKING

USA | Canada | UK | Ireland | Australia
New Zealand | India | South Africa | China | Singapore

Viking is part of the Penguin Random House group of companies
whose addresses can be found at global.penguinrandomhouse.com

Published by Penguin Random House India Pvt. Ltd
4th Floor, Capital Tower 1, MG Road,
Gurugram 122 002, Haryana, India

Penguin
Random House
India

First published in Viking by Penguin Random House India 2019

Copyright © Nikky-Guninder Kaur Singh 2019

ISBN 9780670088621

Typeset in Adobe Caslon Pro by Manipal Digital Systems, Manipal
Printed at Replika Press Pvt. Ltd, India

My rakhi for my bira

Contents

Acknowledgements

Iss bakshash ke iss azmat ke hain baba nanak shah guru
Sabh sees nava ardas karo, aur hardam bolo wah guru!

[So blessed, so glorious, shah guru Baba Nanak
All bow your heads, make humble requests and
Say forever, wondrous Guru!]

'Guru Nanak Shah',
Nazeer Akbarabadi (1740–1830)

I am profoundly grateful to my editor at Penguin Random House, Ambar Sahil Chatterjee, for inviting me to write *The First Sikh*. With Ambar's inspiration 'to appreciate Guru Nanak's legacy from a modern perspective' this project has proved to be a most meaningful and joyous experience. My primary source is the Guru's own oeuvre. Relying on his sublime lyrics I tried to perceive the First Sikh's personality, and his spiritual, philosophical, social and environmental ideals as they intersect with our present reality. So we can discover his enormous relevance for our dangerously divided and polarized world.

My thanks to the many organizers for hosting my lectures on Guru Nanak over the last few months: Dr Chloe Martinez, Mr Chan

Choudhury, Dr Agyapal Oberoi, Dr Rajender Kaur, Mr Harjot Sidhu, Dr Arvind Mandair, Dr Pashaura Singh, Dr Swaranjit Singh, Dr Nicole Ranganathan, Dr Mohinder Singh, Dr Anne Murphy, Ms Margaret Edwards, Mr Lally Marwah, Dr Francesca Cassio, Dr Julie Vig. Their warm hospitality and engaging discussions energized the writing process. My thanks to my excellent research assistant, Mansi Hitesh, who will be missed terribly as she embarks on her graduate studies at Cambridge University. My thanks to my dear Colby alum Fazal Rashid for his thoughtful initiative. And my thanks to President David and Carolyn Greene, Provost Margaret McFadden, Jim and Mary Crawford, and to my students and everybody in the Colby family for their heart-warming support.

I also wish to express my regrets. There is no way to offer a comprehensive study of the First Sikh. How does one convey his biography, his philosophy, his mystical orientation, his revolutionary spirit, his environmental sensibility, his phenomenal legacy in a volume? We can only acquire a tiny sense of his vast vision, his multilayered verse, and his wide-ranging impact. I apologize to the many, many innovative and dedicated *kirtaniya*s, artists, poets, activists, philanthropists, educators, film-makers, scholars and creative writers whom I have not been able to acknowledge in this study. I'm afraid I recount only a handful that I have personally come across.

The Sikh daily routine, writing, imagination, morals, ceremonies and even the five Ks worn on the body are the legacy of the First Sikh. Yet none of them construe exclusionary boundaries for the religion; they are multivalent symbols of our shared human experience, sparkles of the universal infinite One. This is the genius of the First Sikh: by experiencing the wondrous universal *Ikk Oan Kar*, he gave birth to the distinct and dynamically evolving Sikh religion. As we celebrate his 550th birth anniversary, we open our arms wide to embrace our collective humanity. And together, Urdu poet Nazeer Akbarabadi reminds us in the prelude above, 'Constantly say, wondrous Guru'—just as the First Sikh envisioned. At some level, the person and his revelation become one.

Nikky-Guninder Kaur Singh
Colby College
16 April 2019

THE

FIRST SIKH

Introduction

Getting in Touch: Sources and Aspirations

Baby Nanak was born in Talwandi in undivided Punjab 550 years ago, and he subsequently birthed the Sikh religion. Today, over 25 million Sikhs living in different parts of the globe trace their faith to this First Sikh. Though there may not be much factual documentation on him, his biography is deeply imprinted on the Sikh consciousness. We know his mother, Tripta, was a pious woman, and his father, Kalyan Chand, worked as an accountant for the local Muslim landlord. The parents named their newborn after their older daughter, Nanaki. When he grew up he went to live with his sister, Nanaki, and her husband, Jairam, in Sultanpur Lodi, to work for a Muslim employer. He was married to Sulakhni, and they had two sons, Sri Chand (b. 1494) and Lakhmi Das (b. 1497). In his twenties, he had a revelatory experience of the singular divine Being—*Ikk Oan Kar*. Thereafter, he travelled with his Muslim companion Mardana to places far beyond the Punjab. They met holy men from diverse religious backgrounds. While Mardana strummed on his *rabab*, a divinely inspired Nanak would burst into song. Eventually, he settled in Kartarpur, a village he founded on the banks of the river Ravi. A community of men and women calling themselves 'sikhs' (disciples or seekers) grew around him here and created the blueprint for Sikh doctrine and practice. In his own lifetime, he appointed a successor, who was followed by eight more, culminating with the Tenth Guru, Gobind Singh (1666–1708).

For the millions of Sikhs, the First Sikh is the source of their religious worldview, their ethical resource, their aesthetic paradigm. Their daily routine, rites of passage, ceremonies and commemorations all revolve around him. What they say and do and wear and think about is derived from him (as we discuss in the concluding chapter). His birthday is a celebration of their identity. From a wider global perspective, we find in Guru Nanak a modern thinker far ahead of his time who systematized a liberal lifestyle, combining the sacred and the secular aspects. In fact, as we shall see, he is so radical that even today we are not quite prepared to access many of his progressive ideals! In a period of political turmoil and ontological insecurity, he powerfully rejoiced in the wondrous One. There is something absolutely extraordinary about him! What is that? This volume is an attempt to understand precisely *that* extraordinary being of the First Sikh. And what could be more important evidence of his personality, his vision, his emotions, his concerns, his self-awareness, his undertakings than his own voice?

The primary source for this volume is indeed the Guru's vast oeuvre, his 974 hymns meticulously recorded by his fourth successor, Guru Arjan, in 1604. These appear across the 1430 pages of the Sikh scripture, the Guru Granth Sahib (GGS). We hear the First Sikh's voice in each of the three basic sections of the GGS: the liturgical (pp. 1–13), in nineteen of the thirty-one raga chapters (pp. 14–1353), and in the concluding miscellaneous segment (not assigned to any specific musical mode, pp. 1353–1430). His language is essentially Punjabi, which draws upon a variety of local languages and dialects. Besides Siraiki, the language of south-western Punjab, and Khari Boli, the language of the Delhi region, which is the basis of modern Hindi and Urdu, Guru Nanak abundantly utilizes Persian, Sanskrit and Arabic.

Importantly, the First Sikh identifies himself as a 'songster' (*dhadhi*): 'a dhadhi of low caste—*hau dhadhi ka nic jati* (Asa di Var, 9). He identifies himself as a 'poet' or 'seer' (*shair*): 'my breath, my flesh, my very life is Yours, You are my absolute love, and this is what poet (*sairu*) Nanak says, You are our true provider—*sasu masu sabh jio tumhara tu mai khara piara, nanaku sairu ev kahatu hai sache parvadgara*' (GGS: 660). These self-references introduce us to a most humble personality; the living, breathing corporeal figure is before our eyes, with each pore saturated in the Divine. He is the picture-perfect image of his supreme moral value, 'sweet humility, Nanak, is the core of virtues and good deeds' (GGS: 470).

The dhadhis would be a part of the medieval wandering minstrel tradition, and in the Punjab they were loosely associated with the major religions of the region, Hinduism and Islam, and later with Sikhism. Patronized by chiefs and princes, they eulogized religious figures, folk heroes and valorous deeds of the members of the families they served. The term shair/sair comes from the Arabic word for poetry, *al-shi'r*, and according to Islamic scholar S.H. Nasr, its root meaning is consciousness and knowledge.[1] *Kavi* is a seer/poet in Sanskrit whose knowledge, explains comparative philologist Georges Dumézil, 'goes beyond ordinary technical operations, or at least directs them from a higher level'.[2] With his Indo-Islamic literary heritage, the First Sikh's understanding of poetry is a spontaneous awareness, a revelation, rather than a 'making' or 'crafting' that underlies the Greek poesis. His self-understanding transcends divisions of religion, caste, ethnicity or language; he locates himself within a broad South Asian context.

His sublime lyrics conjoin verbal language and musical sound. Poetry is universal to begin with and set in melodies that enhance access to audiences who may not know the language. Cosmic melodies, sounds of nature, musical instruments and biological rhythms of the body reverberate across Guru Nanak's hymns recorded in the GGS. He is so consumed by his awareness and love for the universal Divine that he has no control over his words: '*Jaisi mai ave khasam ki bani taisara kari gianu ve lalo*—as comes to me the Husband's word, that is what I say O Lalo!' (GGS: 722). Paradoxically, the First Sikh's spontaneous speech ends up being most artistic.

The words from that transcendent One come in a gusty speed and are shaped into lovely artistic designs, innovative similes, mesmerizing paradoxes and brilliant metaphors. They create seamless alliteration and rhyme, lyrical assonance and consonance. Their momentum produces geometric patterns, verbal arabesques, stair-like parallelisms and dynamic somersaults that I find more and more captivating since my initial study at Wellesley College, *Physics and Metaphysics of the Guru Granth Sahib*.[3] Guru Nanak's images, symbols, analogies and metaphors draw upon this cosmic universe of ours with its solar system, galaxies and outer space, and upon our planet Earth with its rich flora and fauna and its agrarian rhythms. They draw upon domestic, economic and political spheres. Simple similes from the Punjabi landscape endow familiar sights and sounds with enchantment. His paradoxes break the conventional linear mode of thinking, and his metaphors expand the human experience. Punjab, being a frontier region, resonated with expressions not only from South Asia, but also from the Turkish, Persian and Central Asian cultural traditions. The First Sikh's multicultural diction and phrasing create a rich literary mosaic. His embodied voice in the most direct and immediate way harmonizes with the nineteen musical measures (ragas) it is set within, and thus its sonic energy becomes even more intense.

For me, neither the First Sikh's personality nor his message can be understood without a literary appreciation of his works. His ideology is entirely woven into his poetic syntax. There are no narratives or deontological prescriptions that we can clutch on to. Each reader/listener must decipher the lyrics for themselves. The poet/songster wanted to reach each person individually and relate with them intimately. Guru Nanak's artistic poetry endows his philosophy with emotive power and his Sikhs their existential communitas. The Guru sought to awaken his community, and revitalize their senses, psyche, imagination and spirit. To cite the distinguished Sikh scholar Professor Harbans Singh, 'Guru Nanak's genius was best expressed in the poetical attitude. No other way would have been adequate to the range and depth of his mood.'[4]

Regrettably, the Academy has not given much attention to the Guru's sublime repertoire. As noted by Professor Christopher Shackle, the foremost expert on the study of Guru Nanak's language and literature, 'Guru Nanak generates a wonderful variety of poetry of the most astonishing literary quality which shows him to be a master equally of moving expression in his lyrical hymns and of the clearly articulated exposition of complex spiritual realities in his remarkable longer compositions.'[5] Professor Shackle's compelling tribute underscores the need for an aesthetic appreciation of Guru Nanak's literary output. Scholars in India have also lamented the neglect of poetic aspects of the Guru's verse. Half a century ago Professor Attar Singh commented on the wild enthusiasm with which Guru Nanak's fifth centennial was celebrated, but the focus, he observes, was on the Guru's message and teachings:

> Aesthetic evaluation of the poetic art of Guru Nanak as also his place in the literary history of the Punjab or India were relegated to a minor position in academic discussion. . . . the academic dilettantism in the language avoided engagement with the theoretical as well as practical aspects of literary evaluation of the works of Guru Nanak. For the most part, the scholars were engaged in projecting the message without any attempt to correlate it with the medium.[6]

Our primary material for this volume will be the First Sikh's prolific output, which is lyrical and beautiful, and structurally consistently coherent. But stylistically it varies richly, and thematically extends widely, altogether offering us important insights into the inner being of the author, his worldview, the initiatives he took, and his legacy that lives on.

Guru Nanak's wide-ranging works emerge in different metres, rhymes, stanzas and compositional styles. The building blocks of his compositions are essentially short half-verses of three or four words. These brief units take on the form of four-stanza compositions (*caupada*), eight stanzas (*ashtpadi*), four stanzas of six verses (*chhant*), and even sixteen-stanza compositions (*solaha*). Many of these go on to form longer compositions. Guru Nanak's melodious ensemble is full of vibrant spiritual, emotional, social and political resonances. Each simple, brief passage is so richly packed that it can be utilized to navigate any aspect of life at any stage. His timeless verse infiltrates precise historical moments and emotions to generate new values, new attitudes, new orientations and new social and cosmic relationships. The First Sikh has given us an inexhaustible literary reservoir that generations across cultures can keep drawing upon.

I want to begin with a brief introduction to a few of his works. We will be returning to them in subsequent chapters of this volume.

These give us the first impressions of the First Sikh. In each bit of these compositions we get to hear his tone, see the world through his eyes, get a feel for his language, a sense of his personality. Our dhadhi/shair's words bring us face to face with him. I have cited some original verses so we can savour their beauty and rhythm. The translations are all mine. Of course no translation can ever replace the original. Robert Frost said it right, 'Poetry is what is lost in translation.'

The Japji is regarded as his 'single greatest composition;'[7] 'the quintessence of Guru Nanak's achieved vision and art'.[8] This opening hymn of the GGS designed for personal contemplation is not set in the musical framework. Its thirty-eight stanzas (*pauri* in the original means the 'step' of a ladder) in different metres form the sequence of the composition. Encircled in alliteration, assonance and consonance, the thirty-eight stanzas in breathtaking images systematically develop the First Sikh's ontology, epistemology, ethics, aesthetics and soteriology. Chapter 3 in this volume focuses on this quintessential composition.

Guru Nanak's Pahare ('hours', *pahar* is about a three-hour period) draws upon the traditional poetic form based on the Indian time frame in which the night and the day were each divided into four quarters or watches (pahar). With his focus on the passage of time, the Guru in this lyrical composition laments the failure of precious human life (GGS: 74–75). The atrophied 'roving friend' is the restless mind allured by worldly delights. 'Roving friend' or *banjara* (in the original) evokes long-distance traders. Descendants of Roma Gypsies, they migrated from Europe to the Middle East and South West Asia, supplying goods across India. Engaged in the fluctuations of time, the itinerant does not settle on the everlasting Divine.

The first quarter returns to the lodging in the uterus while the fourth forecasts the moment of death. The Guru vividly depicts the first, the entry into this world, but he proclaims the utter mystery of departure and what happens afterwards. He mentions no heaven, no hell. In the first quarter, though, he distinctly photographs the foetus turned upside down rapt in meditation, leaving his readers/listeners with a very positive perspective on this first period of gestation in the mother's body. In the second, he captures the love and affection showered on the child, evoking the iconic baby Krishna bounced from arm to arm (*hatho hath nachaiai*, literally, danced from one hand to another). The third quarter is lived in oblivion of the divine One. Building upon syntactical units such as *dhan sio rata* (consumed by wealth), *joban mata* (drunk on youth), the First Sikh imparts a tragic rhythm and haunting quality to his memorable composition.

His Thitin (GGS: 838–40) is composed in the poetic form based on the monthly cycle of lunar days, *thitin* (dates), which are different from solar days (*var*). Guru Arjan and Bhagat Kabir also composed hymns in this genre (GGS: 296–300 and GGS: 343–44, respectively). Guru Nanak's hymn vividly conveys his fascination with time, and its relationship with the motions of the celestial bodies of the sun and the moon. It starts with *ekam*, the first day of the waning half of the lunar month, and proceeds to *amavas*, the last day of the dark half of the month. While praising the transcendent One, the First Sikh rejects conventional Indian notions of certain days being more propitious than others because of their astrological or astronomical positioning. Since the universal Divine is the creator of all gods, goddesses and scriptures, to serve them separately is meaningless. Denounced here are fasting, ritual bathing, pilgrimages, ascetic practices and their coordination with specific days, contingent on the movement of the planets. He mentions the *ekadasi* ('ten+one') fast on the eleventh day of the month, which is observed by many Hindus and Jains by not eating beans and grains:

Ekadasi ikk ridai vasavai
hinsa mamta moh chukavai
fal pavai barat atam chinai
pakhand rach tat nahi binai

Eleventh bring the One in your heart
Violence, craving, and lust take off
Attain the fruit of ritual fast
—See your very self
The Real is not seen by pretentious acts

GGS: 840

The rhyming antonyms and synonyms create an emphatic rhetoric. He urges his readers to lodge in (vasavai) the divine One in the heart, get rid of (chukavai) violence, craving and lust, and recognize the true self. This Real self (tat), the essential self within, is not visible through any pretentious acts. All days are thus equally sacred, and the fruit of the fasting is immediately available. Guru Nanak's Thitin in twenty stanzas is a paean to the divine glory felt intensely each day of the month.

His Barah Mah or Barahmasa (GGS: 1107–10) stands out in Sikh literature for its poetic splendour and philosophical import. The genre of the Barah Mah (twelve months) was popular in the romantic and devotional literature of medieval India going as far back as the late eleventh-century Persian composition 'Mahha-i Farsi' (Iranian months) by Masud Sad Salman. Leading scholar of South Asian literature Francesca Orsini considers the Barah Mah as 'one of the chief carriers of a shared poetic language of emotions-and-the seasons in North India . . .'[9] Besides the twelve-month cycle, songs in cycles of four, six and eight months were also sung in diverse languages and tunes. Guru Nanak's Barah Mah synthesizes the universal and personal dimensions of lived time in the psychological and spiritual passage of a young woman longing for her Beloved over the twelve months of the year. Nature at times mirrors her feelings, at others its lush landscapes and soundscapes augment her pangs of separation. Through her ardent search for the Beloved, cameos of the changing reality are captured in vivid, poignant images and fitted harmoniously into an integrated system with enormous existential import.[10]

The Indian calendar begins with the month of Chet or Chaitra (mid-March to mid April), so the Guru begins with the spectacular sights and sounds of spring. Hearing the bumblebee buzzing beside the blossom boughs and the koel bird singing happily in the mango grove, the separated lover aches in pain. After the blazing heat of Asarh comes the month of Savan, bringing welcome rain showers. The earth is cooled and quenched, but not the young woman, for 'her Beloved is still in distant lands'. She lies alone on the empty bed. Along with the pain of solitude is the fear: the lightning amid the monsoon clouds terrifies her. Having lost her sleep and appetite, the lover in the month of Savan lives a deathlike life. Her yearning integrates the polarities of life and death, the lightning in the skies above and the bed on which she tosses and turns on land.

Bhadon (August/September) is the month of abundance, and the poet Nanak brings out the roaring revelry of the season: 'Frogs croak and peacocks screech, babiha-bird cries "beloved, beloved", and snakes go biting about; mosquitoes are stinging, lakes are flooding, but without Hari, where's the joy?' In the month of Kattak (October/November) when the days begin to shorten and lamps are lit, an illuminating simile conveys her psychological state: 'As oil to the lamp so the Beloved to the bride.' In the month of Maghar (November/December) she realizes the healing power of art: 'She listens to the praise of her Beloved through song, music, and poetry, and her sorrow departs.' The month of Vaisakh (April/May) is the month of harvest when farmers negotiate business deals, and so commerce enters the young woman's vocabulary: 'Without You I am not worth a penny, but if You are with me, I become priceless.' Over the course of the twelve months, she pulls the timeless Beloved into her personal, historical and cosmic context.

In his Barah Mah, Guru Nanak's images and ideas, the external world and the inner being, philosophy and poetry perform a live intersection of time and timelessness. The twelve months, the six seasons, the lunar and the solar days, the hours, the minutes, the seconds are all *bhale* (blessed), for it is sometime now, somewhere here that the ontological Beloved pervading all time and space is instantaneously discovered. Nature pulsates with life. Its sweeping imagery, ever so variegated, enhances the existential power of the First Sikh's composition.

His acrostic Pati Likhi in thirty-five stanzas initiates the Gurmukhi script, and as each stanza introduces a letter of the alphabet, it discloses the oneness of the Creator in exquisite artistic constructions. This is how the First Sikh introduces the letter 'urai': '*upma ta ki kijai ja ka ant na paia*—how can we find a simile for One whose limits cannot be found?' (GGS: 432). Simile (*upama*) in Sanskrit literature is considered to be the most important semantic poetic figure; likewise in the West, Wittgenstein famously described it as 'the best thing in philosophy'. Ironically, the First Sikh expresses the failure of this 'best thing'. There is nothing against which the object can be compared, and so he brings home the sheer impossibility of any description.

But soon the infinite Absolute is imaged playing Chaupar, a board game! This game is displayed in a delightful painting from Basohli, Jammu (1694–95) at the Metropolitan Museum of Art in New York. Here we see Hindu god Shiva and his wife Parvati playing the game together. However, the Chaupar game unfolding in Guru Nanak's Pati Likhi has no partner; the sole transcendent Creator it is. The cross-shaped design of the Chaupar board with four arms metamorphoses into the four ages:

B began to play the Chaupar game
On the game-board made out of the four ages
With all created beings as pieces
The One rolled the dice across

This playful scene memorably shows the majesty and power of the Creator. It was Wittgenstein too who said, 'Philosophy ought really to be written only as a poetic composition.'[11] Rightly so, Guru Nanak's doctrine of the divine Will (*hukam*) rolls out in three dimensions across his poetic composition.

But we pieces are completely oblivious of our Creator's sport. The Guru hauntingly reminds people, '*Mammai moh maran madhusudan maran bhaia tab chetvia kaia bhitar avro paria mamma akhar visraia*—Mohu (attachment), Mortality, Madhusudan, we remember this when we die; with so much else packed in the body, the letter "m" slips away' (#28). The dialectic between stuffing ourselves with illusions and lacking a sense of reality is convincingly written out in his Pati Likhi. Interestingly, Pati (a flat wooden board) was used by children till recent times; coated with clay, it would be refreshed daily for writing. The First Sikh's imaginary draws the Chaupar board game on the writing board, leaving his readers imagining exciting new arabesques.

Dakhni Oankar is another acrostic (GGS: 929–38) in fifty-four stanzas, based on a southern (*dakhani*) melody. This longer composition has more acoustic space for Guru Nanak's alliterative aesthetic and stair-like parallelisms. It begins with a profuse celebration of Oankar, the primal source of all creation—the cycles of time, natural phenomena, scriptures. The syllabic totality Oankar then fuses into *ekankar*: '*ekankar avar nahi duja nanak ek samai*—there is the one Being, no other; Nanak, we merge into this One' (#5). The euphonic flow is an emphatic calligraphy of the oneness of our supreme Creator, and simultaneously, it hearkens us to our ultimate destination—we return to this very One. In alluring rhymes, the acrostic extols the sole alpha and omega of all beings and things; it extols the Unity embracing all pluralities.

Guru Nanak's imperative, 'Write the divine Name—*likh ram nam*' is logically appropriate for an acrostic. Children learn by writing on their writing boards. Writing is an intriguing multi-faceted process, though. We cannot merely copy down words. Don't we need to think about a subject before we write it out? We must first discover (*khoj*) the Name (#19). The Guru renders it in aesthetically beautiful and precious images, and he endows us the agency to 'choose the gems and pearls—*chun lai manak moti*'. When we write we voice the subject from the individual perspective, so writing the beautiful Name resonates with each of us personally; we make the intangible Divine tangible for ourselves. Writing helps us to remember better, and so the process serves as a valuable mnemonic device as well.

What is written is read out. Guru Nanak ends his acrostic with an appeal. We must read (*pariai*) with a true mind (*sach mann*) the holy word (*sabad*) on the true board (*sachi pati*):

> *sachi pati sach mann pariai sabad su sar*
> *nanak so paria so pandit bina jis ram nam gal har* (#54)

The true mind is clear of prejudices, stereotypes and all sorts of scratches; it isn't sullied by lies or illusions. The true writing board is this vast pluralistic creation on which the quintessential Reality (*su sar*) of the holy word is calligraphed. The parallel line below acknowledges the true reader (*so paria*) or the wise intellectual (*so pandit bina*) as the person who wears the divine Name around his/her neck (*gal har*). The perfectly rhyming '*su sar*' and '*gal har*' create an intriguing semantic relationship, for '*su sar*' is the utterly insubstantial reality, while '*gal har*' is a material, substantial garland (*har*) draped around the neck (*gal*). The colliding worlds come together harmoniously. The transcendent holy word is embodied; the human body is adorned by the beautiful precious jewel of the divine Name. Such poetic sounds subliminally deepen the philosophical richness of Guru Nanak's acrostic.

Siddha Gosht is a dialogue along the lines of the Upanishads and Socratic discourse. Its seventy-three stanzas are discussions (*gosht*) with a group of Siddhas (GSS: 938–46). Technically, the Naths and the Siddhas were two different yogic sects, but they appear interchangeably in the Guru's works. Members of the Nath sect are also called Kanphat yogis, distinguished by their split (*phat*) earlobes (*kan*). The Naths were influential in medieval Punjab (displayed in a scene from a Mughal album on display at the Chester Beatty Museum in Ireland where a Kanphat yogi sits with a dog; the painting illustrates the parallel between the dog's devotion to his master and the yogi's for Shiva). The Siddha Gosht hymn recounts Guru Nanak's conversation with their leaders. In addition to Adinath, the original master, Lord Shiva, there were believed to have been nine other Naths who had attained immortality through the arduous *hatha yoga* techniques. The text mentions only two historical interlocutors—Charpat (#4) and Loharipa (#7)—both of whom predate Guru Nanak by several centuries. The location of the dialogue, its time frame, and its typography are not too explicit either; nevertheless, Guru Nanak's philosophy comes out clearly in this dialogical format. The Siddhas raise questions about creation, the holy word, breath, yoga and guru, which the First Sikh consistently answers in a polite and respectful manner, but entirely from his unique personal perspective. Later Sikh works (like that of Bhai Gurdas and the Janamsakhis) frequently bring up Guru Nanak's discourse with these world-rejecting ascetics.

The genre of the Var (ballad) depicting heroic events was widespread in Punjabi folk poetry. Professional singers with hand-held drums (*dhad*) travelled around singing praise chronicles in popular tunes. Guru Nanak adapted the narrative style of the folk ballad, but he transformed the dynamics of the historical battlefield into a meta-historical spiritual sphere. His successor Gurus adopted his model, and there are altogether twenty-two Vars in the GGS. Though these long compositions are attributed to a primary author, they include the lyrics of the other Gurus, each poetically interacting with and building upon the central themes taken up by the main author. The three Vars by Guru Nanak appear in Raga Majh, Asa and Malar, and in all three of them he refers to himself as a dhadhi. His Asa di Var (GGS: 462–75) is particularly popular, and in many places of worship this twenty-four pauri composition has become a part of the daily morning liturgy. It is prescribed to be sung in the tune of the local ballad of 'Tunda As Raj', the maimed (*tunda*) king (*raja*) called As, glorified in folk poems for defeating his evil brother.

Guru Nanak begins with praise of the creator, giver, knower and taker of all. This One whose doing is everything is now 'seated, watching with delight—*kari asan ditho cao*' (GGS: 463). Divine pleasure forms the atoms of our multiverse. His overture sets the tone for his composition. It is followed by nine verses in melodious repetitions extolling the manifold attributes of Truth (*sach*) and culminating with the Nanakian equation 'Those who reflect on Truth are true themselves.' In this pattern of rhythmic repetitions the Guru continues to hymn the glory of the greatness of the great (*vadi vadiai*), the wondrous (*vismad*) multiverse, and all phenomena—physical, intellectual, emotional—as the nature (*qudrat*) of the singular Noumenon. He then discloses the workings of the universe under the supervision of the divine One; the moral degeneration of society blind to the presence of that One; and the futility of rituals, codes of purity, book learning, insipid talk and hypocrisy. To cite #9 as an example:

We may read cartloads of books
We may read caravans of books
We may read boatloads of books
We may fill up caverns with books we read
We may read year after year
    We may read month by month
We may read through the entire course of life
We may read with each breath we take
    Nanak, one item alone gets recorded
The rest is vain pompous froth

The First Sikh's emphatic rhetoric is most effective. The finale returns to the 'greatness of the great One, no telling can tell; to the Creator who gives us our daily bread . . .' The morning Asa di Var is a cadenced circle offering both subtle metaphysical ideals and practical advice on right and wrong. The chime of its moral guidelines impacts the actions listeners/singers choose to do over the course of the day.

Kuchaji and Suchaji are unique Nanakian compositions. Kuchaji is a depiction of the incompetent bride/wife who received gifts of gold, silver, colourful pearls and jewels from her divine Groom. Sadly, she fell for their trappings and forgot her Husband. Centred on her ego, hers is a fragmented and inauthentic mode of existence. Her old age and looming death are both allegorically expressed: 'Now the cranes cry out in the skies above, white herons have appeared, my friend—*ambar kunja kurlia bag bahithe aejio*' (GGS: 762). Her antithesis is the Suchaji who leads a full and successful life: she enthusiastically decorates her new home, delights to be in the proximity of her Husband, and enjoys hearing spiritual melodies. However, the Guru does not hold on to these polarities, for once the incompetent gets rid of the five psychological afflictions that were robbing her of her essential selfhood, she becomes the local chief and administers justice. Even though he is living in medieval India, the First Sikh acknowledges how women can engage in politics and government. His is an optimistic religiosity; we may do wrongs, but they are deleted as soon as we flush out egoistic self-centredness.

Babarvani hymns are historical in nature. They tell us that Guru Nanak witnessed Babar's conquest of the relatively peaceful regime of the Muslim Lodi Sultans. The Guru composed four hymns that have collectively come down in Sikh literature as Babarvani (Babar hymns that declare Babar's rule in India): three in Raga Asa, and the fourth in Raga Tilang. There are extremely few historical allusions in the 1430 pages of Sikh scripture, so Guru Nanak's description of a crucial historical event is noteworthy. In his narration of dates and places and accounts, he is not giving us a 'historical' account of the establishment of the Mughal Empire in 1526 as such. What he accomplishes instead is a poignant synthesis of the particular socio-political conditions of medieval Indian history with universal transcendent values. We will take up his Babarvani in the fourth chapter when we discuss the revolutionary spirit of the First Sikh.

Solahas are hymns in sixteen stanzas (*solaha*), found only in Raga Maru. There are altogether sixty-two of these sixteen-stanza hymns in the GGS out of which twenty-two have been composed by Guru Nanak, twenty-four by Guru Amar Das, two by Guru Ram Das, and fourteen by Guru Arjan. The length of Guru Nanak's Solahas provides him the poetic space to express his inexpressible feel for the infinity and infinitesimality of the Divine, and so paradoxical and multivalent images speedily flow out offering readers myriad possibilities of recollecting the Divine without letting the mind halt on any one. The Guru seems to spell out more details in this format. For instance, he usually refers to pilgrimage sites in general, but here he describes specific holy places thronging with pilgrims from diverse traditions in different corners of the Indian subcontinent—Kashi, Kanchivaram, Puri, Dwarka. Against the backdrop of Raga Maru's desert heat (its name is derived from *marusthal*, meaning dry land), we can hear the music of cool, lapping waves beside the bustling locations. Temporally, too, he goes way back into the past when there were 'no species, no languages, no air, no water/There was no creation or destruction, no coming or going.' These sixteen-stanza hymns spotlight Guru Nanak's pluralistic and expansive vision.

Miscellaneous segment: In the final section of the GGS, there are thirty-two short poems by our First Sikh. These are the extra lyrics (*vadhik*) from the longer Vars ('Lyrics, Ballads, and Extras', GGS: 1410–12). These final poems demonstrate his far-reaching knowledge. They leave us with a strong feel for his awareness of myth (allusions to the Ramayana, #25), of history (Emperor Babar's invasion of Lahore, #27), society (if a Brahman discerns the ultimate being, he is worthy of veneration, #16; a Kshatriya who performs acts of charity and philanthropy must be honoured, #17), economics (inspect the product before making the deal, #2), body (why must we mourn and wail? #6; why put our poor body through arduous yogic exercises? #18), and psychology (none of us reach all our goals, and how ironic the way life goes on only to take us away, #31). The recurring beat is, of course, the infinite Divine in each and every heart (#9). Resonating throughout his corpus, the various themes expressed in these concluding lyrics embrace the audience in his expansive consciousness, and in turn play upon their consciousness so they participate fully and fearlessly in all spheres of life. Like the opening Japji, the First Sikh's finale opens up for his readers/ listeners a joyous possibility of becoming 'one with the perfect One'. A most fitting conclusion in itself.

Overall, the First Sikh's compositions reveal his familiarity with the idioms and practices of Hindus, Muslims, Buddhists, Yogis and Naths; importantly, they also relay his intention to reach out to a wide audience and relate closely with his diverse contemporaries. We discern a threefold pattern in his literary strategy. (1) He transforms external practices into internal processes: the sacred performances of *arati* (Hindu worship) and *sama* (Sufi mystical concert), decorating deities with sandalwood paste, or yoga exercises are all metamorphosed into mental experiences. (2) He shifts any sacred space—be it the temple or the mosque or the monastery or the cave—to the social world where everyone must equally carry out their human responsibilities. (3) He expands an adored deity to the transcendent infinite that cannot be incarnated in any tangible shape or form, or else he intimately pulls in the almighty Allah to pulsate within the individual body. The Guru uses familiar motifs and customs of his contemporaries to convey his specific ideals in a way that would affect his listeners emotionally. Often he employs satire to jolt people out of blind faith and routine practices.

In his artistic verse, we palpably feel the First Sikh's phenomenal presence. In fact, the body–poetry link is tellingly made in an early Janamsakhi account where he is seen bathing with a jug of water while his successor, Guru Angad, watches him (illustration 56 of the B-40 Janamsakhi, more in Chapter 2). Pointing to his blue-black skin on his ribcage, the Guru explains to Angad that the night before a young shepherd was reciting his Arati Sohila where the terrain happened to be thorny, so he brushed against some of the bushes and was bruised. That the First Sikh was somatically present in his verse is strikingly conveyed in the illustration and its narrative. Along with Guru Angad, the viewer witnesses the porous nature of Guru Nanak's body—its fusion with his intangible word. The 'body as poetry' is not some plain old simile; it is not a figurative trope either, and it is not a literalist slip. His sonorous verse is the actual breathing Guru. Shattering the tyrannical opposition of body and mind, language and reality, a new vision of being in the world is brought forth by the First Sikh. Personally, for a Sikh academic like me, aesthetic appreciation of his poetics is the way to absorb his innermost private world and be in touch with him intimately.

~

Along with Guru Nanak's own compositions found in Guru Arjan's superbly documented archive, this study of the First Sikh draws upon the ballads of Bhai Gurdas and the Janamsakhi narratives. Bhai Gurdas was an important figure in early Sikh history. He was born only twelve years after the passing away of Guru Nanak in 1551, and he died in 1636 at the age of eighty-five. His long lifespan made him the contemporary of the First Sikh's five successors—Guru Angad (Nanak 2) through Guru Hargobind (Nanak 6), and he also taught Tegh Bahadur (son of the sixth, and the future Ninth Guru) classical texts and philosophies. Bhai Gurdas was chosen by Guru Arjan as the scribe for the momentous compilation of the Sikh canon, the first recension of the Sikh holy text installed in the inner chamber of the Harmandir Sahib in 1604. Thus, he not only witnessed but also participated in the origins and crystallization of the Sikh faith in a vital way. His literary works are revered as a 'key' (*kunji*) to the treasury of Sikh theology and history. His Vars (ballads) in Punjabi are very popular, as Sikhs memorize and quote them with regard to belief and behaviour. His Var 1 (Cantos 23–45) is especially useful to us as it illuminates the person and role of the First Sikh.[12] The opening chapter will make substantial use of Bhai Gurdas's poetic testimony.

Janamasakhi literature is yet another rich archive, and the second chapter of this volume will focus on it. Shortly after Guru Nanak passed away, mythic narratives (*sakhis*) about his birth and life (*janam*) came into circulation and have been very popular in the collective Sikh imagination. Many of the narratives construct concrete scenes to render Guru Nanak's universal message. Those that are illustrated evoke lingering emotions through their symphony of colours and compositional elements. The written Janamsakhis are the first prose works in the Punjabi language using the Gurmukhi script. The dominant motif of the Janamsakhis is not chronological or geographical accuracy. Professor Harbans Singh explains, 'These accounts were written by men of faith. They wrote for the faithful—of a theme, which had grown into their lives through the years as a real, vivid truth. Straightforward history was not their concern, nor was their description objective and conceptual.'[13] The Janamsakhis have been circulating orally, in writing, and in paintings and illustrations. In the language of poetry, colours and simple prose, they depict the First Sikh in three dimensions and help us get a real feel for him. As many set the stage for his scriptural hymns, they bring out the nexus between the biography of Nanak and his compositions. Together, Guru Nanak's verse, the ballads of Bhai Gurdas, and the Janamsakhi narratives reflect a vibrant portrait of the First Sikh.

Besides these basic sources, I will also utilize several later primary and secondary texts. I grew up in a Sikh home resounding with his hymns, teachings and images, and teeming with scholarly works on him. Professor Harbans Singh, my father, wrote a major biography for his fifth birth centennial entitled *Guru Nanak and Origins of the Sikh Faith* which has been formative in my approach. He also chaired the first department of religious studies at Punjabi University in Patiala, held symposiums on the first Sikh Guru, and later edited the *Encyclopaedia of Sikhism*. Guru Nanak was all around me at home and in my wider Punjabi society. Starting from my undergraduate years, the First Sikh has been the focus of my own research and scholarship. I have written on Guru Nanak from various perspectives and presented my work at diverse venues. Over the last few years, I have been devoted to translating some of his works. This volume draws upon my numerous publications over the decades. Years of my research, thinking, translating and writing turn up in these pages.

Half a century ago, for the First Sikh's fifth birth centennial in 1969, Guru Nanak University was established in Amritsar, Guru Nanak chairs were established at several universities, two Guru Nanak institutes were set up, seminars and symposia were held at various university campuses. Guru Nanak studies received a major boost transnationally. Endowed Sikh chairs in North America have been established at the University of British Columbia, University of California at Santa Barbara, University of California at Riverside,

University of Michigan at Ann Arbor, Hofstra University on Long Island, and more recently at the University of California in Irvine. There is a growing number of professors in the USA, Canada, the UK and Europe whose teaching and research focus on the legacy of the First Sikh. The scene is very different from my graduate school days when there were barely any books or scholars or teachers of the Sikh tradition. The overall interest and collaborations between scholars in India and in diasporic communities have generated a large corpus of published materials on the First Sikh. For his fifth centennial, several English biographies were published, including *Guru Nanak and the Sikh Religion* by Hew McLeod (Oxford: Clarendon, 1968), *Guru Nanak and Origins of the Sikh Faith* by Harbans Singh (Bombay, 1969), *Guru Nanak: His Personality and Vision* by G.S. Talib, and *Guru Nanak in History* by J.S. Grewal (Punjab University, 1969). In their own and different ways these eminent historians have made important contributions to the understanding of the Guru Nanak of history.

My goal here is a more personal one. I want to rediscover the First Sikh from my perspective of a Sikh woman academic located in a global twenty-first-century world. I have been intrigued by him for decades, and especially during the last several years he percolates deep in my being as I translate his verse. His simple, pithy style tends to be extremely subtle and sophisticated and I find myself constantly wondering about the meaning behind his enchanting lyrics. I am several generations apart from the First Sikh, and live thousands of miles away from Talvandi where he was born, or from Kartarpur where he gave birth to the first Sikh community. Yet his presence is an intrinsic part of my life, and what I observe of my fellow Sikh men and women, and one that is steadily entering the consciousness of non-Sikhs outside the Indian subcontinent as well. It is with a desire to meet this unique person as closely as I possibly can and introduce him to a global audience that I take up this project.

There are five chapters in this volume. Chapter 1 is an attempt to understand the phrase 'First Sikh'. What does 'first' signify? And 'sikh'? What did 'sikh' signify for our First Sikh? What implications does it have for us today? Chapter 2 explores the First Sikh's life story through the Janamsakhis as they zoom in on his pluralistic personality and corporeal metaphysics. Chapter 3 analyses his ontological, epistemological, aesthetic, ethical and soteriological worldview from his philosophical-mystical stance. In Chapter 4, we encounter the First Sikh as a revolutionary thinker who champions human rights and feminism, and in Chapter 5 we engage with him as a modern environmentalist; his sublime poetics galvanizes us to fight against racism, classism, sexism, fanaticism, orientalism and exploitation of natural resources. The 'inconclusive conclusion' surveys his vast legacy in the personal and collective life of the Sikhs, along with his tender mnemonics by non-Sikh poets Firoz Din Sharaf and Shiv Kumar Batali. His rich and enduring reality is so alive. These chapters are not mutually exclusive; they are simply a framework to grasp a few facets of the kaleidoscopic First Sikh.

1

The First Sikh: Continuing Reality

The Sikh religion begins with the First Sikh, Guru Nanak (1469–1539). 'Religion' as we all know is a modern Western concept, with no equivalent in the Indian context. But its classic definition by anthropologist Clifford Geertz, 'A system of symbols which acts to establish powerful, pervasive, and long-lasting moods and motivations', is very pertinent.[1] In medieval north India, Guru Nanak set in motion spiritual moods and ethical motivations which continue to inspire and sustain millions of Sikh men and women worldwide.

According to the Sikh Gurdwaras Act, 1925, 'Sikh means a person who professes the Sikh religion.' The official Sikh ethical code known as the Rahit Maryada defines a Sikh as: 'Any human being who faithfully believes in (1) One Immortal Being, (2) Ten Gurus, from Guru Nanak Sahib to Guru Gobind Singh Sahib, (3) The Guru Granth Sahib, (4) The utterances and teachings of the ten Gurus and (5) The baptism bequeathed by the Tenth Guru; and who does not owe allegiance to any other religion, is a Sikh.'[2] The foremost 'One Immortal Being' is quintessentially Guru Nanak's precept, but the other four are not applicable to him. The First Sikh precedes nine Sikh Gurus (Guru Angad to Guru Gobind Singh, from 1539–1708), he precedes the compilation of the Guru Granth Sahib (1604), he precedes the baptism bequeathed by the Tenth Guru, and with his universal vision of ultimate Reality the First Sikh would not have stipulated any exclusivist claim. With him (1469–1539), we are at a moment *before* the dynamic crystallization of the title 'Sikh' over the subsequent centuries.

What then does 'First Sikh' signify? What is 'First'? What is 'Sikh'? What was Guru Nanak's understanding of the word 'Sikh'? Did *he* see *himself* as the First Sikh? What meaning do these terms have for the community? How did these evolve? How do they envisage the continuing reality of Guru Nanak? These are some of the questions that form the subtext of this chapter. We may not come up with absolute answers; nonetheless, to seek answers is important. These questions set us on a fresh and more personal approach to the Sikh religion, and thereby help us discover the immediacy and individuality of Guru Nanak.

Firstness of the First

Guru Nanak was born in pre-modern, pre-partitioned Punjab, the gateway to the Indian subcontinent. For centuries the fertile Punjab, land of the five (*punj*) rivers (*ab*), had been attracting people of different religions and ethnicities. The soil Guru Nanak grew up on was layered by the Greeks, Scythians, Sassanids, Huns, Afghans, Persians and Turks. Closer to his times, Babar established the Mughal empire. The region resonated with the songs of Bhagats and Sufis, the lovers of god from a variety of Indic and Islamic traditions. Bhakti, a theistic devotional movement within Hinduism that started in the south of India in the sixth century, was abloom in the north by the time of Guru Nanak's birth. Meanwhile, as a result of the Muslim conquest of northern India, charismatic Sufis from Afghanistan and Central Asia had established their orders and sanctified the medieval Indian landscape with Sufi shrines (dargahs), retreats (*khanqahs*), community kitchens (langars) and mosques.

Guru Nanak inherited this culturally, linguistically and religiously diverse world. Even our brief introduction illustrated his abundant knowledge of texts, myths, ideologies, social codes, musical measures and practices current in medieval India. We hear him in conversation with people from different faiths in different places, communicating with them in their dialect. His prolific compositions bear witness to his familiarity with literature, sacred spaces, pilgrimages and prescriptions from multiple religious traditions. He is as familiar with the Muslim *takbir* prayer or the *darud* blessings for Prophet Muhammad as he is with the *gayatri mantra* of the Vedic tradition; he is well versed with the Vedas and the Qateb. He has a nuanced understanding of Hindu puja, Muslim namaz, Siddha techniques, yogic breath control, asceticism of the Digambara Jains, Tantric sahajyana, and so forth. He mentions death rituals of the Hindus (cremation), Muslims (burial) and Parsis (offering to nature), and is well versed with holy figures from different Hindu, Muslim, Jain, Buddhist, Nath, Tantric and Yogic schools. He also had an extremely refined musical ear, for most of his compositions are set in musical measures from the classical Indic raga classifications, along with folk musical patterns with simpler beats. He made ample use of regional Bhakti and Sufi forms with their rhythms and melodies, and he was innovative too. We are told ragas like Majh and Tukhari were invented by him.[3]

The astounding breadth and depth of Guru Nanak's knowledge of medieval Indian religious traditions that we recover from his oeuvre reveal his openness to and acceptance of others. His passionate love for the divine One and his humility that saturates his self-references, along with his at-homeness in the pluralistic soil and spirit of north India, I would say, are the defining features of the First Sikh. His is not mere tolerance of others but a real engagement, understanding and appreciation of diversity and difference. Across his compositions we hear him praise people who have sincere devotion for their respective deities, scriptures and rituals. He urges people to be who they genuinely are—Hindu, Muslim, Siddha, Yogi or whatever they choose to be; he wants everybody to match their internal and external selves, their beliefs with their practices. Unquestionably, he denounces pretentious practices and authoritarian claims to theological knowledge and superiority. We hear him pungently criticize elite custodians of various Indic and Islamic schools who exerted their control over the masses by reinforcing religious divisions and imposing rules and regulations that only led people astray from a genuine experience of the all-encompassing Divine. Condemning external costumes and customs adopted in the name of religion, the First Sikh celebrates the universal One and Its infinite expressions. As he exuberantly rejoices in the wondrous beauty manifest all around, he viscerally infects his readers and listeners, whatever tradition they may belong to. He expresses his belief in the formless divine One in multiple ways—it can be the Islamic Khuda, Buddhist Nirvana, Upanishadic Aum, Vaisnhnava Hari or Ram, Yogi's supreme Nath, Bhagat's Madhusudan; the First Sikh's boundless imagination goes beyond all divisions and barriers, be it aniconic Islam, representational Hinduism or atheistic Buddhism.

But we must be absolutely clear that he is *not* affiliated with any particular religion—nowhere in his vast oeuvre does he acknowledge following any spiritual teacher or school of thought. Regrettably, historians of religion classify him in pre-existent traditions and deny Guru Nanak the rightful category of being the *first* for a new mode of thought and praxis. Beginning with H.H. Wilson in 1828, several scholars generally declared Guru Nanak as a follower of Kabir, the forerunner of the Hindu school of Nirguna Bhakti.[4] Others viewed him as a figure who combined teachings from Hinduism and Islam, and produced Sikhism, the prime example of 'syncretism'. Refining this line of thought, the leading Western scholar W.H. McLeod has repeatedly postulated his 'admixture' theory which denies Guru Nanak as the rightful 'founder' of a new ontological and existential reality, and instead categorizes him as 'reworking the Sant tradition'. McLeod defines the Sant tradition essentially as 'a synthesis of the three principal dissenting movements, a compound of elements drawn mainly from Vaishnava Bhakti and the hatha yoga of the Nath yogis, with a marginal contribution from Sufism . . .' His theory:

> . . . affirms a basically Hindu origin and holds that Muslim influence, although certainly evident, is no-where of fundamental significance in the thought of Guru Nanak. The religion of Guru Nanak, and so of Sikhism as a whole, is firmly imbedded in the Sant tradition of northern India, in the beliefs of the so-called Nirguna Sampradaya. The categories employed by Guru Nanak are the categories of the Sants, the terminology he uses is their terminology, and the doctrines he affirms are their doctrines.

McLeod claims the Sant tradition as the basis of 'Guru Nanak's thought, and inheritance which, like Kabir, he reinterpreted in the light of his own personality and experience'.[5] Likewise, W.C. Smith, a pioneer for the study of comparative religion, writes, 'To call him [Nanak] "the founder" of Sikhism, as is often done, is surely to misconstrue both him and history.'[6]

There are important methodological issues here which deserve to be examined. To what extent should the existence of 'historical influence' call into question the uniqueness of any religious thinker or religious tradition? These scholars seem to neglect the most vital resource—Guru Nanak's own works. Nowhere in his 974 hymns does he acknowledge following any spiritual 'Sant' teacher or upholding any Sant doctrine or principle. We do not see him emulating any specific mystic or school of thought or reworking ideas anywhere; in fact, we hear the First Sikh criticize hatha yoga and the other Nath perspectives posited in McLeod's 'admixture' theory. What his works repeatedly demonstrate is his intense personal experience of Reality, common to all people—Hindu, Muslim, Yogi, Buddhist and Jain—and reinforce his enduring relationships with people of other faiths. By refuting Guru Nanak as the founder of the Sikh religion, scholars refute his status as the *first*, and frame Guru Nanak as one who replicates, reproduces, reinterprets, refines and reforms elements from existing traditions. They may even use superlatives for his works: 'There is in them an integrated and coherent system which no other Sant has produced; there is a clarity which no other Sant has equalled; and there is a beauty which no other Sant has matched . . .'[7] This praise makes Guru Nanak a unique Sant but a Sant all the same. Dr Nripinder Singh cogently argues against such claims:

> To see Guru Nanak allied to, or participant within, an earlier ongoing tradition however rich and variegated is to misconstrue not only the mission of a man but also the phenomenon of prophecy and the religious experience of a multitude of people over a course of five centuries.[8]

The genetic approach of Western scholars like Hew McLeod and W.C. Smith deflects research from the First Sikh's vision and text to that of his antecedents. The academic focus is shifted from a study of his worldview to Sant parameters. Rather than giving him a fresh look, he is determined by pre-existing traditions; rather than recognizing his *firstness*, he is deemed secondary. That Guru Nanak's vision was merely a continuum or a rejuvenation of a prior tradition drastically diminishes his primaryness. Going against the Sikh faith as practised over the past five and a half centuries, such intellectual compromises do injustice to the prescience of the First Sikh's innate perception and initiative. Of course, Guru Nanak did not operate in an intellectual vacuum, as we fully acknowledge; he belonged to a rich cultural and religious milieu.

But he was the *first* to experience something distinctly universal—his and his alone—which he intentionally and formally set into motion. This is something we cannot ignore, for it is the cornerstone of the Sikh faith. Evidently, the belief in the One immortal Being professed by Sikhs today in the Rahit Maryada definition goes back to Guru Nanak's palpable experience. As we will explore, the 'all-inclusive One' envisioned by him is quite different from the prevalent monotheistic notion of the 'One God' of the Abrahamic traditions. The First Sikh's prolific oeuvre and the institutions of *seva*, *sangat*, langar and guru established by him prove beyond a doubt that he was the founder of Sikhism. Professor Harbans Singh strongly affirms:

> Attempts have been made to split Guru Nanak's doctrine into various strands and to trace their origin to preceding schools of thought. But to understand Guru Nanak fully, we have to look at the totality of his tenet and at what impact it made on history. In this perspective, we shall see that Guru Nanak is historically the founder of the Sikh faith. His precept was definitively the starting-point. In many significant ways, it signaled a new departure in contemporary religious ethos.[9]

By dismissing his firstness, we dismiss Guru Nanak's personal spiritual experience and his original contributions; we miss out on his historical significance, we miss out on the independent origins of the Sikh religion, we miss out on the pioneering groundwork of the institutions he set up, we miss out on his revolutionary impulse.

His Firstness in His Own Words and in Early Sikh Sources

Guru Nanak's firstness is evident in his autobiographical passages recorded in the GGS. They capture his mystical experience of the transcendent One, corroborated by later Sikh sources. In the final envoi of Raga Majh, Guru Nanak identifies himself as a dhadhi three times as he describes his divine encounter. He is summoned by the transcendent One, given an outfit, is fed and employed by his Patron. The Var Majh self-references mark the first moment in Sikh history, and we will be returning to them in subsequent chapters as well. The First Sikh's testimony:

> I was a hopeless songster (dhadhi) till I was put to work
> I was ordered to sing divine praise night and day
>> Right from the start.
> The Owner in the true palace called for this songster:
> I was dressed in the robes of true praise and glory,
> I was offered a meal of the true (*sach*) ambrosia (*amrita*) of name (*nam*)
> Those who partake guru's wisdom to their fill
> Attain happiness.
> This songster will resound the holy word (*sabad*) and spread it far
> Says Nanak, by exalting Truth (*sach*)
> We attain the absolute One
>
> GGS: 150

Guru Nanak here is not mentioning Kabir or any other sant, he is not singing to any king or hero or leader, he is not engaged in reforming any current ideologies, he is not blending any disparate traditions to reproduce his own hybrid religion. What he is going through is a spontaneous and sensuous experience directly from/of the transcendent Divine. The First Sikh's personal testimony overturns McLeod's assumption that 'we can hardly accept the claim that it was delivered by direct, unmediated inspiration from on high'.[10]

Guru Nanak embodies the phenomenon of firstness, defined by philosopher Charles Pierce:

> It is not in being separated from qualities that Firstness is most predominant, but in being something peculiar and idiosyncratic. The first is predominant in feeling, as distinct from objective perception, will, and thought.[11]

'The first is predominant in feeling' and Guru Nanak is feeling the presence of the infinite One intensely. He wears the outfit of true praise and glory, he consumes the meal of the true elixir of the Name, and he is excited to take up his new assignment to play the holy word. The First Sikh sees the absolute One and absorbs the all-encompassing reality into his bloodstream. The garments worn by people externally mark their religious sect, and so his dress of *sachi sifat salah* (of 'true praise and glory') is his new identity marker. The holy word (sabad) is the same as the name (nam)—the designation of the singular reality Guru Nanak praises, wears and drinks. In his meta-historical encounter the songster Nanak bursts into sublime verse on the 'isness' of the One Being, the owner of the transcendent Palace. Distinct from objective perception, will and thought, his is a peculiar and idiosyncratic reflex, a reflex which is the nub that holds together the community of Sikhs, whatever part of the world they may live in. In his own words, '*dhadhi kathe akath sabad savaria*—the songster adorned with the holy word expresses the inexpressible' (GGS: 149). Not himself any more, but a songster with prophetic power, Guru Nanak starts to 'tell' (*kathe*) the 'untellable' (*akath*). Something radically new came on the horizon.

The First Sikh's detachment from all prevailing schools and masters, and his passionate attachment to the divine Patron is apparent all over his verse. In the dialogical format of the Siddha Gosht (GGS: 938-46) his views become more explicit. It is a discourse with a congregation of Siddhas seated in their yogic postures. They address him as *bale* ('young one', #1) which suggests the meeting took place sometime during Guru Nanak's early years on one of his long journeys. Interestingly, the group is curious to know about the First Sikh's religious heritage, and quite like our modern scholars, they try to classify the youngster. But the First Sikh refuses to be boxed into any religious system or school of thought, and resolutely claims to have derived his identity and status from the divine One: '*sabad guru surat dhun cela*—the holy word is my guru, my consciousness is the disciple of Its melody' (Siddha Gosht, 44). He declares his utter independence: '*Akath katha le rahao nirala*—I live my unique way telling the untellable story.' The First Sikh is fully aware of his own distinct way (*nirala*). By telling something fascinating that cannot quite be told, he is not assuming to give sermons or mandate any specific regimen and religious practices common to his milieu. Rather than put the body through rigorous exercises, he proposes that it be dressed with the divine Name: 'With the holy word on our lips we shine like the infinite light of the moon; when the Name lives in us, our body and mind become holy like the holy verse' (#59, also #68). The dialogue highlights the First Sikh's universal religiosity: to live out the enchantment of the Divine within. The goal of spiritual liberation is thus attained savouring the infinite One midst family and society.

In his discourse he takes on yogic diction. Yogic energy channels *ida*, which lies to the left of the spine, and *pingala*, to the right of the spine, while *susumna* runs along the spinal cord in the centre. The three connect at the circuits of intensity (chakras), and with yogic exercises channel the flow of energy from the lower body to the crown of the head. But instead of a physiological flow brought about by yogic exercises, the Guru advances the holy word full of spiritual energy, one that unites the individual with the universal Divine. He continuously uses clothing and objects typically associated with yogis, like their patched cloak, earrings, cap and begging bowl, to convey his own perspective. The earrings are the holy word worn inside, the cloak is the all-pervasive One draped around the body, the begging bowl is the mind emptied of ego, the cap is woven from the five elements. The Guru does not say; he makes his interlocuters think about the five: air, water, fire, earth, and ether would be the fifth. In his offbeat style he charges his audience to gather the characteristics of each of these elements: impartiality of air, patience of earth, coolness of water, purity of ether, and the ability to burn impurities like fire. Through yogic wording and phrasing, the First Sikh delineates his distinct philosophy and ethical practice: match the external lifestyle with the inner experience of the universal Divine.

He does exactly what he proposed to do during his personal encounter with the divine One recorded in Var Majh. That critical moment is further elaborated in the Janamsakhis. These are the earliest prose accounts, vital for understanding the earliest community (more in Chapter 2). According to the oldest extant Puratan Janamsakhi Guru Nanak had a mystical experience in Sultanpur. At this point in his life he was working at a local grocery store and living in the home of his married sister, Nanaki, and her husband, Jai Ram. Nanak would go for his daily bath in a nearby stream—but one morning he disappeared. Everybody thought he had drowned, but to their surprise he reappeared after three days. Narrative No. 10 from the Puratan Janamsakhi vividly describes the First Sikh's absence as his divine communion:

> As the primal being willed, Nanak, the devotee, was ushered into the divine presence. Then a cup filled with ambrosia (*amrita*) was given him with the command, 'Nanak, this is the cup of name-adoration. Drink it (*pio*) . . . I am with you and I do bless and exalt you. Whoever remembers you will have my favor. Go, rejoice, in my name and teach others to do so . . . I have bestowed upon you the gift of my name (*nam*). Let this be your calling.' Nanak offered his salutations and stood up . . .[12]

The Janamsakhi narrative confirms Guru Nanak's autobiographical reference recorded in Sikh scripture that something momentous took place which transformed him entirely. He is endowed with a new status, and he is commissioned to spread the divine Name. In the Janamsakhi sequence Nanak receives a robe of honor (*sirpao*) as the physical object that marks his special dispensation. Subsequently, he takes on the role of the guru to spread the message 'to attain the absolute One' by no other means except 'by praising Truth (*sach*)'. People started to gather around him to hear and recite the sonorous praise he was gifted by his Patron—to wear and savour.

The foremost Sikh historian and theologian, Bhai Gurdas, who was chronologically and historically very close to the First Guru, goes on to describe the Guru embarking on his mission. Born only twelve years after the passing away of Guru Nanak, he was, as we noted, a contemporary of five Sikh Gurus. Sikhs revere him 'as an integral link between the Gurus and their disciples . . . as the very first apostle who . . . educes an understanding of that [Sikh] community's faith and religious life during a very crucial phase of its development'.[13] In Canto 27 of his Punjabi ballads, Bhai Gurdas captivatingly captures Guru Nanak's advent:

As Guru Nanak made his appearance, mist lifted, light filling the
   world
Like the stars vanish and darkness recedes as the sun rises
Like the deer scatter in panic as the lion roars
Whichever spot the Baba set his foot upon that became the seat of
   worship
Seats sacred to the Siddhas now laud the name of Nanak
Every home has become a Dharamsal, joyously resonant with the
   sacred chant
Baba reclaimed all the four corners and all the nine regions of the
   Earth
Bestowing upon them the gift of True Name
In the age of darkness the holy Guru made his appearance

These vibrant images and metaphors underscore the divine dispensation
of Guru Nanak; they illustrate him as the founder of a new and different
religion. The medium of Divine revelation and the revelation itself are
closely linked.

Bhai Gurdas's depiction of the primal occurrence of Guru Nanak's
appearance stresses the contrast between the cosmos prior to Guru
Nanak and the one after his advent. The metaphorical moment is the
early morning when darkness ends. The stanza begins with the visual
simile of the rising sun and the disappearance of fog and darkness.
Guru Nanak's radiance ends mental fog, intellectual nescience and
emotional obstructions; just as the dark skies with twinkling stars give
way to brilliance and effulgence, so transparency and clarity spread.
Although night and day are strikingly different from each other, there
is no harshness or hostility between them. For Bhai Gurdas, just as the
rising sun does not acrimoniously strike out the dark, but rather most
delicately and harmoniously brings in light, so does Guru Nanak on the
horizon of fifteenth-century north-west India. His aural image is loud:
hearing a lion roar, a pack of deer scatters in panic, and so Bhai Gurdas
accentuates the sonorous significance of Guru Nanak's message. We
may recall, Lord Buddha's first sermon in the deer park is popularly
known as the 'roar of the lion'. Whether Gautama the enlightened one
proclaims Dharma, or Nanak the founding Sikh Guru communicates

the divine Word, the analogy in both instances is that of a lion's roar. Overall, Bhai Gurdas's juxtaposition of the visual and aural images expresses the person of Nanak, bringing forth a verbal message charged with such power and vigour that it shakes the multitudes to their very depths. Hearing the new message of the First Sikh people are jolted from their lassitude. His is a historic entry on the world stage.

The First Sikh's Consciousness of His Firstness: Script and Scripture

At some level, the Guru must have been conscious of his firstness. We hear him voice his intention with commitment: 'This songster is going to resound the holy word widely—*dhadhi kare pasau sabadu vajaia*', and he carries out his role most effectively. He travelled widely with his Muslim companion, meeting people, visiting their sacred spaces, and discoursing with them. But he also took important steps to systematize and formalize the vision he was vouchsafed. That he initiated a new alphabet (Gurmukhi) and appointed a successor (Guru Angad) during his own lifetime demonstrate his resolve to establish his legacy. Both of these are a vital testimony to his conscious engagement in the process of inaugurating and establishing a new and distinctive religious community.

His acrostic (GGS: 432-4) introduces the new Gurmukhi alphabet. Literally 'from the Guru's mouth', Gurmukhi evolved from the *lahndi/ mahajani* business shorthand the First Sikh used during his apprenticeship in storehouses. His successor, Guru Angad, developed and standardized the script, and it is widely used by Sikhs. The process of 'writing' occupies profound significance in Guru Nanak's philosophical worldview. It serves as an expression for the Divine, the all-embracing ontological and existential principle: 'You are the writing board, You are the pen, You are the writing on the board' (GGS: 1291). His composition *Pati Likhi* in thirty-five stanzas underscores the oneness of the Creator. Most of these stanzas begin with letters of the Gurmukhi alphabet, in the very form that they are in use today. The acrostic starts out with praise of the universal Creator: '*Sassa soe sarisat jin saji sabhna sahib ek bhaia*—S Sole Sahib over all is the one who designed this creation.' Each component of this acrostic is a poetic gem. The current Punjabi alphabet follows the order of stanzas nine to thirty-three. The need for a special script goes to show the First Sikh's aspiration for a systematic preservation of something 'new' for writing his new revelation. Parallel to the Arabic script for the holy Quran and Sanskrit for the sacred Vedas, Gurmukhi would be the script for his community.

Literary and visual sources show him carrying a small volume of his compositions. Bhai Gurdas depicts him 'with a book under his arm—*kitab kachh*' (I: 32). Likewise, early Sikh paintings depict him holding a small volume in his hand, or with a small book placed beside him.[14] Though little is known about the 'first' volume belonging to Guru Nanak, these are indications of the First Sikh's aspiration for a 'new' text in a new script to foster the self-identity of his new community. A Sodhi family from the village of Guru Harsahai claimed to have inherited it, and therefore it has been called the 'Harsahai Pothi'. Unfortunately, it was stolen in 1970.[15]

The verses carried under the First Sikh's arm were subsequently embodied in the GGS, with a canonical status by 1604. The GGS enshrined in the Harmandir Sahib by Guru Arjan was a decisive factor for the self-definition of Sikhs, both individually and collectively. Guru Nanak's successors continued on his spiritual legacy, adding their individual contribution to the development of the canon. The second, Guru Angad (1504–52), valued its aesthetic and epistemological power: 'Ambrosial holy verse expressing reality came with knowledge and contemplation' (GGS: 1243). Adding his own writings to the volume he had received from Guru Nanak, Guru Angad passed it on to the third Guru, Amar Das. The epilogue of Guru Nanak's Japji is attributed to Guru Angad (GGS: 146). It depicts our variegated world, playing in the lap of female and male nurses day and night, with air as our guru, water as the father, and Mother Earth our matrix. But in fact we catch this memorable scene in Guru Nanak's own sixteen-stanza composition (Solaha 1:10). The striking similarity between them suggests that the Second Guru was reproducing Guru Nanak's passage from his opening solaha. Its imagery must have deeply resonated with the Fifth Guru as well, for during the making of the canon, he set it as a finale to the Japji, the inaugural hymn of the GGS. Such instances demonstrate the power of poetry. It is through their enjoined cadences of words and rhythm,

their warm sense of kinship and their spiritual joy that the different
Gurus become one voice of Nanak.

With the Third Guru (1479–1574) there is actual evidence of a
sacred anthology in the making. Two extant volumes (*pothi*s) were
created under his supervision in the town of Goindval founded by
him. These Goindval Pothis include the compositions of the first
three Sikh Gurus, along with the works of eight medieval saints. They
were inscribed by his grandson Sahansram, son of Baba Mohan, and
therefore they are also called the Mohan Pothis. These were written
in the Gurmukhi script, and during the compilation of the GGS, the
Fifth Guru utilized them.[16] Guru Amar Das also produced his own
lyrical hymns. Present-day Sikh rites and ceremonies conclude with the
congregation reciting sections of his 'Anand' (meaning 'bliss').

For his successor, Guru Amar Das chose his daughter Bibi
Bhani's husband, Ram Das (1534–81). Guru Ram Das continued to
compose hymns and foster the self-consciousness of Sikhs through the
medium of their distinct poetic legacy. To strengthen the individual
and collective identity of the evolving community, the Fourth Guru
instituted simple ceremonies and rites for birth, marriage and death.
His composition 'Lavan' (GGS: 773–74) forms the nucleus of the
Sikh wedding ceremony.

It was Guru Ram Das's son, the fifth Sikh Guru (1563–1606), who
produced the authoritative collection, the GGS. Arjan had spent the
first eleven years of his life with his parents, Bibi Bhani and Guru Ram
Das, in the home of his maternal grandfather where the two Goindval
collections were being made. He naturally would have absorbed the
inclusivity and precision involved in the textual compilations. The
fellowship of Sikhs from the Kartarpur days of Guru Nanak had
increased numerically and spread geographically, so there was a need for
a central canon for their spiritual and moral life. The community (*panth*)
needed a text (*granth*) to concretize its distinctive 'Sikh' worldview. The
problem of 'counterfeit' works was also prevalent. Since the Fourth Guru
had bypassed his older sons and appointed Arjan as his successor, the
eldest son, Pirthi Chand, was estranged from him. Pirthi and his gifted
son Meharban began to compose works under the name of Nanak. It
was with a view to fixing the seal on the sacred word and preserving it

for posterity that Guru Arjan began to codify his literary legacy into an authorized volume in 1603.

Guru Arjan chose Bhai Gurdas to be his amanuensis and the bards Balvand and Satta of the Mardana lineage to ensure continuity in the singing and musical style. A picturesque spot on the outskirts of Amritsar was selected for the compilation process. Today, a shrine called Ramsar marks this site. Since there was an enormous amount of poetic material in existence, selections had to be made from the works of the preceding four Gurus, as well as his own. Guru Arjan was a superb poet with an expansive repertoire. Adhering to Guru Nanak's discourse, Guru Arjan reiterated the singularity of that source: 'Some call it Rama, some call it Khuda; some worship it as Vishnu, some as Allah' (GGS: 885). In order to crystallize the founder Guru's universal vision for perpetuity, he collected the verses of the Sikh Gurus, Hindu Bhagats and Muslim saints from different social and geographical backgrounds. The infinite divine One common to all—Sikh, Muslim and Hindu alike—experienced by the First Sikh are embodied harmoniously in the GGS. No demarcations of any accent or that of Guru, Sufi or Bhagat are made. The Sikh sacred text brings together Abrahamic monotheism and polyphonic Indic worlds. Through his profound personal sensibility, Guru Arjan heard the essential human language; he did not get stuck on external differences in accents, intonations, grammar, vocabulary or imagery. With great insight he recorded the spiritual lyrics spanning the Indian subcontinent over half a millennium, and thus 'a unique work was created: the world's largest original collection of sacred hymns organized on the basis of 31 ragas in which they are to be sung and played'.[17]

Guru Arjan certainly did not aim to blend 'a syncretic text', for that would only deny the rich distinctions he respected. Such presumptions fail to see the originality of the Sikh poetic horizon birthed by the First Sikh. Guru Arjan did not try to add two disparate traditions to reproduce a hybrid Sikh text; he did not assemble their passages and market it as a new product. What he did seek was a vertical expansion of the spiritual consciousness shared by Hindus, Muslims and Sikhs. And what he created was a literary text scripted in an enduring relationship with people of other faiths. His predecessors treasured the speech of holy people filtering through the past: 'The sublime holy verse of devoted people resounds throughout the ages,' proclaimed the Third Guru (GGS: 910), who played a major role in bringing together their verse in Goindval. Starting with the First Sikh, it was important for his successor Gurus that people familiarize themselves with difference and diversity. The 'other' could not merely be tolerated; the 'other' had to be engaged with, understood and appreciated. So in the making of Sikh scripture, Guru Arjan collected the voices of Sikh, Muslim and Hindu poets and gave them equal status. He even set their poetry into musical measures so readers and listeners could aesthetically experience That One conceived in different forms and expressed in different styles. The pluralistic spectrum was important for the intellectual, emotional and spiritual development of his religiously diverse society. The Fifth made Guru Nanak's ideal of the singular Divine into a concrete reality.

Textual scholars provide important details of the formation of the Granth, and the editorial skills displayed by the Fifth Guru.[18] On 16 August 1604 the holy volume was ceremoniously installed in the inner sanctuary of the Harmandir (modern-day Golden Temple). Guru Arjan appointed the esteemed Bhai Buddha as its custodian (*granthi*). According to the Sikh tradition, the inaugural verse read by Bhai Buddha happened to be a hymn praising the Divine as the source of all actions and accomplishments (GGS: 783). Guru Arjan's installation of the GGS has been a vital moment in the construction of the personal and communal identity of the Sikhs. Interestingly, this first anthology of sacred Punjabi verse appeared just when Emperor Akbar was adopting Persian as the lingua franca of his administration. His progressive outlook forms the social, political and religious backdrop of the Sikh volume. As recorded in *The Akbarnama of Abu-l-Fazl*, the Mughal emperor even paid a visit to the Sikh Guru.[19]

Guru Gobind Singh (Nanak 10, 1666–1708) strengthened the authoritative status of the GGS. He prepared a volume based on the Kartarpur version compiled by Guru Arjan in 1604 and expanded the sacred text by including hymns of his father, Guru Tegh Bahadur (1621–75). It was inscribed by his gifted devotee Bhai Mani Singh. Since it was produced during Guru Gobind Singh's stay in the place called Damdama after he was forced to leave Anandpur, it is called

the 'Damdami Bir'. As noted by W.H. McLeod, this version closed
the canon of the GGS.[20] However, scholars have not yet been able to
trace when exactly the Ninth Guru's hymns and couplets were added
to the GGS. Unfortunately, many important sources were destroyed
during the partition of India in 1947, as were several rare manuscripts
in the Sikh Reference Library at Amritsar during the Indian Army's
Operation Bluestar at the Golden Temple in 1984.

Just before he passed away, the Tenth Guru in 1708 terminated the
line of personal gurus and transferred the succession of guruship to the
Granth itself. In the context of his own departure and the politically
precarious situation of his community, the appointment of the Granth
as the Guru was to empower his Sikhs. Their historical and spiritual
past was embodied in the Granth. The guruship of the Granth would
also resolve any problems of succession posed by schismatic groups. As
Sikhs remember, Guru Gobind Singh followed the precedence of the
First Guru. He placed a five paise coin and a coconut before the Granth
in veneration, and to the gathered Sikhs he instructed they henceforth
acknowledge the Granth in his place; there would be no other Guru.[21]
His widow Mata Sundari strongly pronounced the identity of the guru
and the granth: 'The guru is lodged in the word—*guru ka nivas sabad
vichu hai.*'[22] Containing the divine–human encounter of their ten Gurus,
Sikhs henceforth were to derive their guidance and inspiration from
their sacred text. Ever since, the GGS has unequivocally been their
sole sovereign. Every morning and evening Sikhs recite their liturgical
prayer (Ardas), and, standing up, in unison, assert:

> *Agia bhai akal ki tabhi chalaio panth*
> *sabh sikhan kau hukam hai guru manio granth*
> *guru granth ji manio pragat guran ki dehi*
> *jo prabhu ko milibo chahai khoj sabad main lehi*

> [When the timeless One gave the charge, the community came to be
> All Sikhs are ordered to own the Granth as their Guru
> Know the revered Guru Granth as the visible body the Gurus
> Those who want to meet Prabhu, they do so in the holy word]

Professor Harbans Singh commemorates Guru Gobind Singh's accomplishment, inaugurated by the First Sikh:

> This was a most significant development in the history of the community. The finality of the Holy Book was a fact rich in religious and social implications. The Guru Granth became Guru and received divine honours. It was owned as the medium of the revelation descended through the Gurus. It was for Sikhs the perpetual authority, spiritual as well as historical. They lived their religion in response to it. Through it, they were able to observe their faith more fully, more vividly. It was central to all that subsequently happened in Sikh life. It was the source of their verbal tradition and it shaped their intellectual and cultural environment. It moulded the Sikh concept of life. From it the community's ideals, institutions and rituals derived their meaning. Its role in ensuring the community's integration and permanence and in determining the course of its history has been crucial.[23]

The closeness between the First Sikh and his volume described by Bhai Gurdas and the Janamsakhis foreshadows the ultimate equation between the Guru and the sacred text made by the Tenth. It marks the fulfilment and culmination of the assignment given to the First Sikh by his divine Patron. The scriptural Guru constitutes the core of Sikh ethics, philosophy and aesthetics, and presides at all public and private ceremonies, rituals and worship. Most Sikhs aspire to have a room in their house to enshrine the GGS. At home or in formal places of worship (gurdwaras),[24] the GGS is draped in silks and brocades. Each morning it is ceremonially installed (*prakash*) and closed at night for rest (*sukhasan*). A canopy hangs above it, and when the volume is open, a person holding a whisk attends to it, a cultural marker of respect. Devout Sikhs open the GGS at random and read (or hear) the passage on the top left of the page as their personal message for the day from the divine One. At Sikh weddings, no vows or rings are exchanged, nor anything legal recorded; the bride and groom circumambulate the GGS four times, and after each circle they simultaneously touch their foreheads to the ground in front of the holy book as their acceptance of and commitment to each other. For their children, families choose a name beginning with the first letter from the page that the GGS fortuitously opens at. For special occasions, an unbroken reading (*akhand path*) is organized.[25] The primary devotional practice of the religion is *kirtan*, the singing of scriptural hymns. From rural Punjab to metropolitan centres around the world, Sikh celebrations include processions with colourful floats displaying the GGS. The sacred volume has acquired the status of a juristic person, accorded even by the Supreme Court of India.[26] It is the sovereign who presides at all Sikh ceremonies, rituals and rites of passage. The centrality of the holy volume in Sikhism is a unique phenomenon in the history of religion. Conceived in the mystical experience of Guru Nanak, it gestated in the spiritual matrix of the next four Gurus, was delivered by Guru Arjan in 1604, cradled in the newly built Harmandir, and appointed as the Guru for perpetuity in 1708. Sikh scripture is calligraphed in the First Sikh's spirituality; he is the defining figure of Sikh personal and corporate life.

The First Sikh's Consciousness of His Firstness: Guru and Guruship

Equally important was his appointment of Guru Angad as his successor. Vividly described in the GGS, it is celebrated in the ballads of Bhai Gurdas and later Sikh sources. Mindful of his new existential modality, the First Sikh installed Guru Angad and ensured a new leadership for his community. Guru Angad was made the Second Guru with the intention to carry on and 'crystallize his teachings and his followers into a formal structure'. I would therefore disagree with W.C. Smith's claim that 'Nanak could well have lived the life he did and preached the message that he preached, with yet nothing for us to call Sikhism emerging in Indian history, if later generations had not produced an Arjun to crystallize his teaching and his followers into a formal structure . . .'[27] The First Sikh was fully conscious of his new message and praxis, and therefore, I argue, he started an infrastructure that would provide momentum for later generations. The Sikh community came to be because of the visionary *first* Sikh. It was *his* aspiration to safeguard his revelation for future generations. He is unequivocally the founder of the Sikh religion, and his successors were essential in building upon the foundations set up by him.

In their compositions, Satta and Balavand describe the succession of guruship. These two grandsons of Bhai Mardana were bards at the Sikh court. They begin with praise for Guru Nanak as the originator of a spiritual 'empire' (*raj*), a builder of a 'true' (*sach*) 'fort' (*kot*) with strong foundations:

> Nanak established his empire—
>> Building his true fort on firm foundations
> He placed the canopy on Lahina's head
>> As he praised the Divine, sipped ambrosia
> He handed the strong sword made from
>> The instruction of spiritual wisdom.
> The Guru bowed to his disciple during his own lifetime
> He put the *tikka* while still alive.
> Now Lahina succeeded Nanak
>> —He deserved it so
> It was the same light, it was the same manner
>> It was the body that was changed.
> The immaculate canopy waves over him
>> He has occupied the throne in the Guru's trade . . .
>> GGS: 966–67

In political syntax and royal tropes, Satta and Balvand depict Guru Nanak as the inaugural leader who appoints his disciple as his successor during his own lifetime. The transference to the Second Guru is vividly choreographed: Guru Nanak places the canopy (the cultural marker of honour) on his successor's head, he puts the tikka (ceremonial mark, another cultural trope for respect) on his forehead, and he bows respectfully to him. Guru Nanak performs these acts in the accompaniment of Divine praise and drinking of ambrosial amrit—something he had done during his own revelatory experience. As noted above, Guru Nanak also passes the strong sword (*kharag jor*) to Guru Angad, a symbolic representation of the 'instruction of spiritual wisdom' (*mat gur atam dev di*). Interestingly, one of the five symbols given by the Tenth Guru to his Sikhs is the sword. In consonance with Bhai Gurdas and the Janamsakhis, this scriptural passage confirms that Guru Nanak made Lahina more than his successor: he made him equal with himself. Poetic statements from Bhai Gurdas and the GGS marvel as the First Guru is physically, intellectually and spiritually absorbed into the Second.

Bhai Gurdas narrates the succession of the Second Guru with his own artistic talent:

> He promulgated in the world the authority of the Divine Order
>> And created a community purged of the pollution of selfish ego
> While still in this world he installed Lahina as his successor
>> And bestowed upon him the umbrella of Guruship
> Kindling another light with his light Guru Nanak changed his form
> None can describe the marvellous deed of the marvellous one
> He changed his body into that of Angad, who reflected his own light
>> Bhai Gurdas, Var I: 45

Self-conscious about his mission, Guru Nanak at the close of his life installs his successor. Not opting for either of his two sons, his devout follower Lahina is made Angad. The First Sikh absorbs Lahina into his own person and renames him Angad, literally, a limb of his body. Light passed on from Guru Nanak to Lahina is like one flame kindling another (*joti jot milai kai*). Bhai Gurdas then goes on to narrate that Angad (Nanak 2) left Kartarpur and retired to the town of Khadur where he passed the light he had received from Guru Nanak to Amar Das (Nanak 3) who then raised the town of Goindval (Var I: 46). Our primary Sikh historian and theologian validates the scriptural portrait of Guru Nanak as the intersection between a historical person and a timeless reality.

The transition of Guruship started by the First was repeated successively by his nine successor gurus. Each of the Ten historical Sikh Gurus played a crucial role in the development and reinforcement of Guru Nanak's ideology and practice. The content of their instruction was the same One, the poetic method they utilized was also similar.

The same voice spoke though the Ten. They personified the same light. They held the same vision. They clearly perceived Guru Nanak's legacy as a new way of experiencing the divine One. To signal their corporeal and spiritual continuation, the Guru authors of the GGS signed their compositions with the name 'Nanak'. Nevertheless, the authorship in the GGS is clearly distinguished with the use of the word 'Mahala' and a numeral for identification. It is 'Mahala 1' if the composition belongs to the First Guru, 'Mahala 2' if it is by the Second Guru, and so on. The word 'Mahala' could mean either 'woman', implying the Guru is the spouse of the Divine, or 'palace', implying that the sacred word lives in the guru. Each Guru valued and nurtured the literary inheritance from his predecessor, and adding his own compositions to the collection on the very model set up by Guru Nanak, he would pass on the poetic legacy to the next. The Tenth ended the line of personal Gurus by passing on the succession of Guruship to the scriptural volume. The identity of the book and the guru concretized Nanak's spiritual legacy for all time. According to Professor Harbans Singh, the presence of Guru Nanak for his successor Gurus 'was a constant reality, an inspiration and the norm in the exercise of their spiritual office . . . in both utterance and deed later Gurus, Nanaks themselves as the followers believe, were acting out the inspiration mediated to them from Guru Nanak'.[28]

The First Sikh's way of life, with its stress on the divine Name, became the paradigmatic mode of existence for his followers. Family and home are lauded; asceticism and otherworldly orientation are spurned. A new community with its unique vision and practices is born. Bhai Gurdas's entire focus is on the new religion. His ballads open in a celebratory spirit:

Greetings to the Guru who resounded the mantra of the True Name . . .
All who have come to the Guru's feet
    Receive the True Word, they are liberated
They have given themselves to loving devotion
    To celebrating the Guru's festival,
        To cherishing the divine Name, and to charity and ablution . . .
                                              Bhai Gurdas, Var I: 1

A group of followers becomes attached, literally, to the feet of Guru Nanak—'*caran gahe gurdev de.*' Once the seekers claim him as their Guru, they are imparted the True Word (*sat sabad*). A definite starting point can be discerned here. The disciples begin to seek the Guru, and the Guru gives them the Word. The followers become imbued in loving devotion, and they begin to celebrate the Guru's festival. The term '*gurpurab*' is ambiguous, for it literally means 'day of the guru', and so it could denote the Guru's birthday or death anniversary or any other important event pertaining to his life. The overall import, however, is quite clear: for his followers, Guru Nanak begins to mark their history. In Var I: 23 Bhai Gurdas uses the term '*ulta khel*' (opposite play) to convey the revolution brought about by the First Sikh: 'The four castes are turned into the same one—*cari varan ikk varan karaia*;' 'The rich and the poor become equal—*raja rank barabari.*' The age-old division of Indian society into the four castes is done away with. Yet again 'Ganga is made to flow in the opposite direction—*ulti ganga vahaion*' (I: 38) poetically replays the revolutionary spirit unleashed by the First Sikh. His way of life with its stress on the divine Name, generosity and routine of cleanliness (inner and outer) becomes the paradigmatic mode of existence for his followers. A new pattern starting with Guru Nanak is unambiguously identified.

In Canto I: 38 Bhai Gurdas offers a valuable snapshot of the daily customs of the earliest community of Sikh men and women. The place is Kartarpur. The Guru has returned from his travels. He has taken up his regular routine. He has installed Angad to Guruship. The scene overflows with his visual and aural magnificence:

> From his lips flows the holy verse that
> > Turns darkness into light
> Spiritual discourses flow
> > Unstruck holy verse resonates
> They sing Sodar and Arati
> > And Jap in the ambrosial hour
> The gurmukhs are free from the burden of the Atharva Veda
>
> Bhai Gurdas, Var I: 38

Guru Nanak utters the holy verse and darkness disappears. Light with its varied energies—creation and sustenance, knowledge and elucidation, radiance and beauty, ultimate joy and liberation—fills the air. The Guru's verse has become the sole devotional and ethical avenue for the nascent community. To this day, Sikh homes and their formal places of worship maintain the routine of reciting the Jap hymn in the morning, and the Sodar and Arati hymns in the evening. With these hymns as a part of their daily liturgy, Bhai Gurdas astutely notes that Guru Nanak's followers are liberated from the heavy weight of the Atharva Veda (*gurmukhi bhar atharbani tara*). The Atharva Veda is a metonymic marker for the traditional Indic ritual prescriptions and burdensome duties scheduled for different castes and genders. With the advent of the First Sikh, customary texts and practices and rituals are gone; the community adopts his liberating new egalitarian message.

The First Sikh steers his people away from traditional cultural rites. His 'Alahnian' hymn is a striking example. Traditionally, dirges were sung by a chorus of women eulogizing a dead person as a part of the mourning custom. The group of women would gather at the house of the dead person for several days, and wail beating their breasts and thighs (a custom that lasted till quite recent times in the Punjab). Guru Nanak shifts the entire scenario. Movingly utilizing the folk genre, he exhorts people to come together—to mourn the emotional separation from the Divine, not physical death; to remember the Divine, not the dead person; to rejoice in the splendour of this world and not lament any loss. An authentic death, he claims, is the union between the individual and the Divine; it is a life lived in the transcendent palace, revelling in radiant colours forever. But an inauthentic death follows a life of oblivion to the Divine and to the wondrous magic of human existence. Such a dead mode of existence only brings individuals back into the womb, spinning them into the cycle of life and death. Guru Nanak makes readers squarely confront death and helps them overcome the much-feared phenomenon: 'Death would not have a bad name if only people knew what death is' (repeated in the 'Alahnian' hymn, GGS: 579). Praising the Guru's new and heroic impulse, Professor Harbans Singh writes:

Such language was unique in an age dominated by timidity and apprehensiveness. Death was not to be regarded as the unspeakable dread that crippled every moment of life, but the portal by which men entered a new realm of God's wisdom and love.[29]

The First Sikh's verse is the vital ingredient that feeds Sikh identity. Sikh funeral rites end with his second successor's 'Anand', the hymn of bliss. Its opening stanza resounds, 'Jewel-like melodies with their families and fairies (*parian*) from afar have come to sing the holy word within.' From Bhai Gurdas to contemporary historians, Guru Nanak is treasured as the starting point of a new spiritual and ethical mode of being. The respected Sikh historian Dr J.S. Grewal compellingly states: 'Guru Nanak installed Angad as the Guru in his lifetime to carry forward the egalitarian Gurmukh Panth on the highway of the Name, Gurbani, congregational worship, and community meal.'[30]

In fact, the Second Guru, in Sikh scripture itself, attests to a new teaching initiated by the First. Guru Angad's short verse is part of the concluding stanza of Var Majh, very closely placed with Guru Nanak's depiction of his numinous encounter discussed earlier. Referring to Sikh men and women, Guru Angad says:

> They heard the teaching
>> They're absorbed in the praise of Truth
> Who could give them any more?
>> They received their teaching from Guru Nanak Dev

GGS: 150

As early as Guru Angad then, the community had absorbed the teachings Guru Nanak had set to spread. There is a consciousness of a new spiritual lifestyle promulgated by the First Sikh. Such historical references challenge scholarly presumptions about the secondary role of Guru Nanak. Guru Angad's verse discloses the profound impact Guru Nanak had on the very early Sikh community, so there has to be something religio-sociologically new about his teaching, and the way Guru Nanak shaped and systematized his institutions of seva, sangat, langar and guru. In light of such scriptural verses, how can we denounce the First Sikh as a 'founder' and claim 'had it not been for later generations, the Fifth Guru Arjan or the Tenth Guru Gobind Singh, we might never have heard of Guru Nanak'?[31] But W.C. Smith rightly reminds us that we cannot underestimate the role of Guru Arjan who 'congealed' the tradition. The Fifth Guru, who compiled the GGS, placed the Second Guru's observation just before the First Sikh's initiation by the Divine One and his resolve to resound the holy word widely. Here we find exact verification: What the First set to do in the future is already being accomplished by the time of his immediate successor. Guru Arjan's editorial enterprise but firmly confirms the First's firstness. The following analysis of 'sikh' shines more light on his firstness.

Sikh

Etymologically, the term is traced to the Sanskrit *shiksha* and *shishya*. But as Wittgenstein reminds us, the 'meaning of a word is its use in the language',[32] so we must go beyond the lexical meaning to grasp how the word 'sikh' functions in Guru Nanak's verse. The Guru uses it as a derivative of the Sanskrit shiksha—an abstract feminine noun, meaning teaching or learning. However, Guru Nanak also initiates its use as a verbal adjective (gerundive) going back to the Sanskrit shishya— someone to be taught, and so 'sikh' becomes a noun, meaning a student or learner. For example, he says, '*seve sikhu so khoj lahai*—the *sikh* who discovers is the one who serves' (GGS: 1328). The synergy between the 'teaching' and the 'learner' signifies 'sikh'.

We hear it for the first time in Guru Nanak's Japji, the inaugural hymn in the GGS:

> *Mat vichu rattan jawahar manik*
> *je ikk gur ki sikh suni*

> [Wisdom shines with jewels, rubies, and pearls
>   If we hear one teaching from the guru]

Japji, Stanza 6

Here we find a nuanced definition of 'sikh' forming the very matrix of Guru Nanak's metaphysics, epistemology, ethics, aesthetics and soteriology. It is reiterated in the 'Prabhati', the final GGS raga: 'The guru's teaching is full of jewels and pearls; seekers (sikh) find it, they serve the guru' (GGS: 1328). Paradoxically, his short verse opens up several vital dimensions of thought and praxis that identify Sikh and Sikhs.

A feminine noun, 'sikh suni' is a teaching that is heard. Therefore, what is critical is its sonorous dynamic (*suni*). 'Hearing' actually is a part of Guru Nanak's triple maxim, *sunia, mania, mani kita bhau*, and we will think through them individually. Literary philosopher Hans-Georg Gadamer underscores the importance of 'hearing': 'Whereas all the other senses have no immediate share in the universality of the verbal experience of the world, but only offer the key to their own specific fields, hearing is an avenue to the whole because it is able to listen to the logos.'[33] Hearing opens us up to the profound dimension of language and puts us in touch with our past, for it is through hearing that we absorb our tradition and belong to history. So forceful is this sensibility that we have no control over it: we turn away from seeing something by looking in another direction, but we cannot 'hear away', says Gadamer. Ancient Indian philosophers knew this well! *Shruti* (what is heard) is their body of revealed literature, the sacred, unalterable Vedic canon. What is heard (shruti) is different from *smriti* (what is remembered), which therefore is uncanonical literature, susceptible to change. Orality is regarded as the dominant mode of transmission; the Vedic seers heard the revealed knowledge and it was passed down the generations by the priests who recited them and the worshippers who heard them.[34]

Guru Nanak would have known the importance of hearing from his rich Indic past. However, there is a major difference in the process he espouses: whereas shruti is a set of fixed Vedic corpus transmitted orally across generations, sunia for Nanak is a universal human faculty open to each person and each generation. Instead of the specific texts heard once upon a time, the First Sikh emphasizes the ongoing activity of hear-*ing*. There is no stress on the exactness of pronunciation and recitation as mandated by a shruti text; rather, the First Sikh stresses the sensuous expansion of the individual, as each person hears it in their own distinctive way. The Guru even implores his somatic self to hear the teaching, '*Hau tudhu akha meri kaia tun sun sikh hamari*—listen, my body, I am telling you, hear the teaching' (GGS: 155). His successors build up on the First Guru's practical orientation and urge that the teaching be received in a direct, sensory and corporeal manner. 'Sikhs hear with ears the instruction given by the true guru,' says his successor (Nanak 4, GGS: 314). Men and women are admired for their sensory acuteness: 'Blessed, blessed are the guru's Sikhs for they hear with their ears the guru's divine instruction' (Nanak 4, GGS: 590). Clearly, Guru Nanak gives agency to the men and women around him: they hear the teaching themselves with their own two ears. The role of an intermediary—Brahmin or mullah or Nath master—is done away with. Something radically new is brought into practice by the First Sikh.

What is heard is the universal '*anahad*'. Guru Nanak appropriates this Sanskrit term, meaning 'soundless sound' or 'unstruck' self-producing sound, and correlates it with the transcendent Word (anahad sabad, GGS: 237). Thus it appears across the GGS, as Verse (anahad bani, GGS: 231), as Melody (anahad *dhun* GGS: 236), as Music (anahad *vaje*, GGS: 578) as Drum (*mridang* anahad, GGS: 1271), as the ancient instrument of the Veena (anahad *beena*, GGS: 767). According to the Guru, from the very beginning of time, this transcendent sound vibrates through our entire multiverse: 'from primal time the unstruck melody beats night and day in each and every heart . . .—*ad jugad anahad andin ghat ghat . . .*' (GGS: 1020). The 'soundless sound' or the 'unstruck sound' (anahad) is the subtle self-producing sound, vibrating the blissful melody in the multiverse, chiming again perfectly with the Guru, and with the Guru's pure holy word, which is but the Name, the revelation of the transcendent One. These sonorous synonyms share a fundamental similarity in that they are present in every body (*dehi*); they vibrate in each and every heart (*ghati ghati*).

In their collaborative work, *Sound and Communication: An Aesthetic Cultural History of Sanskrit Hinduism*, Annette Wilke and Oliver Moebus offer a comprehensive study of sound as primal and existing prior to matter.[35] They provide a valuable historical development: 'In many forms pure Nad became an aesthetic and soteriologically powerful awareness—transforming reality, all the way to the Guru Granth, the holy book of the Sikhs.'[36] I wish Wilke and Moebus had applied their sonic expertise to the Sikh holy book; nevertheless, their discussion of the unicity of sound helps us understand its philosophical appeal for Guru Nanak. Since sound always retains its unity, the unstruck sound serves as an aesthetic attribute of the transcendent One.

How is it heard? The First Sikh gives no analogues to the numerous Indic sonic techniques authors Wilke and Moebus elaborately discuss. Nowhere in Guru Nanak's works do we find any stipulation for the performative reciting and hearing of Vedic mantras. There is no visualization of divine deities such as 'the great benevolent god' 'said to be the embodiment of Nada'. There is no 'strict meditation of the Yogis and their inner sounds whose range only includes booming, thundering or rushing . . . only for people who exercise the greatest effort in order to achieve deliverance'.[37] There is no perception of a Kundalini snake coiled in the body, nor any attempt to raise its serpentine energy up the body's channels (*nadi*) and Yogic chakras, which was the religious practice among many of Guru Nanak's contemporaries. If anything, he dismantles all such prescriptions.

For the First Sikh the sensibility of hearing is patient and attentive listening. It requires self-cultivation. To hear the primal soundless sound pulsating all over, we have to be in balance and equipoise, back to our original naturally still and effortless state (*sahaj*). With tantric antecedents, 'sahaj' practices were popular amongst Nath yogis, Vaishnava Sahajiyas, and Indian Buddhist Sahajyanis, both Indian and Tibetan. Guru Nanak's usage draws upon the term etymologically. The compound *sah* (together) and *ja* (born) denotes 'born together', therefore 'sahaj' in Guru Nanak's vocabulary refers to the original, natural state—the state of oneness which we are essentially born with. Sahaj is the feeling of serenity, when there is no hostility, anger, resentment, craving or anxiety. In this quiet serenity all restlessness has been arrested. But caught in the dualities of I–me (*haumai*), we run around chasing our selfish goals, completely deaf to our real self. Only by freeing ourselves from egoistic and illusionary dualisms can we open ourselves to hear the soundless sound. For Guru Nanak, we get to this stage not by sitting in any specific posture or putting the body through any rigorous techniques, nor by intellectual debates or mantra recitations, nor by fasting or ritual actions, nor going on pilgrimages or such actions; rather, we live our ordinary life, doing our everyday actions, constantly tuned into the One—the soundless sound, the unstruck melody. It is living an active life in rhythm with the universal primal soundless sound, it is being a harmonious wholistic self while engaged in various facets of daily life.

Stanzas 8–11 of the Japji explain the process. Such hearing leads to the faculties of all the gods—one gains knowledge of all the continents, one acquires the import of all the ancient texts, one learns all the techniques of meditation, one masters the experience of all the sages of Hinduism and Islam (and by implication all religions), and through listening, all suffering and anxiety are annulled. So forceful and tactile is this sensibility that 'by hearing, hands can fetch and clasp the unplumbed reality—*sunieh hath hovai asgah*' (Japji stanza 11)! The teaching heard is most comprehensive, at once physical, spiritual, historical, scriptural, disciplinary. Transcending all borders and boundaries, it propels the mind towards an all-inclusive realization of the infinite Reality. Hearing connects the conscious with the unconscious, the exterior with the interior, and the learners—his Sikhs—were to refine their sensibility so they would embrace not only the infinite knowledge of the multifarious Hindu and Muslim past but also the temporal countless vibrations of the multiverse constantly all around them. The goal: to hear day and night that timeless, soundless sound beat in each and every heart (*ghat ghat*).

'Hearing' (*sunia*) in his threefold maxim is followed by 'embracing' (*mania*) the holy word, and this sequence is maintained by the First Sikh in his Japji hymn as the four stanzas on 'embracing' come right after the four on 'hearing.' Like many other Nanakian terms mania (from *mann*, mind or heart) is a multivalent term, endowed with endless semantic potential. It connotes trust, faith, receiving, keeping in mind, remembering, accepting, following, embracing. The Guru admits:

No words can say what's to embrace[38]
Attempts to explain are later regretted
No paper, pen, or scribe can describe it
Nor any philosophizing help to realize it

Japji, Stanza 12

Despite its utter ineffability, he devotes four passages to mania (Japji 12–15). It is by 'embracing' that our mind and intellect awaken, we become cognizant of knowledge beyond what we see and hear, and the more knowledge we gain, the more our mental attitude changes, the more open we grow, the more confidence we gain, and the more virtuous we become in our existential dealings:

> Embracing we walk on a clear path
> Embracing we advance in honor and glory
> Embracing we do not stray down lanes and byways
> Embracing we are bonded with righteousness.
>
> Japji, Stanza 14

The climax of Guru Nanak's maxim is a heart beating with love (*sunia mania mann kita bhau*). This state goes beyond hearing and embracing the teaching; it is being in love with the knowledge of the infinite One. Indeed, love is passionate; love is transformative. It takes lovers to the depths of richness and fullness where there is freedom from all kinds of limitations of the self. Again, the Guru stipulates no particular way: 'Countless are the ways of meditation and countless the avenues of love,' he says in his Japji. This love 'comes with the knowledge of the infinite One' (GGS: 61). Hence, love and knowledge, emotion and cognition, are intrinsically connected, and even the same term mann is used for both 'heart' and 'mind'.

The First Sikh consistently applauds love as the supreme virtue:

> Those who hear, embrace, and nurture love in their hearts,
> They cleanse themselves by bathing at the sacred fount deep inside
>
> GGS: 4

The result is aesthetically powered: '*Mat vichu rattan jawahar manik*—wisdom shines with jewels, rubies, and pearls.' Precious material objects sparkling in the mind evoke enormous joy. This knowledge doesn't imply any distant eternity akin to Plato's ideal forms or of some theoretical formulations, but of intense beauty and wealth belonging to this very multiverse of ours. In another verse, Guru Nanak maps out the daily temporal rhythms of such people: 'Gursikh piare dinasu rati—these sikhs are loved by the guru day and night' (GGS: 1170). The intrinsic emotion of love is reciprocal, and his successors repeatedly note how 'the faces of the Sikhs radiate— gursikha ke mukh ujale' (GGS: 590); 'The faces of the Sikhs glow because of the beloved Divine—gurskiha ke muh ujale kare hari piara' (GGS: 308). So intense is their love that it displays somatically. They realize the non-dualized One, and in turn are loved by the divine Beloved. There is no Cartesian mind–body split; learning gives Sikhs a wholistic experience at once interior and exterior, sacred and secular, cognitive and sensuous. Sheer bliss and total freedom becomes their mode of existence in this life and beyond for they merge into the infinite One Itself. Those who live out the teaching are Sikhs.

In his Japji Guru Nanak says, 'Sunieh sat santokh vichar—by hearing we gain truth (sat), contentment (santokh), and reflection (vichar),' and I believe at some level the Fifth Guru compiled the canon to concretize this very Nanakian ideal. In his finale (mundavani) to the Guru Granth Sahib we hear Guru Arjan's rationale:

> Thal vichu tinu vastu paio
> sat santokh vichar…
> je ko khavai je ko bhuncai
> tis ka hoe udharo
>
> [In the platter lie three things:
> Truth, contentment, reflection . . .
> Those who eat, those who savor
> They are liberated]

GGS: 1429

The Fifth Guru conjoins the sense of hearing with that of tasting, so the sacred volume is a thal (large metal dish) which holds the food of truth (sat), contentment (santokh), and reflection (vichar). These three dishes made up of epistemological ingredients are not intellectually conceived or logically argued; rather, they are swallowed and digested by the body in the company of others. Just like any hearing makes its way from the outside into the inner self, so does everything we eat. The sonorous and the sapiential ingredients feed the psyche. Conceptual knowledge of the Absolute (sat) flows in two directions: coming inwards, it gathers joy and contentment for the individual (santokh, from the Sanskrit *sam/* together, and *tush/*happy or content), and it spreads out towards others (*vichar* from the Sanskrit *vi/*out or spread, and *char/*go). The personally fulfilling quality of Being is reflected upon—thought through—in the company of others. The First Sikh's successor carries the First's momentum forward: sonorous and sapiential elements received from the scriptural platter would bring knowledge that would nourish the individual and unite them with fellow companions.

As we have been observing all along, the First Sikh has a whole new role for the guru who imparts the teaching. Rather than a particular figure or a sacred book or a mantra as such, the guru is a vital mechanism that brings the ever-present Being into consciousness, an awakening to the forgotten dimension of the singular Reality. Speaking in the cultural idiom of his milieu, Guru Nanak opens up a wide horizon of instructors: '*Gur isar gur gorakh barmah gur parbati mai*—the guru is Shiva, guru is Vishnu, guru is Brahma; the guru is Parvati, Laxmi and Sarasvati' (Japji, Stanza 5).[39] Earlier, he said, 'Through the guru comes the mystic sound *nada.*' Clearly, 'guru' is not confined to any one master, deity or gender; the realm of knowledge is no longer confined to Goddess Sarasvati. Traditionally, the iconic goddess with her veena in one hand and the Veda in the other represents knowledge inclusive of sound and word, music and language. Along with and besides goddess Sarasvati, the First Sikh appoints goddesses Parvati and Laxmi—the quintessential Hindu models of fertility and wealth. These are equally the instructors of knowledge and enlightenment. Guru Nanak's perspective on teaching is again very expansive, for genuine recognition can come through any medium—teacher, divinity, text, temple or refuge—as long as it elucidates the divine One, the common denominator. In another scriptural verse, he explicitly says, '*Sikh mat sabh buddh tumhari mandir chhava tere*—all (*sabh*) teaching *(sikh)*, wisdom *(mat)*, discrimination (*buddh*) belong to You (*tumhari)*, Yours (*tere*) are the temples (*mandir*) and places of refuge (*chhava*, literally shade)' (GGS: 795).

What the guru imparts, then, is awareness of the divine One. The non-dualistic One (ikk) is at the heart of the stylistically epigrammatic Nanakian verse *ikk gur ki sikh suni*. Dispensing with conjunctions and prepositions, the First Sikh's statement opens up exciting possibilities, and somehow endows each of these tiny words with an endless semantic potential. Fusing into one another, they become synonyms. Initially, I was faced with my translator's anxiety: Does the ikk refer to the guru? Or does it refer to the teaching? His compact literary artistry spells out that the One (ikk) is the teaching, the One (ikk) is the guru, and the One (ikk) is the mechanism—the sense for hearing, common to all living beings. 'There is the One alone without any second,' Guru Nanak repeatedly asserts. Sonic experts inform us that sound retains its unity even when separated, and therefore primal sound becomes the perfect metaphor for Guru Nanak's universal ikk (One). And we heard him take up the divine order: 'The songster will resound the holy word and spread it far.'

In Asa di Var he identifies his guru as the true guru (sat guru). This One has no gender, no material form. Yet, only after he 'meets' his true guru does Nanak begin to treasure the universal Sovereign of this multiverse. Ecstatically, he says:

> I joyously circle around the true guru
> Meeting the true guru made me treasure the One
> I learnt to line my eyes with knowledge
> And at once the whole universe was before my eyes

Asa di Var, 13

There is no difference between the true guru and the sovereign One. The true guru, therefore, is simply the channel that brings the timeless Sovereign into consciousness. That One was always there, is and will be forever. It is the recognition that makes us cherish the One, which too is a divine gift. Paradoxically, the Guru with his numinous epiphany circles joyously around his utterly transcendent sat guru! Eyes lined with the knowledge of the singular Sovereign see and treasure total unicity. Dualities and divisions disappear. In every face the imprint of the divine One is seen. In all the sounds of the world, all the languages used by the various species, in all the heartbeats, the vibrations of that soundless sound are heard. The First Sikh says over again, '*Guran ikk deh bujhai sabhna jia ka ikk data so mai visar na jai*—the guru gave me one realization, all beings have the same One creator, may I never forget' (final verses of Japji Stanzas 5 and 6). This is the teaching (sikh*)* the First Sikh received, and he installed Lahina as his successor with his verse in the new script precisely to safeguard it. The guru is the spiritual guide to inspire us to imbibe the universal One; the guru is the inspiration itself. Says Guru Nanak '*Bhule sikh guru samjhae*—the guru gives insight to the lost sikhs' (GGS: 1032).

Bhai Gurdas celebrates Guru Nanak as a unique communicator—*Jis mantra sunaia* (the one who brought forth the 'mantra'). Grammatically, the verb 'to hear' is put in the causative form, 'He made us hear' (*sunaia*). The Divine Name is transmitted by Guru Nanak through the primal sense of hearing, so it could reach the innermost being of his people. His mantra has no bearing on any previously existing traditions. Without being esoteric or secretive, the mantra is simply the timeless True Name (Sat Nam). Guru Nanak's epiphany of the Divine, encapsulated in the Mul Mantra (the root mantra), begins with 'Ikk Oan Kar, Sat Nam'. As the preamble to his Japji, it forms the opening of the GGS, the starting point of the Sikh tradition launched by the First Sikh. Disclosed to all, this core formula asserts a singular, genderless, timeless and spaceless Reality. The numeral One at the outset proclaims the existence and the unicity of the ultimate Reality. Space and time do not limit It in any way. It has no colour, it has no form. Nobody gave birth to it. Nobody brought it into existence. It has no fear. It has no enmity. Guru Nanak's Mantra of Sat Nam is full of negations that characterize the absolute, unconditioned self-existing nature of Reality (Sat). It does not belong to any existing contexts; it does not hold on to any existing form of god or goddess; it does not claim inheritance to any established Hindu or Islamic or Buddhist or Jain precept or concept. Bhai Gurdas does not cast Guru Nanak in any historic lineage or mould. He is not seen as the disciple of any ancient or medieval saint. Nor is Guru Nanak perceived as an incarnation of any god or goddess, or of any angelic figure. Autonomous and independent, the First Sikh is esteemed as the momentous Bringer of an aural gift that frees people from burdensome prescriptions, definitions and accents from the past. Those who absorbed his teachings, the Sikhs, were free to hear the soundless sound in their profoundly sensuous way.

The condensed 'self-existing, gift of the guru—*saibhan* (self-existent) *gur prasad* (gift of the Guru)' concludes Guru Nanak's Mul Mantra. The finale returns to the opening, the ever presence of the infinite One, and as it recapitulates the suis generis attributes, it thrusts the circle forward towards flesh and blood recipients. A nexus is established between the universal Being and those subjects who recognize it in their own particular historical, social and personal reality. Guru Nanak's usage of the term 'prasad' with its synonyms 'clearness' and 'gift' is meaningful: the self-existent is of course absolutely evident, but it is banished from memory; its disclosure therefore is a 'gift' from the Guru. The Guru is the epistemological medium that brings the ever present Being into consciousness so that life may be lived authentically here and now.

For me, it reinforces the role of the guru as a midwife. This Socratic analogy from *The Theaetetus* works out well in the Nanakian context, especially because of its corporeal dimension. Each individual is pregnant with the knowledge of the timeless, self-existing Creator. But we live obliviously, walled in by our selfish dualistic ways. Like the midwife who brings new life into the world, the guru brings us new awareness. The gift of the First Sikh was the new identity he birthed from the body of the transcendent One: his Sikhs were to palpably recognize the universal One, going way back to the beginning of time. The joy of the First Sikh's revelatory experience echoes through the body of the Guru Granth Sahib and bounces back in the lives of the Sikhs: 'The guru's sikhs in love tightly hug the guru—*gursikh parit gur milai gallate*' (GGS: 164). His gift to his Sikhs is liberating, it is enchanting, it is experienced here and now.

And, importantly, the First Sikh oriented his sikh towards *others*. The First Sikh did not retire into isolation away from society for his own spiritual benefit. He travelled to various religious sites, he discoursed with people of various faiths, he married, he had children, and he installed a successor for his community to nurture the collective spirit and reinforce social commitment amongst his people. Like him, his learners were not to opt for an isolated or ascetic lifestyle. Aligned with knowledge of the universal One, without divisions and hierarchies, they were to be responsible members of society and work for the collective welfare. In his own words from the Japji, '*Manai tarai tare gur sikh*—the guru's sikh embraces the One, attains liberation, and frees others along' (Japji 14). The First Sikh's religiosity has a congregational setting. That expansive, sparkling wisdom has no space for narrow, self-centred attitudes, and Sikhs were to live ethically in harmony with one another. Guru Nanak set up the institutions of sangat (congregation), seva (selfless labour) and langar (community meal) to foster the spirit of communitas.

Seva is voluntary manual labour in the service of the community. Seva means a deed of love and selfless service for fellow human beings. It is presented as the highest ideal. By doing seva one cultivates humility. By doing seva one overcomes the obsession with the egotistic self and extends beyond individuality. Seva is an essential condition of spiritual discipline. The First Sikh says, 'By practicing deeds of humble and devoted service alone does one earn a seat in the next world' (GGS: 26).

Langar, the community kitchen, asserts social equality and familyhood of humanity. This fundamental institution started by Guru Nanak involves the process of preparing meals together as well as eating together. The term denotes both the meal and the place where it is prepared and served. The food served at langar is vegetarian. Both men and women, irrespective of race, caste, and religion engage themselves in one task or another—chopping vegetables, kneading dough, rolling it out and fluffing it, cleaning utensils. And without any consideration of caste or rank, they sit in rows and partake of the meal. Don't we experience a togetherness with people we dine with? Thanksgiving and Christmas dinners, Seders and Id celebrations are shared with the people closest to us. Guru Nanak's establishment of langar is a fundamental step towards bonding humanity, regardless of the differences in race, gender, caste and class. As an instrument of social transformation langar continued to gain importance during the time of his successor Gurus. In Guru Angad's day, his wife, Mata Khivi, was compared with 'a thickly leafed tree' that provides shade for everyone, because she used to serve rich food in the langar. Guru Amar Das insisted visitors first enjoy the langar meal with others before meeting with him: 'First *pangat* [the row in which all sit together to partake of the langar meal] and then meeting with the Guru' (GGS: 967). Since the time of the First Sikh, preparing, eating together and serving langar is considered meritorious.

Sangat refers to a communal gathering. It is best understood as 'togetherness', a feeling of kinship with people we are with. It highlights three important elements. Firstly, the importance of the community. Rather than individuality and isolation, comradeship and company with others is prized. Guru Nanak thus paved the way for an active and fruitful engagement with community members, implying a full acceptance and celebration of this very world. Secondly, sangat (like langar) is open to all, therewith liberating men and women from social, religious and gender restrictions. In Sikh congregations, members sit on the floor as a statement of equality, and together sing hymns, listen to expositions of the holy text, and make supplications. Thirdly, sangats provide spiritual and moral inspiration. 'Through sangat, one obtains the treasure of the Divine Name . . . Just as iron rubbed against the philosopher's stone turns into gold, so does dark ignorance transform into brilliant light in company of the good,' said Guru Nanak (GGS: 1244). Participation with others is a catalyst for moral and spiritual growth.

These institutions were instrumental in living out the universal Reality envisioned by the First Sikh. Transcending divisions, hierarchies and supremacies, they affirm equality and inclusivity. Bhai Gurdas appropriately compares Guru Nanak's new faith to a needle that sews materials ripped asunder, bringing harmony to the torn and conflicting groups of Hindus and Muslims (Var 33: 4). Bhai Gurdas's diction, 'sharp as a razor' and 'fine as a hair', concretizes the value of the new way of life (Var 9: 2) which eliminates doubts and dualities and questions concerning what, why, where and when, and leads to the bliss of complete Oneness (Var 9: 11). He avails of numerous similes as an attempt to describe and explain something new and special, commencing with the individual experience of Guru Nanak. From those early times to this very day, Sikhs around the globe recite, reflect and live their life on his mantra of Sat Nam, and practise the democratic and emancipatory institutions inaugurated by their founder Guru.

In Raga Asa, Guru Nanak's own verbal camera zooms in on a community gathering:

Sikh sabha dikhia ka bhau
gurmukh sunana sacha nau
nanak akhanu vera ver
itu rangi nacau rakhi rakhi pair

[In the concert of sikhs, lovers of learning
Face the guru to hear the true Name
Nanak says this over and over
Let's dance in colours, our feet on the beat]

GGS: 350

I believe this is what the First Sikh imagined for the community he gave birth to, and his own words too relay its import: 'Nanak says this over and over.' Each time I enter a Sikh shrine or sit with the congregation, the above Nanakian image flashes forth. Sparkling jewels and rubies and pearls illuminate the space where Sikhs, the lovers of learning, gather! No dancing or clapping in this new concert of Sikhs, so the dance is Guru Nanak's metaphor for a poised balance of the physical and the spiritual self. With and among fellow beings, we hear the true Name, the beat of the primal sound. And we dance, that is, we *do* actions for the good of humanity by utilizing our human faculties—always in tune with the universal melody, the mind coloured by the beauty of the jewels, rubies and pearls within. The aesthetic enjoyment of hearing the teaching with fellow lovers of learning is no different from the soteriological goal of living colourfully and blissfully in *this* world midst our families, communities and our magical cosmos. So we lead a life of truth, contentment and reflection.

~

The First Sikh projected these 'powerful, pervasive, and long-lasting moods and motivations . . .' into the future, and today they form the very foundations of the Sikh religion. A Sikh is one who appropriates, interiorizes and lives by the First Sikh's teaching, an awakening to the common divine One, open to everybody, through various channels. What is incredible about the First Sikh is that he draws no boundaries, he makes no exclusivist claims—the absolute One is the common ground—and yet he splendidly triumphs in launching a distinct religious tradition remarkably vibrant centuries later in every corner of the world. The Sikhs have their own form of worship, their sacred space, their sacred text, their physical identity, their socio-religious institutions—all grounded in the legacy of the First Sikh. Guru Nanak indeed had to be a great artist to give birth to a unique and distinct Sikh religion which is 'set in the heart of the universal'. For the Nobel Laureate Rabindranath Tagore such accomplishment is 'Not through the peculiarity which is the discord of the unique but through the personality which is harmony.'[40] For sure Sikhism is not a monolithic, static, reified system; it is a 'cumulative tradition'; nevertheless, it is the consequence of the envisioning and doing of the First Sikh. The *firstness* of the First Sikh is critical for understanding the philosophy, ethics, institutions, scriptures and doctrines, and historical development of the dynamic and ever-accumulating religion of the Sikhs.

2

Janamsakhis: Remembering the First Sikh

The continuing reality of the First Sikh hinges on his historical memory, and though memories return to the past, they are vital to the making of the future. The Sikh community continues to be shaped and strengthened by Guru Nanak's memories. Elie Wiesel famously said, 'Without memory, there is no culture. Without memory, there would be no civilization, no society, no future.' The community birthed by the First Sikh started to share narratives (sakhis) of his birth and life (janam). This genre of the Janamsakhis has been very popular in the collective Sikh memory. The narratives are read and told by the young and the old alike, and many of them are also painted and brightly illustrated. Parents and grandparents read them as bedtime stories to young children. The Janamsakhis provide Sikhs with their first literary and visual introduction to their heritage, and they continue to nurture them for the rest of their lives.

Through the years, they have come down in a variety of renditions such as the Bala, Miharban, Adi and Puratan. Narratives from epics like the Ramayana and the Mahabharata have been popular for centuries on the Indian subcontinent. A mixture of mythology, history, philosophy and geography, these texts narrate events which actually happened, thus they are known in India as *itihasa* (the Sanskrit for 'history'). By the time the Janamsakhis came into circulation, miraculous stories (*mu'jizat*) about Prophet Muhammad and about Muslim saints (*karamat*) had also become widespread in the Punjab through Sufi orders. The Janamsakhi writers were influenced by what was current in their milieu, and they took up the pattern in which great spiritual figures were understood and remembered. Despite the personal loyalties and proclivities of their various authors, the Janamsakhis invariably underscore the importance and uniqueness of the First Sikh's birth and life. Some of the stories incorporate verses from his works to illuminate his theological and ethical teachings in a biographical framework. Written in the Gurmukhi script, they are the first works of prose in the Punjabi language.

The earliest expressions of Sikh art are actually pictorial representations of the Janamsakhis. Wherever sizeable and influential communities developed, the familiar stories were put in easily identifiable forms for them. These happened to be not only in religious centres in the Punjab like Amritsar, Anandpur, Damdama, but also Patna in Bihar where Guru Nanak's ninth successor, Guru Gobind Singh, was born, and Nanded in Maharashtra, where he breathed his last. Patrons from these centres commissioned local artists, and consequently numerous Janamsakhi renderings have come down from different regions and different periods. This wide dispersion makes the dating and exact place of production difficult for many of them. Nevertheless, it lends a fascinating variation. The First Guru is depicted in the Guler and Kangra styles of northern India, just as he is in the eastern Murshidabadi or southern Deccani styles. The artists who painted him were also Hindu, Muslim, Buddhist or Jain, and they presented the Sikh Guru through the lens of their respective religious beliefs. The stories they chose to paint depended upon their personal interest, and much was contingent on their individual talent.

The quantity of illustrations varies in the manuscripts. The first extant Janamsakhi is the Bala with twenty-nine illustrations dated to 1658 (owned by P.N. Kapoor of New Delhi). The next illustrated extant Janamsakhi collection has forty-two illustrations. It is dated to 1724, and it is held by Bhai Sikandar Singh of Bagharian in the Patiala district. The B-40 Janamsakhi (dated 1733) is considered to be very important because it has extensive historical documentation.[1] It has fifty-seven illustrations whereas some of the later versions have over a hundred. The quality varies too: some artists are preoccupied with the contents and hastily move the narrative forward, while others linger on subtle details to evoke aesthetic sentiments. The paintings from the Nainsukh family of artists are especially lauded for their refined work. The recent discovery of a creased sheet filled with thumbnail sketches of seventy-four events in Guru Nanak's life has proved the speculation that templates were used by different groups of painters and scribes to retell Guru Nanak's biography, for we find very similar depictions of particular scenes in manuscripts from geographically distant regions.[2] And so, in bright colours and dramatic sequences, they paint the parables, allegories and miraculous happenings and evoke lingering emotions. The Janamsakhi tradition continues as they are being retold by modern artists and writers.

In the language of myth and allegory, the Janamsakhis depict the divine dispensation of the First Sikh, his concern for kindness, social cohesiveness, and his stress on divine unity and the consequent unity of humanity. However, their mythic and allegorical dimension does not in any way reduce their importance for Sikh history. I follow Mircea Eliade's phenomenological perspective, and have all along analysed Janamsakhis as sacred history, which is 'true history', because myths always deal with *realities*.[3] Anthropologist Bronislav Malinowski describes myths as 'charters' of social norms, customs and beliefs. In her axiom, American poet and political activist Muriel Rukeyser said, 'The world is made up of stories not atoms.' Mythos leads to ethos; stories are the animating forces which give direction to our lives. They are, to use James Jarrett's term, the 'ur-phenomenon' which predates our categories of literature, science, philosophy, religion and dreams but from which these very distinguishable activities arise.[4] The founder Guru's mythic depictions not only reflect the core values of the Sikh tradition, but also shape and crystallize them for future generations. The Janamsakhis are a hidden treasure for the Academy as they provide useful clues into earlier scholarly debates about Sikh origins, and open up new directions for historical research.

For the most part, however, they have been neglected by scholars. The exception is Professor Hew McLeod's substantial study of the Janamsakhis,[5] and his translation of the historic B-40 Janamsakhi.[6] Both these are most valuable contributions. In a highly sophisticated typology, McLeod categorizes the narrative anecdotes into moralistic, chimeric fairy tales, devotional and aetiological legends.[7] What resonates most with me, a Sikh academic at an American liberal arts college, is the corporeal and pluralistic imaginary of the Janamsakhis. Their biological emphasis subverts the patriarchal preoccupation with the soul, death and the other world, and promotes a life and living here on Earth.[8] Likewise, pluralism is an essential paradigm for contemporary society assaulted by the forces of homogenization. We need to sew together diverse cultural, religious, linguistic, ethnic and biological relationships that are rapidly ripping apart. Whatever way we choose to categorize the various Janamsakhis, they unanimously celebrate the greatness of the First Sikh, and somehow through their focus on his biography they expand emotional and spiritual horizons that link us with fellow humans, species and the wider cosmos *here and now.*

This chapter explores the literary and visual Janamsakhi materials as they unfold and reinforce the First Sikh's image and message down the centuries. It is not a search for empirical certifications of his birth and life, rather, an attempt to understand and appreciate the events narrated by the storytellers and illustrators. Through their allegories and descriptions they present aspects of the First Sikh's personality that were meaningful to them, and by analysing them we get important insights into his identity formation, social relationships, moral attitudes and spiritual disposition. We will draw upon several Janamsakhi collections, the main ones being the Bagarian, the historic B-40, the Puratan and the Kapany collection.[9] I do avail myself sumptuously of the visuals because they literally illustrate the Guru's biography. The rudimentary accounts are amazingly refined; they generate 'long-lasting moods' and offer a multifaceted sensory richness of human existence. Questions that form the subtext of this chapter: What is the 'physical' depiction of the first Sikh and his biocultural rhythms in the Janamsakhis? The impact of his biographical events for Sikh identity formation and construction? The contemporary global relevance of the Guru's presence and engagement in a multiethnic, multireligious and multicultural medieval India?

Corporeal Metaphysics

That magic lies in temporal daily motions and emotions is the fundamental motif of the Janamsakhis. In this section we see it replayed in the Guru's corporeal representation and the rites of passage he goes through; we see it replayed in his rejection of actions he deems not quite natural. Conversely, the miracles we deem supernatural are disclosed by the First Sikh as attributes of daily life. Overall, then, the Janamsakhis form a very interesting archive, affirming each moment, all space, and every being around us.

In full validation of the human body, Janamsakhis portray the First Sikh in a normal way. He is not too tall, nor too large, and he does not occupy any more space than anybody else. I would disagree with scholarly observations that 'the area covered by Guru Nanak is always more than any other person'.[10] Rather than any exaggeration of external features and spacing, what spectacularly emerges is the Guru's inner power and spirituality. In the early illustrations he is not depicted with even a halo. Yet, the First Sikh's simple pose, whether standing, sitting or lying down, and his gentle gestures addressing people from various strata of society and personal orientation spell out his greatness. As we see robbers and demons and religious leaders bow before the First Sikh, we feel tremendous force exude from this sage-like reservoir of spiritual wisdom and personal peace. He fights no battles. He shows no anger. He is not dramatic. No matter what the setting may be, there is a perpetual calm and at-homeness in the world about him. Without making him look big or placing him apart or without a halo (which only appears in later Janamsakhis), we sense something profoundly wondrous about him. The narratives depict his growth from a baby to a little boy to a teenager to a dark-bearded youth into grey-bearded middle age, and subsequently to a full white-bearded elderly man (baba). Guru Nanak is firmly located in this temporal, historical world of ours. His physical growth is a sign of an organic and authentic mode of existence.

Birth

Many of the Janamsakhis zoom in on the illustrious advent of his birth to a Hindu Khatri couple. Guru Nanak's father, Kalyan Chand, worked as an accountant for the local Muslim landlord; his mother, Tripta, was a wise and perceptive person. In their central concern and luminous descriptions, the First Sikh's birth narratives have a great deal in common with those of Christ, the Buddha and Krishna (collected by Otto Rank in his study, *The Myth of the Birth of the Hero*).[11] The prophets told the Buddha's father, King Sudhodhan, that his child would be a great king or a great ascetic. The three Wise Men followed a bright star to honour the baby Jesus, born in a stable in Bethlehem. And just as that stable was lighted by the bright Star of Bethlehem, the humble mud hut in which Nanak was born was flooded with light at the moment of his birth. The gifted and wise, both in the celestial and terrestrial regions, rejoiced in the momentous event and bowed to the exalted spirit, which had adopted bodily vesture in fulfilment of the Divine Will.

But unlike the 'virgin' births of Sakyamuni and Jesus, Nanak has a normal birth. The midwife Daultan attests to Mother Tripta's regular pregnancy and birth. Mother Tripta's body entrusted to a Muslim Daultan symbolizes the respect and the close connection the First Sikh's family had with the adherents of Islam. The Janamsakhis show Mother Tripta happily holding the baby in her arms, while Daultan proudly and excitedly reports that there were many children born under her care, but none so extraordinary as baby Nanak. Affirmation of the natural powers of conception, gestation and birth underlie their rejoicing.

Rejection of 'Unnatural' Rites of Passage

Missing in the Janamsakhis are rituals such as *mundan* and circumcision commonly practiced in his society. In fact, we get an especially vivid picture of Nanak refusing to participate in the *upanyana* ceremony, reserved for upper-caste Brahmin, Kshatriya and Vaishya boys. Young Nanak disrupts this crucial rite of passage that had prevailed for centuries. His denial is framed within an elaborate setting arranged by his parents. A large number of relatives and friends are invited to their house. Pandit Hardyal, the revered family priest, officiates at the ceremonies. Pandit Hardyal is seated on a specially built platform purified by cow-dung plaster, and the boy Nanak is seated across, facing him. Pandit Hardyal lights up lamps, he lights up fragrant incense, he draws beautiful designs in flour chalk, and he recites melodious mantras. When the priest proceeds to invest the initiate with the sacred thread (*janaeu*), Nanak interrupts the ceremonies, questions him as to what he was doing with the yarn, and refuses to wear it. At this point, the narrative juxtaposes Nanak's criticism of the handspun thread to his ardent proposal for one that is emotionally and spiritually 'woven by the cotton of compassion, spun into the yarn of contentment, knotted by virtue, and twisted by truth', recorded in the GGS (p. 471). Contrary to being draped externally, the *janaeu* is an internal process. 'Such a thread,' continues Nanak, 'will neither snap nor soil, neither get burnt nor lost.' His biography and verse are thus blended together by the Janamsakhi authors to illustrate his rejection of an exclusive rite of passage antithetical to the natural growth of boys from all backgrounds alike. A young Nanak interrupts a smooth ceremony in front of a large gathering in his father's house so that his contemporaries would envision a different type of 'thread', a different ritual, a whole different ideal than the rebirth of upper-caste Hindu boys into the patriarchal world of knowledge. That everyone treat one another equally every day is the subtext. There are many such vignettes in which the First Sikh vividly dismantles the prevailing societal hegemonies of caste and class, and reinforces an egalitarian perspective on human growth.

Often, his denunciation of rites and rituals is disclosed in interesting ways. Sharp and witty, the Janamsakhis can be very effective. Coming across some Pandits offering waters to the rising sun, the Guru begins to sprinkle palmfuls of water in the westward direction. When asked about his contradictory act, he simply responds that he is watering his fields down the road. This tiny story raises a loaded question: Is taking care of crops and other honest work any less than feeding distant dead ancestors? He draws the attention of his contemporaries to matters of living a collective responsible moral life. Whatever the setting, he conveys the futility of rituals and highlights truthful living midst family and society on a daily basis.

Schooling

In lieu of the manifold life-cycle events current in medieval India (varying by caste and gender, and the timing of each ritual determined by astrological charts), the Janamsakhis emphasize a common routine sequence: the Guru's first day at school. In the Bagarian collection the little one is wrapped up cozily, carried by Father Kalu and accompanied by Mata Tripta. But most of the time he is depicted as a four- or five-year-old escorted only by Father Kalu. He holds a wooden board with a tiny handle, a metonymic marker that its holder would write up a new script, a new morality. His Pati Likhi acrostic flashes in our mind. The wooden board clutched by him in this very first illustration of the B-40 Janamsakhi would inscribe the First Sikh's semiotic reflex, and eventually concretize into the 1430-page Sikh scripture, the Guru Granth Sahib. The youngster's grip reveals the intrinsic bond between the timeless Sikh sacred text and Guru Nanak's corporeal matrices.

In the B-40 set of illustrations, young Nanak on his first day of school wears a yellow full-sleeved robe coming down to his ankles with an elegant reddish sash neatly tied around his waist, and a matching turban over his head. The *chooridar* (literally 'bracelet forming') trousers peep out from below his robe, as do his curly locks from the turban on either side of his face. It is a most endearing portrait. His formal dress and upright demeanour are markedly different from the rest of the kids who are meagerly dressed and romping around. The turban customarily donned by Mughal princes, Sufi saints and Rajput nobility imparts Nanak a maturity beyond his years. He confidently greets his moustached teacher dressed in the typical upper-caste Brahmin outfit of a pleated dhoti tucked around his waist with one end of it draping from his right shoulder down his bare chest. Caught at the liminal threshold between 'home' and 'society'—behind him stands his father and across sits his teacher on a pedestal with food and books—Nanak displays phenomenal dignity. Virginia Woolf aptly said, 'It is clothes that wear us and not we them.' Again, Guru Nanak's clothes may not be fancy in their fabric, but their design discloses his respect for his own body and elicits the same response from his viewers. Without giving him any supernatural qualities, the Janamsakhis tellingly portray his inner authority and self-assurance.

Growing Up

The Janamsakhis continue to offer a substantial sketch of the Guru's life. We see him growing up in his village, Talvandi. He is close to his sister, Nanaki, and has friends with whom he plays. But he also has a search for something more; there is a sense of discontent about him. He needs to figure things out. So the Guru leaves home to travel, and it is in the stories of his travel that one finds evidence of the greatness of the Guru, his tenderness. Particularly touching is his closeness with Nanaki and Tripta.

During his travels, the itinerant Nanak meets up with his parents, as narrates the B-40 Janamsakhi. He and his companion do not go home, because this second parting would have been much too painful for the family. When the mother comes over to see him, Nanak bows at his mother's feet. His humility and love pour out. How deep his bond with Mother Tripta! She in turn is flooded with tears. She kisses her son, exploding in boundless joy. Then 'witnessing his mother's love Baba is filled with grief—*tab mata ke het kari ke baba lagga bairag karan* (B-40).[12] Full of love and tenderness, the First Sikh breaks the masculine typology. The love from the mother and for the mother has to be a vital impulse in his profound passion for the Divine and his compassion for society. Mother imagery would later play significantly in the First Sikh's theological vision. The infinite Divine is *both* father and mother.

A delightful scene from the Kapany collection captures the meeting between the brother and sister in her married home (object no. 1998.58.24). Affection pours out as their arms reach to greet each other. In this equilateral triangular scene, the viewer moves briskly from the wide floral patterns along the rhythmic designs of the 60-degree interior-angled walls to the ever-narrowing distance between the siblings. The two face each other: Guru Nanak is with his companions, Hindu Bala and Muslim Mardana; Nanaki is with her female relative. The architectural backdrop and the physical setting of the protagonists reinforce the emotional union between the siblings. The divine nature of the Guru becomes ever so visible through such human encounters. In this way his verses recorded in Sikh scripture like 'Mori run jhun laia bhaine savan aia—peacocks have burst into melody, O sister, the monsoon has arrived' (GG: 557) are tangibly accessed. We can see the verbal embrace flowing from the Guru's deep unconscious, 'O sister' (*bhain*).

Wedding

The Janamsakhis continuously celebrate the unity of the sacred and the secular intrinsic to the First Sikh's religious worldview. They portray his infinite spirituality in his human body and temporal locus, and with great festivity depict him going through the wedding rite of passage with bride Sulakhni. The Kapany collection contains four colourful paintings. In entrancing pinks, yellows, oranges and golden-brown, they cover the major north Indian wedding ceremonies: the procession of the groom's party to the bride's home, their reception by the bride's family, the wedding nuptials and the departure of the bride with the groom from her natal home. In Guru Nanak's wedding procession (object no. 1998.58.8), the young groom with only a moustache (no beard yet!) is confidently riding a white horse. The miniscule detailing of designs on the horse heighten its ornamental vigour. The men walking beside the groom on horseback are all in a festive mood. Some blow trumpets, some play the drums, some light fireworks while others sparklers, and some dance excitedly. The groom in a golden-brown outfit is decked in an ornamental turban with a plume, and he has a halo. His marriage and divinity are not antithetical by any means. As the 'Lavan' hymn from the Guru Granth Sahib describes, marriage is a rite of passage into more and more intense cycles of existence. Though the procession is moving forward, several protagonists are turning back to see the groom, the centre of festivities. The closest to him, turning back, is perhaps Bhai Bala, attending to the needs of the groom-Guru. We also recognize the turbaned Jairam, the brother-in-law of the Guru (sister Nanaki's husband). In keeping with the traditional custom of the wedding party (*barat*), only males accompany the groom to the bride's house. No women are seen in the painting.

Next in the sequence a prenuptial moment is captured (object no. 1998.58.7), and once again only men are present. The young groom sits across a white-bearded gentleman in pink who is perhaps Bhai Chona, the father of bride Sulakhni. We see the priest in another frame (object no. 1998.58.9) where he is dressed in pink like Bhai Chona and also has a beard, but his chest is bare, and he wears a dhoti typical of a Brahmin priest. Face to face in object no. 1998.58.7, the bride's father (we think) and the groom each has his own attendant waving a fan, though the Guru's appears more fervent because of the way he stretches out and arches over him. Stylistically, the painting is extremely refined. The son-in-law and the father-in-law are greeting each other in an interior space made up with *qanats* (tent panels) under a bright red canopy. The bilateral symmetry of their reception extends to other members on each side, and it is rhythmically repeated beyond the enclosure into the garden reaching outside the main gate. The central carpet is made up of red and pink stripes that run diagonally across, and as these stripes strike the green hexagons with red circles on the yellow panels of the surrounding tent, they fill the air with tremendous joy. This space is ideal for the acoustical effect of trumpets, tablas, dholaks, rabab and cymbals of the enthusiastic performers. Between the enclosure and the outside gate is thick foliage from which emerge four elegant horses. Though we actually see only one rider, we get the impression that many more guests are arriving, and acoustically, the galloping sounds seem to merge with the musical melodies. The lively visual and aural tones amplify our anticipation for the wedding ceremony.

In the third wedding scene, we see the bride, Sulakhni, her name meaning 'beautiful' (object no. 1998.58.9). Sulakhni is not wearing any veil. Her eyes are open. Long and fish-shaped, they show her beauty, and they show her as an authentic observant. Sulakhni has a distinctive red scarf on her upper body, but the rest of her dress is golden-brown, just like her groom's outfit. As the couple sit together, their matching attires create a warm intimacy. Even the plume on her head ornament matches his. In the ears of a Sikh spectator echoes the scriptural verse: '*Dhan piru ehu na akhiani bahani ikkathe hoe ek joti dui murti dhan piru kahiai soi*—do not call them husband and wife who appear to sit together; one light in two bodies is called husband and wife' (GGS: 788). The artist touchingly relays the sharing of the spiritual light by the couple.

The finale in this sequence is the return of the husband with his newly wedded wife (object no. 1998.58.10). He is seated in the front, in between the charioteer steering the oxen and the carriage occupied by female passengers. Conventionally on the Indic horizon, the departure of the bride from her parental home is a sorrowful rite of passage (*doli*). But in this instance, the bright colours, the lively gestures of the protagonists, the bounce of the oxen and the bells around their necks, and the spirited horizontal momentum of the composition are all so delightful. The crimson of the carriage is picked up by the varied decorative motifs on the oxen and the shoes of the two men who lead the party—only to be complemented by their dazzling white outfits and the white of the oxen. Sulakhni is midst her companions: an older figure is beside her, and two young women sit across from her in relaxed poses. What is she experiencing as she makes her journey from her natal to her married home? What lies in front of her? What did she leave behind? What does she feel for her husband, the beloved Guru? We can't read her mind; we question, we wonder. This is what the Janamsakhi illustrations are about. Later, two sons were born to the couple.

Last Rites

The Janamsakhis also align the Guru's passing away with the bio-cosmic rhythm of life. As we discussed in the previous chapter, he conferred guruship to his disciple Lahina, making him Angad, a part of himself. The passage of his physical and spiritual legacy is vibrantly recounted in the Guru's final rite. According to the Puratan Janamsakhi:

> Baba Guru went and sat under a withered tree. The tree turned green. Leaves blossomed. Then Guru Angad bowed at his feet. Mataji ached in separation. In the Palace the holy word burst forth. Family members and community all began to weep. Then the hymn in Raga Vadhans began . . .
>
> Puratan Janamsakhi, pp. 128–29

A withered tree turns green! In this final episode, the Puratan Janamsakhi (#57) brings up several of the Guru's verses recorded in the scripture. The central note of the above hymn is '*Nanak runna baba janiai je rovai lae piaro*—Nanak, who weep for divine love, they alone weep, Baba.' Clearly, it is not death but the loss of divine love that we must mourn. The departure of the First Sikh presents him as the embodiment of divine love who came into the world to remind and rekindle that love amongst his contemporaries. The Puratan account continues:

> Then the gathering starts to sing the *alahnian* (songs of mourning). Baba enters the wondrous house (*bismad de ghari aia*). The command is given. Raga Tukhari plays. Baba recites the Barah Mah in the night. Dawn commences as he passes away (*amrit vela hoa, calane de vakhati*) . . .
>
> Puratan Janamsakhi, p. 129

Rather than loss and end, the scene is imbued with life and new beginnings. The dried-up vegetation blooms, the divine Palace bursts with the holy word, the Guru enters the wondrous house, night ushers in dawn, the ambrosial time (*amrit vela*). The First Sikh recites the whole Barah Mah hymn in Raga Tukhari. This hymn, we noted in the introduction, synthesizes the universal and personal dimensions of lived time in the psychological and spiritual passage of a young woman longing for her paramour over the twelve months of the year. In his final hour, the Guru sings of temporality as an integral characteristic of the Divine One and reproduces the closeness between the human psyche and cosmic reality. No moment or event is ever inauspicious. There is nothing negative about death: 'The twelve months, seasons, dates, and days are all glorious as hours, minutes, seconds are naturally ticking towards the true One,' goes the final passage of the Barah Mah. The Guru's own 'Alahnian', songs of mourning in Sikh scripture, are the stage for his final rite of passage. The First Sikh discarded traditional mourning customs.

The Puratan account also attends to the transference of the holy word received from the divine Palace to the Second Guru, to the concern of the Guru's sons for their future without the illustrious father, and to the wishes of the Guru's Muslim and Hindu devotees who wanted to follow up with their own customary rituals—burial and cremation, respectively. Reassuring everyone, Baba Nanak asks the congregation to recite the Kirtan Sohila and Arati verses, after which he recites the epilogue (sloka) to the Japji. Since the sloka is said to be enunciated by Guru Angad, the Puratan account tacitly endorses the first Sikh affirming his successor's spiritual legacy.

After he read the sloka, Baba covered himself with a sheet and slept. The congregation bowed. When they lifted the sheet, there was nothing. The flowers left by both were in bloom. Hindus took theirs; the Muslim took theirs . . .

Puratan Janamsakhi, p. 133

The Guru had earlier asked his Muslim and Hindu devotees each to leave their flowers beside him, specifying each side of his body, left and right. So whichever side the flowers remained abloom would get to follow their custom. Since the flowers on both sides stayed vibrant, Hindus followed up with their cremation rite, and the Muslims with their burial of the blossoms.

These harmonious social, religious and cosmic currents of the first Sikh's corporeal passage from the Puratan Janamsakhi converge in the final illustration of the B-40 Janamsakhi. It is a split narrative. In the bottom scene are three yogis handing ashes to a young fellow, an attendant of the Guru. Youth is the channel to communicate to the Guru about his final moments of embodiment. The attendant has luxurious curls similar to the young Nanak seen in the first scene of his going to school. In the upper plane, the Guru as usual is seated under the tree with Bhai Mardana playing the rabab. He prepares for his cremation in this final scene by asking for a pile of logs, an enigmatic replay of his preparation for school in the opening (#1). No eternity, no disembodied soul, no otherworld; in a this-world oriented finale, finite metaphysics sweeps into sensuous ontology. Mangoes and birds and roses—everything around the Guru—is in vibrant motion. His own departure fits in with this natural momentum of the universe. The Janamsakhis pull together the multifarious sensations, leaving readers and spectators with an intimate presence of the First Sikh in this magical world of ours.

Initiation

Unique to the First Sikh is his initiation as the Guru. This major event of his life from the Puratan Janamsakhi takes place in Sultanpur, where he was employed in a store owned by the local Muslim landlord.

One day Nanak did not return home after his usual morning bath in the river Bein. A wide search was conducted but there was no sign of him anywhere. His clothes were found by the river. Everyone thought he had drowned. The town was plunged in gloom. But the First Sikh reappeared on the third day. During this interval, the Janamsakhi recounts his direct communion with the Divine. This was his personal rite of passage, a symbolic birth that redefined Guru Nanak's social and spiritual identity. Having rejected the upanayana, he goes through an entirely different rite of passage—conforming to the archetypal tripartite pattern of: (a) separation, (b) liminality, and (c) reincorporation. To recap my earlier discussion:[13]

a) Separation: As Nanak goes for his bath in the river, he leaves behind his clothes—indicative of his previous set of codes and signs; he leaves behind his attendant, indicative of his home, family and society at large. He now possesses nothing. The First Sikh has stripped off his cultural conditions and divested himself of society's structures.

b) Betwixt and Between: In this 'interstructural situation', he 'is at once no longer classified and not yet classified:'[14] he is no longer the store employee, nor is he yet the Guru who will attract millions to a new world religion. He is at a dynamic threshold where past borders are gone, and future possibilities are yet to come. During the three days that he is believed to have drowned, he goes through a series of numinous events.

In the multilayered mythic account, the First Sikh is ushered into the divine presence and receives a cup full of amrit: '*Ehu amrit mere nam ka piala hai*—this amrit is the cup of my Name.'[15] Enclosed in the waters of the river Bein, he receives the ambrosial drink. He does not see; he only hears. The phenomenon of hearing we explored in Chapter 1 is crucial to Guru Nanak and the building up of tradition. What he receives is *nam ka piala*, the cup of Name. Nam (the cognate of the English word 'name') is the identity of the transcendent One. This elemental process constitutes the First Sikh's introduction to the Divine: by sipping the universal drink, he gets to *know* the Ultimate Reality. The immortal drink that the First Sikh receives is a sapiential experience of the transcendent One.

After being given the cup of amrit, he is asked to go and instruct others. But there is also the implication in the Janamsakhi narrative that he is put through a test. Before he departs, he is ordered to illustrate his method and technique: 'How does one praise my name? Recite!' Guru Nanak responds with a hymn that was his song—and proof—of praise. We find here a striking affinity between the command the First Sikh receives and the order given by god to the Prophet Muhammad through Archangel Gabriel: 'Recite in the Name of Your Lord . . .' While the Prophet Muhammad hears the Word in the caves of Mount Hira, Guru Nanak hears it in the river Bein. Neither was previously known for his poetic genius, but after passing through the spaces, both of them become the matrix for a voluminous and momentous and most artistic text—the holy Quran and the Guru Granth Sahib, respectively.

In the second phase, Guru Nanak passes the test through poetic syntax and is accepted by the Divine. He recites a hymn, which demonstrates his psychic and spiritual power, as well as his artistic talent. Its final verse:

> If I had a supply of bottomless ink, and could write with the speed
> of wind;
> I would still not be able to measure your greatness
> Nor signify the glory of Your Name
>
> GGS: 13

Nanak becomes a poet. He explodes human language. He uses poignant similes, analogies and metaphors to describe That which is utterly ineffable. After his response, the Voice spoke: 'Nanak, you discern My will.' The Janamsakhi thus attests to the First Sikh's success. He then recites the Japji. Although the Janamsakhi does not produce the entire text of the hymn, it specifies that the First Sikh 'concluded the Jap—*japu sampuran kita*'. Recited at this particular juncture of his spiritual encounter, the Japji acknowledges the Guru's acceptance and gratitude.

In the third phase of his sacred liminality, he is given the dress of honour (the sirpao, more commonly known as *saropa*). The Janamsakhi narrative continues:

The Voice was heard again: 'Who is just in your eyes, Nanak, shall be so in mine. Whoever receives your grace shall abide in mine. My name is the supreme One; your name is the divine Guru.' Guru Nanak then bowed in gratitude and was given the dress of honour from the divine court. A sonorous melody in the Raga Dhanasari rang forth . . . Arati . . .

Puratan Janamsakhi, p. 18

The First Sikh is initiated as the Guru. He is endowed with a new status and identity. The sacrum or the physical object that marks his special dispensation is the sirpao, a piece of material that goes from head (*sir*) to foot (*pao*). Since it is not tailored, it does not carry any male or female codifications. Upon his conferral, the Guru rapturously recites 'Arati', the hymn in which he celebrates the transcendent light permeating every being. In the fecund waters of the river, he recognizes the ontological basis of the universe, and is called upon to share what has been revealed to him.

The written account from the Puratan Janamsakhi of Guru Nanak's revelation corresponds with internal evidence provided by the First Sikh in the GGS (p. 150, discussed in Chapter 1). In Sikh public memory this is the starting point of their religion. Artist Alam in the B-40 Janamsakhi illustration positions the Guru standing in the middle of a panoramic view (#28). Trees and shrubs in a round horizon stretch into infinity, and bunches of little colourful flowers pop up all over the green grass. Bhai Mardana's curled fingers spell out the vigour with which he is striking his rabab, making us see melodious sound waves bursting in the air. In this visually and aurally animated scene, the First Sikh's hands holding the *tasbih*-like rosary are joined together in homage and reach above him. His face is tilted. Extending both below and above, it is an intriguing multi-dimensional perspective. According to the written text, 'Baba Nanak is in the Palace of the formless One— *Baba Nanak nrinakar de mahal vich*' (B-40, 100). The scene reiterates Guru Nanak's autobiographical verse—'The songster was called into the Palace by the Owner—*Dhadhi sachai mahal khasami bulaia*' (GGS: 150). Evidently, the Palace (*mahal*) of the formless One is no different from this world of ours. The figure of the bird in the tree echoes Guru Nanak's human body. The Guru appears in divine ecstasy. With his eyes half closed, his lips in a smile, he stands (stasis) outside of himself (ec), a perfect intersection of the physical and spiritual spheres. Guru Nanak's numinous experience is with and through his own body. His fluid emotional state corresponds with the expansive circular landscape. Demarcations between mind and body, the individual body and the bodies of others, *lok* (world) and *parmarth* (transcendental reality), are obliterated. Without seeing the Divine in any 'form', whether physical or cosmic, Guru Nanak appears to feel the formless One pulsate in each and every form. There are no hints of any Sant mediations, but clear evidence of 'unmediated inspiration from on high'.[16] Guru Nanak's vision of the singular, infinite formless Divine, his moral impulse to connect with everybody around him, and his heightened sensuousness, constitute the First Sikh's revelation. These currents, captured artistically and verbally, crystallized into Sikh metaphysics, ethics and aesthetics.

c) Reincorporation: After his radical experience, the protagonist returns to society as the Guru. In his new status and role, he has gained a new self-awareness. Guru Nanak's initiation does not establish his sexual status, and if at all, his rite of passage shatters the construction of a male identity. Although it was a son, brother and husband who entered the river, the divine initiation endows him with his fundamental humanity. Located in the amniotic waters, he goes through the process of physical drinking, which gives him metaphysical insight into the Divine. He responds in a sensuous, poetic outpour, and is honoured with gender-inclusive clothing from the divine court. Unlike other initiation rites there are no additions to or subtractions from the body; tattoos, circumcision or scarring did not mark his transition. In the First Sikh's case, his new identity is marked by the unity of *bana* (the material cloth) and *bani* (poetry), sirpao (dress) and nam (word).

As he reincorporates into society, 'antistructure' becomes the mode of existence. The earliest Sikh community that developed with Guru Nanak at Kartarpur fits in with the cultural anthropologist Victor Turner's description of 'antistructure' because the neat horizontal divisions and vertical hierarchies of society were broken down. The ancient four-fold class system with its rigid hierarchical codes or male-female gender divisions have no place in the First Sikh's new community. The three important socio-religious institutions of Sikhism: seva (voluntary service), langar (community meal) and sangat (congregation) evolve in which men and women formerly from different castes, classes and religions take equal part.

These institutions established in the first Sikh community at Kartarpur were a practical and existential consequence of Guru Nanak's epiphany recorded in the Janamsakhi. The narrative account may not be factual data, yet it has been essential to the historical development of the Sikh religion. The Tenth Sikh Guru's inauguration of the amrit initiation on Baisakhi Day 1699 is in fact a return to this primal moment of Sikhism. Years later, the 'beginning' of Sikhism embodied in the private, individual and mystical experience of the First Guru was transcreated by the Tenth as a public, social and institutional ritual in Anandpur. By initiating his Five Beloved with amrit, the Tenth Guru extended the vigour of Guru Nanak's amrit into perpetuity: he made the metahistoric drink an essential part of the psyche and practice of the Sikh community. The First Sikh birthed a 'Sikh' consciousness, which has continued to sustain the faith for the last five and a half centuries. His legacy is an enduring and integral part of daily life, and the Janamsakhis are vital for the unity and continuity of the Sikh community.

Miracles

Verbally and visually the narratives portray miraculous events. The Guru can read minds, he can make crops grow instantly, he can stop a huge rock hurled at him with his outstretched hand, he can make the shade of a tree stand still, he can change a ram back to Mardana, he can make a mosque turn around, he can cool a monster's boiling cauldron of oil with a dip of his finger, he can squeeze out both milk and blood from two slices of bread, and so on and on. These are all very interesting. But their renditions do something more. Rather than miracles displaying or communicating the Guru's supernatural grandeur, they strike upon the inner eye and transform the seer. They rupture the habitual way of looking at the world and open up new ways of seeing and being in the world. Professor Margaret Miles aptly warns us, 'If, however, we find our society's public images are governed by a narrow emotional repertoire, repetitive images, and unimaginative narratives, we are not well served.'[17] Highly imaginative and distinctive in their depictions, the Janamsakhis are capable of 'enhancing relationship, community, and society' as Miles would say. These are not miracles in the Western semantic sense. Full of wit and wonder, they wander from the protagonist to the wonders of our own bodies and those that surround us—human or natural—and incite us to expect the extraordinary events in the daily rhythms of ordinary life. The fragmentary little episodes lend themselves to meaningful analysis, and they leave us with a sense of 'vismaya'. From the Sanskrit root *smi*, the word is etymologically related with the Greek *meidian*, to smile, and Latin *miraculum*, to wonder.[18] Rather than describe actualities they offer wondrous possibilities that can take place in this world of ours.

When Guru Nanak goes to Mecca, for example, the mosque moves around—following the direction of his feet. In this popular narrative, the Guru falls asleep in front of the mosque with his feet turned towards the mehrab.[19] The qazi in charge gets upset for the irreverence shown by the visitor, but in response the Guru politely asks the qazi to turn his feet in the direction he felt proper. As the Guru's feet are turned, so does the sacred mosque. Alam illustrates a wonderstruck qazi marvelling at a blue-robed Nanak sound asleep (#12 of the B-40 Janamsakhi). There is no need to consider it a historical fact; the motion of circularity simply shatters rigid mental formulas. That the Divine exists in every direction, that the human body is sacred and all its parts equally so—the head no more than the feet—are effectively communicated. Guru Nanak's act dislocates conventional habits and linear structures and whirls the viewers into a vast interior horizon.

It is the impact of the Janamsakhis which is miraculous, for the various scenarios reveal ways of being wholesome humans. A glance at the First Sikh with crimson blood dripping from the bread offered by a wealthy man in his left hand, and nurturing milk dripping from the bread offered by a humble carpenter in his right, leaves a lifelong imprint on the value of honest labour. Guru Nanak's miracles challenge society to interrogate their innate assumptions, and simultaneously create a 'widening experience', which Gadamer claims is a distinguishing feature of metaphors.[20] The narratives metaphorically promote an understanding, interpreting and application of Guru Nanak's transcendental understanding in our own bodies. The plots and images reinforce the Sikh scriptural message as they translate the First Sikh's aural verses into actions and reactions.

For me, the most miraculous incident is #56 in the B-40 Janamsakhi, the Guru showing his bruises from the thorny terrain he was physically present in, while a shepherd recited his hymn (for details see Introduction). Along with his interlocutor Guru Angad, we viewers witness with our own two eyes the supreme miracle: the fusion of Guru Nanak's body with his intangible verse. Guru Nanak's enchantment with the corporeality of sacred verse is strikingly conveyed:

Mardania, ehu bani jo koi asade piare mere bhagati mera sariru meri deh hovnige tina de muhau pargasu hovaiga

[Mardana, those who love me, those devoted to me, they will be my body, my flesh; revelation will flow from their mouths]

B-40 Janamsakhi, p. 150

The Janamsakhi projects the essential guru–bani identity: '*Bani guru guru hai bani*—the verse is the guru, the guru is the verse' (GGS: 982). The first Guru passed on the sublime verse he received from the universal divine One to Lahina, making him Angad, and so the sequence continued on with his nine successors. Here, the first Sikh is foreshadowing his spiritual legacy: his lovers, his devotees—each would be his body, his flesh, for they would utter the divine revelation from their mouths (*muhahu pargasu hovaiga*). How unfortunate that a meticulous scholar like McLeod would assume the guru–bani identity clearly articulated here as 'uncharacteristically sophisticated for this section of the janam-sakhi'.[21] In their innovative miraculous imaginings, the simple Janamsakhis are for sure highly sophisticated. They resist ordinary vision 'which is attached to the ordinary use of words'. As the French philosopher Paul Ricoeur thinks through, 'The eclipse of the objective, manipulable world thus makes way for the revelation of a new dimension of reality and truth.'[22]

The First Sikh conceived the ontological, orientational and structural guru–bani identity,[23] and gestating in the spiritual womb of the next four Gurus, the scriptural body was delivered by the Fifth Guru in 1604 and invested with guruship by the Tenth in 1708. Ever since, the scriptural Guru continues to be a dynamic agent of Sikh personal and communal life. During their daily liturgical prayers, the congregation recites in unison: 'Know Guru Granthji as the manifest body of the Gurus; those whose hearts are pure find it in the holy word.' Instead of the body and mind split, we receive a new vision of the inclusive divine One and a new way of being in the world and relating with community, society and nature. Centuries later, the lingering image of Guru Nanak's bruises reflected through the primordial mirror opens fresh new possibilities for viewers to experience the sacred and the sensuous in their everyday life. No wonder the supreme miracle is a daily fact of life: each day, very much living on planet Earth, whoever recites his evening Arati Sohila hymns just when the day fuses into the night, is intimately in touch with the transcendent One. But the guru–body miracle cannot merely be parroted or passively assimilated; its ontological novelty has to be palpably felt anew; the Guru must be actively 'searched in the word—*khoj sabad mahi leh*'.

Pluralism

Over and over again the Janamsakhis depict a pluralist Guru Nanak enthusiastically reaching out to people of different faiths. Accompanied by Bhai Mardana, and at times with both Bhai Mardana and Bhai Bala, he travels extensively in all four directions. His geographical journeys parallel his inner search. There is a curiosity in him to know about the foreign and familiarize himself with the distant, the 'other'. He visits the sacred spaces of the many groups of the Hindus, Muslims, Siddhas, Buddhists, Jains; we see him in temples, mosques, viharas and khanqahs; he attends a multitude of fairs and festivals. Full of respect and without any acrimony, he discusses and discourses with people about their respective scriptures, philosophies and practices. To the musically talented Sufi Sheikh Sharaf he requests he sing a ghazal. The First Sikh aspires for understanding and mutuality across lines of difference.

As noted at the outset, his poetics demonstrate his impressive familiarity and knowledge of the doctrines, practices and musical systems of his contemporaries from various religious traditions. The basic common ground of humanity is what he carries to people of various faiths. Rejecting man-made divisive operations, he invites each and every one to be authentically themselves, and thereby makes space for real and different religious commitments. When he meets Muslims, he adjures them to be faithful to the teachings of their faith; when he meets Hindus, he urges them to abide by the tenets of their own tradition. Often quite witty, the Janamsakhis set up scenes in which we see and hear the First Sikh participate in the religious and cultural diversity of his times, while conveying his own distinct existential mode. As he leaves his footprints on distant lands, he leaves his imprint on the hearts of people.

Sikh communities developed in the places he visited. There are tiny populations like those of the Nanakpanthis, found fifteen miles northwest of Pilibhit in Uttar Pradesh, where Guru Nanak is remembered to have discoursed with the Nath Yogis.[24] On the other side of the spectrum, there is a very large Sikh population living in Varanasi. The Gurdwara Gurubagh, located two miles from the city centre, commemorates the visit of Guru Nanak. Its wall inscription records that he visited Varanasi in 1506, and a small garden in the courtyard blooms as a memento of the spot where he sat.[25]

Bhai Gurdas's poetic camera captures the serene manner in which the first Sikh so enriched human history. When Guru Nanak goes to Multan, an important Sufi centre, he is received with a bowl full of milk. This welcoming gesture signified that the region was already full to the brim with religious leaders, and that there would be no place for a newcomer like Guru Nanak. How does the First Sikh react? Without any verbal or physical or philosophical tussle, 'the Baba produced a jasmine from underneath his arm and mixed it with milk in the bowl. It was like the River Ganga merging with the ocean', records Bhai Gurdas (Var I: 44). With the addition of his 'jasmine', the milk did not spill from the brimming bowl; it became more fragrant and colourful. The First Sikh does not impose his views on others. He does not reject existing religious traditions, nor does he intend to replace them with his own. He validates the religious plurality of his day: 'Ram and Rahim occupy the same position—*ram rahim ikk thai khaloi*' (Bhai Gurdas, Var I: 33). The founder Guru fully affirmed and gave equal status to the religious ideals of his contemporaries.[26]

His visuality transcends religious stereotypes current in his milieu. The illustrator of the early B-40 Janamsakhi accomplishes it by utilizing disparate motifs of the tilak and the *seli:* Guru Nanak almost always has a vertical red tilak mark on his forehead, just as he has a woollen cord, seli, slung across his left shoulder coming down to his right waist. Explained by Gadamer, '[W]hat makes a motif is that it has unity in a convincing way and that the artist has carried through this unity as the unity of meaning, just as the viewer understands it as a unity.'[27] Evidently, the bright red line between the Guru's dark eyes or the dark semicircle sinuously clinging his yellow robe go beyond art for art's sake attractiveness: the tilak is saturated with the holiness of the Vaishnava Hindus; the seli with the devotion of the Muslim Sufis. Each has enormous unity of meaning for its own community, and the artist brings them together on the Sikh Guru's body to project his universality. The Muslim Mardana is also painted with the tilak. The visual motifs from two different traditions do not reproduce some sort of a 'composite' or a 'hybrid' model; rather, they convincingly convey to the viewer a figure beyond the either-or religious categories prevalent in medieval India. The more we see the First Sikh in Janamsakhi paintings, the more we realize the origins of Sikhism embedded in *his* uniquely pluralist personality. The Janamsakhi artists uniformly delineate a rupture with the past: their subject is bringing something different and distinctive; he is not a mere participant in the existing north Indian devotional traditions.

In almost all of his adult images Guru Nanak in the B-40 has in his hand a simple circle of beads on a string, ending in a tassel, which is also the leitmotif in the paintings of Guru Nanak by the contemporary artist Arpana Caur. Thought to have originated in Hindu practice, the 'rosary' is a widespread and enduring article used for meditation and prayer by Buddhists, Muslims and Christians alike. In Guru Nanak's immediate historical and geographical context, different Hindu groups used specific types of *malas*. For example, the *rudraksa mala* made up of thirty-two berries (or its double, sixty-four) from the special rudraksa tree was used for meditation on Shiva; the tulsi mala with 108 beads made from the wood of the sacred tulsi shrub was used for the worship of Vishnu and Rama.[28] Similarly, the tasbih with its ninety-nine beads was popular amongst the Sufis for exalting the ninety-nine names of Allah. Actually, these three types are mentioned in the GGS. Guru Nanak's rosaries that we see in the B-40 vary in colour, material and size. Some are black; some white. Their performance varies too: sometimes the Guru holds it in his right hand, sometimes in his left, sometimes with both hands, and sometimes he holds two rosaries simultaneously—one in each hand (#8 and #9 of the B-40 Janamsakhi). The variations suggest that he does not uphold any established norms, and since it is almost always in the Guru's hand, even when he is animatedly conversing, it is more than simply an instrument for meditational practices. Actually, when he is pictured with them in both his hands, he is encountering the demon (#8) and the robber (#9), which indicates that the rosary functioned as the Guru's weapon against evil forces.

For the most part, the First Sikh is dressed in harmoniously flowing robes with a sash, and he wears a turban. Sometimes we even get a peek at his Punjabi *jutti* style shoes, and quite attractive ones too. Overall, he is very much in sync with the cultural trends and mores of his time—a statement of his self-cultivation within a socio-political context. His appearance and gear reveal his affirmation of being in this world. His robes flowing down to his ankles make the strips tightly covering the genitals of the mendicants beside him appear even skimpier. The example of the Digambara Jains, who for centuries have literally been 'sky-clad', is loudly denounced by him. To repeat, not those 'who take off their clothes and go naked like Digambaras' (GGS: 1169), but she who 'wears the clothes of Love' (GGS: 54) is prized. His world-affirming appearance comes across as an antithesis to several of his scantily dressed and shaven-headed Yogi and Nath contemporaries as well. As a sign of 'mastering' their sexuality or 'death' of their body, ascetics from different religious traditions opted to wear little on their bodies, and many smeared themselves with ash. But the Janamsakhis depict the First Sikh engaging with various groups of world-denying ascetics in polite conversations about self-cultivation and performing acts such as feeding them food—gestures to draw them back into society.

The Janamsakhis are practical enough to indicate the challenges of pluralistic ventures. It is not easy to break trends. We see Guru Nanak climbing up a mountain where a conclave of Nath yogis is sitting (#20 in the B-40). The artist paints them with their backs against the world. Some have smeared ash on their bodies as a symbol of their renunciation. Their shaved heads, lengthened earlobes and long earrings (*kan-phat*, 'ear split') signal their rigorous hatha yoga practices and ascetic ideals. A dark-bearded, yellow-robed Nanak, accompanied by Mardana, approaches these venerable men from their back—the life they left far behind. In Alam's composition, the group of shaven-headed yogis is sitting securely together, while the Guru is on the side, standing on the edge of the mountain, accompanied only by Bhai Mardana. Guru Nanak has almost made it to the mountaintop. He is in a precarious locus. But the black-bearded young itinerant seems to have resolved to enter into the circle of these venerable Naths. That it requires tremendous courage and initiative to enter into somebody else's ideological and geographical space is brought home by the narrative.

The spatial gap between the First Sikh and his interlocutors is filled in by a tree. On the tree are perched two little birds pecking their beaks at each other. Yellow and red, they appear to be an extension of the Guru's yellow robe and his red turban. Their play caught in this moment poignantly warbles Guru Nanak's critique of renunciation, which ensued in his lengthy verbal discourse with the Naths, so the scene sets up the stage for the Siddha Gosht discourse recorded in the GGS. Through its sheer forms and colours, the painting effectively communicates that it was so natural for the birds to be aloft on the trees; most unnatural for people to shirk their human responsibilities and sit on the mountaintop detached from society. A viewer of such Janamsakhi painting(s) would outrightly reject the scholarly theories that Guru Nanak was significantly influenced by Nath ideals! Guru Nanak's pictures with the various ascetic groups resonate with scriptural verses: rather than 'smear the bodies with ashes, renounce clothes and go naked—*tani bhasam lagai bastar chodhi tani naganu bhaia*' (GGS: 1127), we must 'wear the outfit of divine honour and never go naked—*painana rakhi pati parmesur phir nage nahi thivana*' (GGS: 1019).

Artist Alam in the B-40, #46 shows Guru Nanak interacting with a group of ascetics who appear to have a different lifestyle, corporeal insignia and spiritual practices from the Naths. They too are 'outside' society, but they are long-haired, they have buns atop their heads, they have long, flowing beards, and some can be seen entering a body of water. The text describes the water in this Himalayan region as icy cold, with many of the ascetics dying after dipping into it. To borrow a term from religious studies scholar Patrick Olivelle, these ascetics are engaged in the process of 'deconstructing' their bodies.[29] The visitor Guru miraculously makes the water pleasantly lukewarm so the sanyasis can comfortably bathe themselves, and with his cupped hands gives out rice, ghee and sugar to feed their famished bodies. Instead of 'deconstructing,' Guru Nanak urges them to nurture their bodies and participate in the natural, social and cosmic processes. The woman sitting next to a male sanyasi across from Guru Nanak in Alam's rendition particularly catches our eye. The Janamsakhi text does not mention any female. Seeing her wholesome figure on Alam's canvas with her long hair coming down to her waist, dressed in a pink garment and pretty earrings, and holding a mala in hands joined together in emotional and spiritual energy, reinforces Guru Nanak's emphasis on the corporeal richness of human existence.

In a painting from the family workshop of Nainsukh of Guler (1710–78), we see the First Sikh and his companions looking upon an ash-besmeared, scantily clad renunciate asleep on the ground.[30] Through this double gaze upon a figure lying listless on an ochre-coloured cloth spread on a tiger skin, the utter futility of renunciation is brought home. The artist displays an ironic contrast not only between the oblivious sleeper and his wide-eyed audience, but also between his lifeless body and the dead tiger's lively tail that seems to curl up from behind. The scene resounds with the question: why would anybody give up this precious human life? '*Hire jaisa janam hai kaudi badle jae*—this life worth a diamond goes for naught' (GGS: 156).

Another Janamsakhi account, *Guru Nanak and the Priests of Kurukshetra*, shows Guru Nanak challenging the rigidity with which vegetarianism was upheld by the orthodox.[31] The Guru is in the historic field (*kshetra*) where the Mahabharata was fought between the Kurus and the Pandavas. The sun above, set in a dark-blue horizon at the centre of the painting, indicates a solar eclipse. From a conventional perspective, the landscape is intensely sacred, both spatially and temporally. In the foreground of the painting, pilgrims are seen bathing in the waters. However, in the middle, Guru Nanak sits under a tree, and behind him deer meat is being cooked in a pot over a fire. A host of perturbed ascetics approach the Guru, pointing their fingers at him for his sacrilegious act of cooking meat in such a holy coordinate of place and hour. But the Guru remains calmly positioned with his legs tucked under him. His hands rest on his lap. His robe is unruffled. The pink shawl remains gently draped over his right shoulder. The golden halo surrounds his serene face. The painting elucidates his message that 'meat is neither prohibited in the Puranas, nor in western scriptures'; 'it is used in ritual feasts and wedding festivities' (GGS: 1290).

Whether in his looks or his outlook, Guru Nanak's interaction with Bhagats, Jains, Yogis or Naths in the Janamsakhi scenes repeatedly leaves us with the impression of the First Sikh deviating from them. In contrast, though, his encounters with Sufi saints underscore real convergences. Even a glance at the B-40 Janamsakhi illustrations evokes an enchanting physical and spiritual proximity between the First Sikh and Muslim holy men. Created in 1733 for a Sikh patron, for the use of the Sikh community, it conveys the Sikh self-consciousness of the late seventeenth and early eighteenth centuries. Serving as an important document, the B-40 Janamsakhi subverts twentieth-century scholarly assumptions that Guru Nanak was 'reworking' the Sant tradition—'a compound of elements drawn mainly from Vaishnava Bhakti and the hatha yoga of the Natha yogis, with a marginal contribution from Sufism . . .', it subverts scholarly warnings that deflect us from remembering and recognizing Guru Nanak and Sufi affinities.[32] The quantity and quality and placing of Sufi figures and imagery in the B-40 manuscript bring out a beautiful intimacy between Guru Nanak and the mystical world of Islam.

In #7 we see Guru Nanak conversing with Shah Abdul Rahman. The Sufi saint is dressed in a rosy pink outfit amidst flora and fauna. Why so much pink, we wonder? It is but the perfect pictorial statement of the physical and spiritual closeness between the Sufi saint and the

Sikh Guru. According to the Janamsakhi text, when Shah Abdul Rahman returns home, his disciple comments on his flushed body, and the saint replies: '*Ajju khudai ka lal milia*—today I met with Khuda's ruby' (B-40, 43–44). The polysemous term '*lal*' denotes the colour red or radiance or ruby or a lover, so the rosiness divulges the Muslim saint's infusion of Guru Nanak's spiritual radiance.[33] The artist translates the Sheikh's words into the language of colours. The encounter is complex: there is the initial seeing, which produces an immediate insight into the Sikh Guru as a radiance/lover/ruby of Khuda for the Muslim saint, and he in turn transforms into a passionate pink. The intimacy between the two spiritual bodies is beautifully emitted.

In another intriguing illustration from the B-40 Janamsakhi Guru Nanak is in conversation with Sufi Sheikh Sharaf (#50). This celebrated figure in the Punjab lived two centuries before Guru Nanak. In Alam's painting he is a young, black-bearded saint ornately dressed like a woman with all her feminine accoutrements. In both content and form, it is a fascinating scene. The background with single, double-storey and some even triple-storey buildings, and a fluted dome reaching up to the skies, gives the impression of an urbanized Muslim town (identified as Baghdad in the text). The balconies and windows are intricately latticed, and the walls are decorated with colourful arabesques. Closer, we get a side view of a mosque set in a compound with its entrance opening up to the right. Its latticed window repeats the pattern of those far in the distance, exhibiting the genius of Islamic art, the conversion of stone into lace. With the dome of the mosque receding into the left horizon and the branches of a vibrant bush across from it into the right, the eye is left wandering beyond both borders. This bush in the compound of the mosque has been rendered realistically, for we can spot eight different birds sitting in a circle on its distinct branches and leaves. Quite unfamiliar in Alam's repertoire of abstract foliage, it immediately evokes the proverbial *Conference of the Birds* by the Muslim mystic Farid ud-Din Attar (after whom Sheikh Farid is named). Rows of tiny shrubs, brownish-pink rocks, and sprightly flowers run parallel to the mosque and the discoursing birds.

Against this backdrop, charged with Islamic aesthetics, the blue-robed Guru and the bride-like bearded Sufi are having their own discourse. As the two figures face each other sitting on their knees on the green grass, the tasbih-like rosary in the Guru's stretched hand appears right in their middle. This rhythmic circle of beads horizontally reaches out to unite them, and vertically extends to the three rose-like flowers and higher to the five daisies and still higher up to the mosque and finally to the houses and buildings in the distance. According to the narrative, the Guru invites the Sheikh to sing ghazals for which he was renowned. The Sikh Guru has the desire to hear with his own ears the Sufi saint sing on the theme of love. The delighted Guru looks upon him, and as the story ends, the saint bursts into bliss. Especially interesting is that Sheikh Sharaf, like Shah Abdul Rahman in #7, palpably feels the impact of Guru Nanak's sight:

> *Babeji di najari bhar dekhne nal sekh tai drib drist hoi gai/rom rom daru divaru masatu hoi gai/hari jame andar har burqe andar brahm hi paia najar avai*

> [With Babaji's look upon him, the Sheikh's sight turned divine. His every pore became ecstatic. Inside every outfit, behind every burqa, all he saw was the Divine!]

B-40, pp. 140–41

The terms *jama* and burqa evoke the human body, and they bring to mind figures of jama-wearing men and burqa-wearing women. The Sufi saint touches the Sikh Guru with his beautiful song of love and in turn is physically touched by the Guru's visual pulsations. His each and every hair literally stands erect in joy, and he begins to see the metaphysical Being in every corporeal figure.[34] This powerful scene of Sikh–Sufi reciprocity is very popular with the contemporary group for lesbian, gay, bisexual and transgendered Sikhs as visual evidence that the progressive Guru Nanak did not condemn cross-dressing or same-sex relationships.[35] The Janamsakhi scenes have great relevance, and if their visceral impact were to reach wider audiences, there could be a real shift in the divisive and oppressive paradigms dominating contemporary society.

The early Sikh self-consciousness is carried forward. In a late-nineteenth-century watercolour at the Government Museum and

Art Gallery in Chandigarh (India) we see the First Sikh wearing a mesmerizing full-sleeved robe.[36] With the patronage of the first Sikh emperor Maharaja Ranjit Singh (1780–1839), Sikh art had reached new heights. In this noteworthy painting, the Guru has a full beard, but in addition to Alam's iconography, he has a halo, and his turban has a high flap and a domed top, and he is framed in a regal setting. One of the Janamasakhis recounts Guru Nanak receiving a cloak of honour during his visit to Baghdad, with verses from the holy Quran embroidered on it.[37] In the watercolour tinted in a golden hue, the Guru's robe is inscribed all over with calligraphy in Arabic characters in the *naksh* script. The Guru, deep in thought, with a rosary in his hands, is seated on a terrace. Some branches in brush strokes on the right echo his profile. In the far background is an impressionist rendering of sizeable foliage. Closer, we get a glimpse of the Mughal-styled balcony balustrade with latticework. Closer still is a big, round pillow-cushion associated with Mughal emperors, and the Guru with his left leg tucked under and the right one placed over the left knee, sits perfectly aligned with his royal backdrop. The rich horizontal folds of his pillow-cushion dynamically intersect with the vertical stripes of his pyjama trousers; the circular designs on his turban rhythmically repeat the circles on the pillow, the necklace around his neck, and the tasbih-like rosary in his right hand; the triangles decorated with yet more triangular florets on his draping shawl join the rectangular border of the Islamicate carpet he is seated on.

In this scene of perpetual motion, the Guru is wrapped in a robe spun with verses from the holy Quran and the sublime Japji that covers his entire front and sleeves. The Islamic invocation '*bismillah al rahman al rahim*' and the Sikh '*adi sachu jugadi sachu hai bhi sachu hosi bhi sachu*' appear together.[38] The diverse threads of the First Sikh's dress powerfully weave the One who is beyond all external designs and forms. In its visual hermeneutics, the work unravels not only the meaning of the term 'text' (derived from *texere*, to weave), but also the singular transcendent matrix from which all the materials emerge. The call for *rahimat* or *rahim* is the perennial womb of truth (sach), has always been through the cycles (*jugad sach*), is (*hai bhi sach*), and will be evermore (*hosi bhi sach*). Without halting the mind anywhere, the painting gives a visual and sonorous push to imagine and intuit That Infinite One, common to everybody, Muslim and Sikh alike.

They may come from different regions and different centuries, but the central message of the Janamsakhis remains the same: the First Sikh reaching out to people across religions, cultures, professions and societal hegemonies, and embracing them in his profound spirituality. In turn, his harmonious personality and beautiful words make their way into the deepest self of anyone he meets. The penultimate sentence of the B-40 Janamsakhi is a breathless account of the variety of men and women who are attracted to the First Sikh's luminous rhyme, and rejoice in his presence: '*Hindu musalman jogi saniyasi brahmcari tapi tapasaru digambar baisno udasi grihasti bairagi khan khaneen umrao karori jimindaru bhumia*—Hindu, Muslim, yogi, sanyasi, brahmcari, ascetic, ascetic leader, sky-clad Jain, Vaishnava, celibate, householder, wandering mendicant, noble, chief, aristocrat, official, agriculturalist, proprietor' (B-40, p. 75). A plurality of 'bodies' drawn to Guru Nanak are enjoying the transcendent One in the fibres of their own body.

~

To sum it up, the Janamsakhis tell the life story of the First Sikh. Their time frame is linear. He travels widely and has meaningful inter-faith conversations. In flesh and blood he *is* the transcendent verse. Everywhere he leaves his imprint on the hearts of people. In various scenarios he shares his views on the importance of truth, the futility of empty rituals, the value of honest work, and the submission to the universal Divine over any other agent. As he carries his progressive message to people from different religious and social backgrounds, he brings them together to enjoy their collective humanity in this magical world. These are the memories we have of our First Sikh. The narratives may not be historically factual but they are far greater than facts. They highlight the very groundwork of the Sikh religion, and invite the young and the old from whatever genders, Sikh or non-Sikh, from east or west, to renew their imagination, thought and experience. These simple, delightful stories open up possibilities to negotiate our complex selves in our complex times.

3

The Mystic Philosopher

Guru Nanak's epistemological, aesthetic, ethical and soteriological perceptions are grounded in his ontological experience of Reality—that of the One infinite reality, 'Ikk Oan Kar'. Whether it is Being, Knowledge, Beauty, Morality or Liberation, the philosopher Nanak approaches these perennial issues as a mystic. In the opening chapter, we analysed his revelatory experience as the starting point of the Sikh tradition, and we discover in this chapter that his philosophical worldview is also framed by that very experience. The word 'method' is a composite of *meta* (after) and *hodos* (way), and in the First Sikh's method, mysticism and philosophy are not at odds with each other. The Guru pursues, interrogates, analyses, criticizes, wonders, intensely feels and tries to express the inexpressible One, and in so doing he combines his divine experience with a keen philosophic pursuit towards an ever-widening Reality.

The Japji, the opening hymn in the Guru Granth Sahib, presents Guru Nanak's philosophy in a powerful and coherent manner. Though it is not set into musical measures, the Japji is extraordinarily poetic in its language, and highly metaphysical. Guru Nanak's art is at its zenith here. The thirty-eight stanzas of the Japji lyrically construct a systematic philosophical system with a built-in ontology, epistemology, aesthetics, ethics and soteriology. The First Sikh anticipates Wittgenstein's maxim that philosophy ought really to be written as one 'writes a poem'. The fundamentals conveyed in his Japji hymn replay across the entire GGS.

In this chapter, we will focus on Stanzas 33–37 of the Japji which describe the spheres of Dharam, Gyan, Saram, Karam and Sach, translated as Duty, Knowledge, Beauty, Actions and Truth respectively. Generally regarded as an esoteric mystical journey, this segment of the Japji has not received the philosophic attention it elicits. If we examine it closely, we find the First Sikh grappling with existential questions: What is Reality? What's out here? Out there? How can we know about It? How do we sense It? How do we relate with our cosmos? What is morality? How can we be free? While thinking through them, the First Sikh somehow morphs them into a training manual as well, which is artistically captured in the final stanza of his Japji (#38). Here, his philosophical views are three-dimensionally presented by a jeweller working in their smithy. The philosophical and mystical aspects have an intricate phenomenological relationship, and by analysing them together we realize the practical implications of the First Sikh's philosophical worldview.

The Philosopher

Ikk Oan Kar

The prelude to the Japji opens with 'Ikk Oan Kar' (One being is), the bedrock of the Sikh religion. It utilizes three modes of knowledge to signify the existence of the One—numerical, alphabetical and geometrical. The primary number '1' is followed by the alpha of the Gurmukhi script and the geometrical arc. While the former two constitute the beginning of the mathematical and verbal languages, the arc is at once without beginning or end. Flying off Guru Nanak's 'Oan', the arc is a dynamic gesture of infinity, of motion and movement. The circle is not closed, it cannot be closed.

The numeral One (Ikk) is a vivid expression of unity shared by humans across cultures. Guru Nanak's fifteenth-century India abounds with eloquent terms and philosophically sophisticated concepts from Sanskrit, Arabic, Persian, and from the Dravidic languages. Yet, Guru Nanak simply utters 'Oan' after the all-inclusive numeral '1'. Oan (from aum) is the primal vocalic syllable of the Indian languages and expresses the totality of Being. Kar (is) proclaims the certainty of that Being. Interestingly, Heidegger's comment on 'is' highlights the power of this tiny word for Sikh philosophy: 'speaks everywhere in our language and tells of Being even where it does not appear expressly'.[1] Since the singular Being *is*, Guru Nanak does not raise any doubts about the existence of the One; philosophical arguments—ontological, epistemological, teleological or moral—would only be redundant.

He goes on to name that One as Sat (Truth or Reality), Sat Nam. Not tautological by any means, 'Ikk Oan Kar Sat Nam' indicates the Guru's inclination to bring Being into language which 'gives us the very possibility of truth'. It is in language, George Pattison explains, 'that the world is disclosed in such a way as to allow it to be a common and continuous world, in which we live together by talking about it over time.'[2] By knowing Its name, the abstract Being can be actively engaged with in the lived context. By giving the name (nam)—sat—a participle of 'as' (to be), the First Sikh identifies that One as 'existing', 'occurring', 'happening', 'being present'. That Truth is not an immutable essence is established at the very outset, and the rest of the Guru's oeuvre reveals Truth as a *becoming*—a flowing in the cosmos, in the human world of motions and emotions. It does not belong to any existing contexts; it does not hold on to any existing form of god or goddess; it does not claim inheritance to any established Hindu or Islamic or Buddhist or Jain precept or concept. And yet it is everything that we can possibly imagine—and beyond!

After introducing Being by the name (nam) of Truth (sat), he expresses Its nature: '*Karta purakh nirbhau nirvair akal murat ajuni saibhan gur prasad*—creator person, without fear, without enmity, timeless in form, unborn, self-existent, gift of the guru.' Known as the Mul Mantra (root creed), this prelude to the 'Jap' recurs in its full or abridged form throughout the GGS and forms the core of the daily prayers and ceremonies of the Sikh community. Without conjunctions or prepositions, it conveys the personal and impersonal qualities of that One at startling speed.

However, conventional theological patterns tend to slip in its epigrammatic style and make it prone to misinterpretations and mistranslations. For instance, the highly respectable UNESCO volume inserts pronouns and prepositions that render the Mul Mantra in a Biblical and masculine diction: 'There is one God/ Eternal Truth is His name/ Maker of all things/ Fearing nothing and at enmity with nothing/ Timeless is His Image/ Not begotten, being of His own

Being/ By the grace of the Guru, made known to men.'³ Such a version distorts Guru Nanak's distinctive theistic understanding by merely reproducing conventional monotheistic conceptions, which do not invite the multiplicity of the First Sikh's numeral One. The language of the Mul Mantra transcends the dichotomy of gender, and its speedy rhythm reveals the dynamic nature of Reality.

Guru Nanak recognizes creation as an expression of the universal True One, hence there is no disruption between 'god' and 'all things'. The creator person *itself is* all the diverse phenomena; Its very being consists of the many. The verbal root (kr, 'create') in *karta purakh* (creator person) evokes the birthing process, which is vastly different from the term 'Maker' that recalls the god from Genesis who makes the world out of nothing. A mother does not make; she creates, she bodies forth. The term purakh, cast in iron masculinity not only in the UNESCO translation but invariably in all translations and exegeses, is defined in the Guru Granth Sahib as *both* male and female: '*Ape purakh ape hi nari*—the One is male; the One is female' (GGS: 1020). In Sanskrit and Hindi '*purusha*' is the word for person in verbs and personal pronouns. In the Samkhya school of Hindu philosophy, however, Purusha, identified as pure consciousness, is antithetical to Prakriti, the physical world of matter. Guru Nanak's karta purakh retains the gender-neutral qualities of Hindi grammar but aborts any dualism between the metaphysical and the physical. The Guru Granth Sahib repeatedly affirms, '*Ap sat kia sabh sat tis prabh te sagal utpat*—Itself Truth, creates but Truth; all creation is birthed by the divine One' (GGS: 294). To repeat, by using the pronoun 'It' I don't mean to objectify or disrespect the all-encompassing Reality, I only want to keep away from limiting and demarcating 'It' with gender-exclusive language.

The various cosmic phenomena are created by and in turn manifest the Divine. Guru Nanak's theology is inclusive, his vista boundless, and the result is absolutely amazing. He powerfully conveys the vast scope of this multiverse—the creation of the sole Creator.

The divine One generated planets, constellations, and spheres below
What was hidden began to show

GGS: 1036

Every bit of creation in and around all over is the Creator's vibrancy. Physical matter including earth, skies and nether regions; psychological states of joy and fear; religious texts of Hindus and Muslims; practical activities like eating, drinking and dressing up; and so is all love—the universal Creator. He frequently uses the Arabic term *qudrat* (in the sense of what is created or natural) as a disclosure for the universal reality:

> What we see is the One's qudrat
>> What we hear is the One's qudrat
> Qudrat is at the core of happiness and fear
> The skies, the nether regions and all that is visible is the One's qudrat
> The Vedas, the Puranas, the Quran, indeed all thought is qudrat
> Eating, drinking, dressing up is qudrat, so is all love qudrat!

GGS: 464

Everything visible is the nature of that utterly invisible One, our first principle. It is the original force, the sole reality. As such, there can be nothing beside the One and nothing outside of the One. The First Sikh offers a coherent and integrated system of the singular One.

That One is then depicted without fear (*nir-bhau*) and without hostility/hatred (*nir-vair*). The use of these characteristics renders a warm persona to the impersonal Being. These are logical characteristics because both fear and hatred destroy unity and hinder the development of relationships. These personality traits signify that Being is not for itself; to the contrary, One is oriented towards Its creation heroically, courageously, wholesomely (opposite of fear), and with love (opposite of hostility). The fearless One evokes love; It does not provoke fear.

In the next sequence of descriptions, *murat* conjures a definite shape (*murati* denotes an idol), and with the preceding word *akal* (timeless: *kal*/ time + *a*/not), the formless quality of the Subject is attributed; similarly, *jun* means birth, and its negative prefix 'a' denotes the One beyond life cycles. Implicit here is Guru Nanak's rejection of incarnation and idolatory, which he explicitly does in the fifth stanza of the hymn: 'The One cannot be moulded—*thapia na jae.*' The infinite One cannot take on any birth; its infinite possibilities are not reduced or confined to any specific form or shape in any life cycle. Nothing verbal or solid or visual, neither male nor female, can ever encapsulate the infinite One.

Yet this timeless, birth-less Being is in close relationship with the cosmos and its natural cycles of birth and death; It is not some static, immutable eternal outside the fluctuations of time as scholars tend to interpret.[4] The First Sikh does not share ontological perspectives that view life in time negatively. He possesses a highly sophisticated awareness of time, and his verse throughout celebrates the flux of time. Temporality is an integral characteristic of Being, and therefore he repeatedly marvels at the lunar and solar systems, the movements making up days and dates, the cyclic rhythm of seasons during the twelve months (see Introduction). Guru Nanak's concept of time includes both linear and cyclic patterns, and therewith joins cosmological happenings with the concrete historical world around us. In the opening line of his Japji he asserts, '*Ad sach jugadi sach hai bhi sach nanak hosi bhi sach*—Truth was in the beginning, Truth has been through the cycles, Truth is, and Truth says Nanak, will be ever more' (inscribed on the robe he was wearing in the Janamsakhi account). Surely in his imagining, the One (akal murat ajuni) is not out of time but actively functioning in and through the various tenses of time. Humans and the Divine share a common horizon of lived time.

Being and Becoming

The end of the Mul Mantra pronounces: *saibhan* (self-existent) *gur prasad* (gift of the guru). The finale thus returns to the opening, the ever presence of the infinite One, and as it recapitulates the suis generis attributes, it thrusts the circle forward towards flesh and blood recipients. A nexus is established between the universal Being and the subjects who recognize It in their own particular historical, social and personal reality. The First Sikh's usage of the term 'prasad' with its synonyms 'clearness' and 'gift' is most fitting: the self-existent is of course absolutely evident but is banished from memory; its disclosure therefore is a 'gift' from the guru. Juxtaposing the plurality of 'all beings' (*sabhna jia*) to the singularity of their One giver (*ikk data*) he goes on to say, 'The guru gave me one insight: all beings have that One giver, may I never forget this' (Japji, Stanza 5). His expression '*data*' (giver/bestower) underscores the generous and beneficent nature of the creator person (karta purakh). Like modern thinkers, the First Sikh knew that memory is not merely a psychological faculty but an essential component of the historical being.[5]

For the mystic philosopher it is essential that Reality be remembered and experienced by individuals. The One named Truth (sat) has to be recognized and life lived in alignment with Its unity and universality. At the very outset of the Japji Guru Nanak raises questions: '*Kiv sachiara hoie*—how to become true? *Kive kure tute pal*—how to break the wall of lies?' Being and Becoming are not two different orders of Reality; rather, they are in constant mutuality. The ontological principle is Sat Nam, 'Truth by Name'. 'Truth' is now framed as an ethical practice: 'How to be truthful?' Guru Nanak repeatedly returns to the relationship between the Divine who is Truth, and us humans who should be living truthfully. He introduces the image of the 'wall' made of false egoism which keeps an individual separated from the divine One. The thirty-eight Japji stanzas delineate ways of breaking free of the I–me egoistic construct and becoming One with Reality. As their finale our mystic-philosopher vividly discloses the intersection of Being and Becoming.

Ontology

Who are we? How did we come to be? What is the meaning of existence? In Stanza 33 Guru Nanak says:

> *Rati ruti thiti var*
> *pavan pani agni patal*
> *tisu vichi dharati thapi rakhi dharamsal*
> *tisu vichi jia jugati ke rang*
> *tin ke nam anek anant*
> *karami karami hoe vicharu*
> *sacha api sacha darbar*

> [Amidst nights, seasons, solar, and lunar days
> Amidst air, water, fire and netherworld
> The earth is placed, the place of righteous action

In its midst beings and lifestyles of all colours
With endless names and countless forms
Each and every action is reflected upon
That One is true, and truly just the Court]

GGS: 7

Immediately, we are made conscious both about our geographical situatedness and about our obligations: we are located on earth (*dharti*), the place of moral actions (*dharamsal*). We begin to live deliberately when we realize the environment we inhabit. The terms dharti and dharam are etymologically rooted in the Sankskrit *dhr*, meaning to sustain, uphold, support. The pan-Indian term dharam is widely used for religion, virtue, duty, propriety, morality, cosmic order and law. In the First Sikh's usage, dharam does not carry any conventional regulations. There is no prescription of the customary four-fold division of Indian society into Brahmins, Kshatriyas, Vaishyas and Shudras. Dharam does not institute any division based on the stages of life—that of *brahmacarin*, *grahastha*, *vanaprastha* and *sanyasin* (*varna–ashrama–dharma*). There are no stipulations for any gender differences or bias, for there is no separate *stridharma* (woman's dharma) as in traditional Indic codes. What we discern here is a cosmic locus. People across castes, classes, religions, genders and ages are equally located in this multiverse—with and amongst all animate and inanimate beings—and have the same moral obligations. No action is singled out or reserved for anyone. Guru Nanak categorically says 'there is only one Dharam—*eko dharam*' (GGS: 1188).

His successors build up on his foundation and firmly proclaim that all four classes possess the one and same mandate: '*Khatri brahman sud vais, updes cahu varna ko sajha*—be they Kshatriyas, Brahmins, Shudras or Vaishyas, the injunction is shared by people of all complexions' (GGS: 747). This message has great relevance for our own day and time because the four classes are based on complexion ('varna' literally means colour or complexion), and though 'castes' may seem a thing of the past, colour and race are vitally important issues that contemporary society needs to face. The divine mandate is thus shared by everyone. Rejecting distinctions and restrictions, the GGS declares: Dharam succeeds 'when the entire earth becomes equal'—literally, one colour: '*Sristi sabh ikk varan hoi'* (GGS: 663). Dharam is definitely not an addendum or an external code of conduct but an emotional response from the inner depths of the self. A scriptural verse poignantly sums it up: 'In the heart of the saint all is Dharam—*sant jana ke hirdai sabh dharam'* (GGS: 294). Rather than follow external codes, morality resonates within saintly people; their heartbeat is goodness itself. Humanity, compassion, truth, justice are shared by saints across cultures and religions. East or West, these are the moral values championed by the Upanishads, Hebrew Prophets, Buddha, Mahavira, Plato, Lao Tzu, Confucius, Jesus, Dogen.

Place is important to our identity. How do we know who we are? How do we remember our past? The places we inhabit are significant to our memories and to the construction of our identity. A place is where we situate ourselves and develop relationships with others. Weaving our situatedness with our moral obligations, Guru Nanak makes us acutely aware that wherever we be located on Earth, in Bhatinda, Kenya, Birmingham or Yuba City, we are a part of the distant planets and galaxies and that our responsibilities extend to the whole cosmos. Temporally too, the interplay between the various planets expands our consciousness of time. The realm of Dharam is made up of nights (*rati*) and seasons (*ruti*) and dates (*thiti*) and days (var). With his distinction between the days of the week and the dates of the month, the First Sikh reminds us of the rhythm of lunar and solar cycles and the harmonious movements created by them. He makes us conscious of the precise moment we are in: What is the date (thiti)? What is the day (var)? At the same time, though, he makes us feel the billions and billions of years behind us and the billions and billions yet to come! Our daily calendars with their narrow standards of measurement acquire a much larger vista, opening us up to the wonderful patterns of our wide universe. The temporal rhythms make us cognizant of the constant flux, diversity and multiplicity—ontologically grounded in the absolute One.

And what are we made of? We are essentially elements—air (*pavan*), water (*pani*), fire (*agni*), earth (*patal*), and their compounds, specifies the Guru. His scientific perspective refuses to separate humans from other species, or even the living from the inanimate. The physicality of individual existence is conjoined with the wider environment. Guru Nanak's basic principle that we are made up of the elements like everything else around us prefigures the Big Bang Theory. For the First Sikh, we have all emerged from the basic matter of the universe, we share the singular source, and we are a part of the reality of the diverse chemical, biological and material shapes and forms. Our sensibilities are common to the various species of our multiverse.

Simultaneously, he rejoices in the diversity of our planet Earth: 'In its midst are beings and lifestyles of all hues, with endless names and countless forms.' No two bodies are alike. He is fascinated by the wondrous variety: 'How many species, how many languages, and how many rulers and kings? How many mystics, how many devotees, O Nanak, there's no end to their end!' (GGS: 7) Against homogenization and uniformity, the First Sikh celebrates the cosmic, cultural, linguistic and political diversity. In his encounter with people of various faiths, Hindu, Muslim, Jain or Yogi, he urges each one to be authentically who they are; his message to everyone is to live sincerely by synchronizing their inner values with their outward behaviour. His respect for the diversity of human experience is an important lesson for modern society bent on killing species for its own use, and imposing economic, political and cultural hegemony on all others. Unless we appreciate diversity, we cannot feel an affinity with others. We cannot coexist harmoniously with other people and species which happen to be different from us. The appreciation of kinship comes with the realization that all particularities palpitate with the indwelling same one Divine—'all species and languages come together in You', says the First Sikh (GGS: 1021). His evening hymn 'Arati' celebrates '*Sabh mai joti joti hai soi*— there is a light in all and that light is the One' (GGS:13, GGS: 663).

The hallmark of the First Sikh's philosophy is pluralism, and the Janamsakhis illustrated it sumptuously. Actually, the Sikh canon, incorporating the voice of Sikh Gurus, Hindu Bhagats, and Muslim Sufis alike, is itself a perfect illustration. The numerous GGS authors vary considerably in their philosophy and expression. For example, Sheikh Farid's religious prescriptions, his rigorous asceticism, his intense anxiety in this world, his fear of judgement, and his eschatological perspectives are all so different from that of the First Sikh and his successors' all-embracing philosophy and their joyous tone. Yet, they are consciously included in the Sikh sacred book with full acknowledgement of their distinctiveness and difference. There are even several scriptural instances where Sikh Gurus (Guru Nanak, Guru Amar Das and Guru Arjan) directly respond to and enter a dialogue with the Muslim Sheikh. We have here a fine example of an effective engagement with diversity.

Similarly, the Bhagats add their own special spiritual ingredients. They too image the Divine, but from their polyphonic Hindu imagination they offer a different hue and vibrancy. Just as Sufi Sheikh Farid opens readers to the West Asian, Hindu poets like Namdev and Ravidas introduce the indigenous Indian worldview. Guru Nanak did not propagate any theory of incarnation or any mythological notions of creation. In fact, the Japji categorically states that the One cannot be installed into any form; no myth explains when or how creation came to be. But it was his broad-mindedness that attracted him to people with views different from his own. As we found in the preceding chapters, there is a genuine intention to know and interact with people of other faiths and overcome any sense of alienation or fear of the other. If Bhagat Namdev relates to the One in the form of Krishna or Ram, there is no reason to exclude him from the Sikh sacred text. Since nothing, nothing whatsoever, could be excluded from the Infinite One envisioned by the founder Sikh Guru, his successor Guru Arjan confidently included a multitude of West Asian and South Asian concepts and images and accents. Their presence in the Sikh sacred text highlights its inherent pluralism and offers a true understanding and praxis of the First Sikh's Ikk Oan Kar.

Inseparable from the home of righteousness (*dharamsal*), the earth (dharti) provides everybody equal opportunity to act ethically and purposefully. This 'body itself is Dharam—*eh sariru sabhu dharam hai*'. Our sense of duty is developed with and through our body and senses while enjoying our diverse complexions, features and accents. There is no body and no thing on Earth which is bad or polluted: 'The earth is not tainted; water is not tainted—*juth na dharti juth na pani*' (GGS: 1240). Cartesian dualisms have no place in Dharam Khand. In order to acclaim the supposedly perfected immateriality of the soul, our sensuous body is not vilified; in order to glorify eternity, our life in its tiny and precious instants is not denigrated. No *thing* we see and hear and taste and touch and smell is denigrated to Plato's pure formless essence, nor are the nitty-gritty aspects of life usurped by some heavenly Lord. This body is sanctified. A magical locus, it is in and through our body that we develop our aesthetic, cognitive, moral, emotional and spiritual capacities.

The First Sikh subverts conventional Indian and Greek philosophies that view the cosmos as a mere appearance of reality or aspire to disentangle the transient physical forms from the immutable spiritual essence. His ontology seeks the union of the temporal with the timeless, thought with emotion, and truth with true living. Individual life or the cosmos is no mere shadow of Kant's phenomenal self (*ding an sich*); it is not the maya or illusion of Samkhya philosophy. It is Truth itself. Guru Nanak exalts human existence as Truth, Reality; he does not denigrate it as a condition of imperfection or falsity.

He does bring attention to the two poles of the moral axis: the *gurmukhs* and the *manmukhs*. The gurmukhs are the 'guru-centred' who literally face (*mukh*) the guru, and they live in harmony with the infinite One they see. In contrast to these enlightened ones, the 'self-centred' split from the universal One, face (mukh) their individual egoistic personality (mann, which in Punjabi means both mind and heart). Whereas the guru-centred use their senses to live free, like the infinite One, the self-centred abuse their senses, trapped by their insatiable obsession with their egoistic self. The gurmukh–manmukh antithesis is central in Guru Nanak's ontology.

So whatever we do on Earth has an effect. The universal injunction plays out: as you sow, so shall you reap. The law of cause and effect applies to each and every action: '*Karami karami hoe vichar*—each and every action is reflected upon.' The First Sikh's Dharam Khand opens up the scene of the true court (*sacha darbar*) too, where nothing anybody does goes unnoticed by the true One (*sacha ap*). We find out the judgement on our good and bad actions (the metaphor of raw and ripe is used) only when we reach the divine court. It is in the divine court 'that the accepted five are adorned—*tithai sohani panc parvanu*.' But who are these 'five' (*panc*) welcomed in the true court? His reference is ambiguous. Translators and exegetes interpret these as 'saints', the 'self-elect, the self-realized Saints'.[6] For me, such self-elect 'saints' are much too elitist; the five are ordinary physical doers, and therefore I believe these are our five senses. The 'five' (panc) emerge frequently in Guru Nanak's verse with both positive and negative connotations. The five senses can turn into virtues; they can turn into vice. On the one hand the 'five' can develop into truth (sat), contentment (santokh), compassion (*daia*), righteousness (dharam), and patience (*dhiraj*); on the other hand, the five senses can regress into lust (*kam*), anger (*krodha*), greed (*lobhu*), attachment (*mohu*) and pride (*ahankar*).

The earth is the stage for righteous action. The earth first offers existence itself and then the opportunity to engage in moral and ethical action. In an alliteration of '*ds*', Guru Nanak reiterates: '*Dharat upai dhari dharamsal*—the earth was created to establish the home of Dharam' (GGS: 1033). In yet another explanation, 'For the sake of good people the true One embellished the earth—*gurmukh dharti sachai saji*' (GGS: 941). The earth is beautiful, and humans are created to do good. The First Sikh charges us with a moral responsibility. We must all work together to maintain the beauty and splendour of the earth, not only for ourselves but also for our future generations.

We build up our home of Dharam (dharamsal) not in isolation but only in and through relationships with others grounded in and on the earth (dharti). Marriage and children, friends, and family, help us build it up. Since the entire earth is the home of Dharam, there is no special spot demarcated for our duties. Morality is not fostered in some distant cave or faraway forest, rather it is practised in the immediate world of family and profession. The Kshatriya is not obligated to take up arms for justice, nor the White Man to carry out 'his burden'. Guru Nanak tore up all those mutually exclusive scripts that had been enforced on people simply on the basis of their biological birth. His Dharam Khand does not set up a strict deontology or draw up a list of rituals. It is not prescriptive; it is not proscriptive. It situates each one of us on our planet Earth and organically puts us in touch with our mothers, our families, our friends, our pluralistic society, our variegated cosmos, our temporal rhythms, and our singular Divine. Significantly, it leaves each one of us to figure out and live in such a way that our daily conduct, moral behaviour, ethical theories, social obligations and political interactions are in harmony with the world around us. The First Sikh liberated people from the traditional millstone around their neck. His ontology celebrates the multiplicity of existence, bonding the individual with the cosmic, the micro with the macro, being with becoming. Thus, in his own unique way, the First Sikh places special possibilities and elicits moral responsibilities so we share the cosmos with infinite species. That we forge constructive relationships and do actions that are not divisive or endangering for anything or any being we reckon is 'the duty of the sphere of realm of Duty—*dharam khand ka eho dharam*'.

Epistemology

Epistemology elicits questions. 'What do we know?', 'What is knowledge?', 'How do we acquire knowledge?', 'What are the necessary conditions of knowledge?' Guru Nanak begins with his own question: 'Tell us about the actions of the realm of knowledge—*gyanu khandu ka akhau karam . . .*' His interactive style motivates readers to search for themselves. The Guru does not assume beliefs or submission or justification for any particular epistemic system. Instead he incites us to think about the choices we make and perform actions with mindfulness. For him, epistemology is inseparable from ethics. Reflecting on knowledge is a philanthropic act (*vidia vichari ta parupkari*, GGS: 356). Like his ontological understanding, epistemology for the Guru is not propositional but an actual *doing*; he subtly trains us to use our intellectual gifts and discover new tracks so we can enact in broadminded ways.

Gyan Khand, the region of knowledge, stretches our mind and imagination. Away from books, teachers and deities, away from rituals and sacred places, we are ushered into a magical planetarium. Without letting the mind halt on any one thing, the Guru flashes 'countless varieties of atmosphere, water, and fire—*kete pavana pani vaisantar*'. His epistemological sphere consists of countless inhabited planets like Mother Earth (*ketia karam bhumi*), countless mountains (*mer kete*), countless moons (*kete cand*), suns (*sur*), and constellations (*mandal des*). The First Sikh's artistic genius is stunning. How do we even begin to imagine the sheer immensity, the geometry of this multiverse he opens for us? In this ever-widening horizon, terrestrial and celestial worlds are not split asunder, the earth is not put under the skies. The Guru prompts us to unveil the astonishing links of our cosmos which have subtle, complex and often mathematical structures. Mental clogs begin to dissolve as the individual becomes cognizant of the vast glory of creation. His breathless recounting makes one hungry to explore the scientific mysteries of the universe. We get excited about the discoveries being made by physicists and astrophysicists.

This sphere also mentions innumerable gods and goddesses, preachers, teachers, saints, and masters:

. . . kete kan mahesa
kete barme gharati ghariahi rup rang ke ves . . .
kete siddha buddha natha kete kete devi ves

[. . . how many Krishnas and Shivas
How many Brahmas were created in millions of forms
Countless siddhas, buddhas, nathas, and so many, many goddesses . . .]

The First Sikh acknowledges multifold figures from Indian religious history. There is no shunning of any school of thought, no phobic reaction of any sort. His epistemology fully accepts the disparate Vaishnavites, Shaivites, Buddhist and Natha systems along with countless male and female deities. Earlier in his Japji he affirms numerous ways of meditation, avenues of love, ways of worship, prayers and austerities, texts and reciters, yogis, renunciates, 'countless the devout reflecting on virtue and knowledge, countless the pious and countless the patrons . . .' (Japji 17). The Guru embraces the manifold diversity because it all belongs to the sole Reality: '*Sikh mat sabh buddhi tumhari*—all teaching, wisdom, discernment are Yours' (GGS: 795).

But every person must grasp it for themselves. No deity, no text, no teacher can give out the instruction. 'Knowledge is not found in words—*gyan na gali dhundiai*,' says the First Sikh unequivocally (GGS: 465). Of course 'we all talk about knowledge all the time, and yet all our talking and arguing brings only distress—*gyan gyan kathai sabh koi kath kath badu kare dukh hoi*' (GGS: 831). Superficial talk and discourse get mired in illusion. All teaching, wisdom and discernment belong to the infinite One, and each individual has to cognize that One for themselves, through their own faculties. 'Without actual tasting there is no liberation—*bin ras rate mukt na hoi*' (GGS: 831). Just as a midwife helps bring out the baby, so can any teacher/master/scripture help us recognize the universal matrix present deep inside and everywhere out and beyond. The responsibility lies on us individuals; we must train ourselves intellectually to recognize the Reality. We need to cultivate ourselves to be able to experience the infinite One. Knowledge is not some objective factual conception that can be memorized; it is not a belief system that can be faithfully followed or ritualistically mastered. The Guru poignantly asks, 'What can the poor Veda or Qateb do when nobody recognizes the singular One' (GGS: 1153)? He empathizes with the Indic and Abrahamic texts which convey the message of the divine One; regrettably, the problem lies with us readers and listeners who neither reflect (*bicarai*) on them nor recognize (*bujhehi*) the singular one (*ikk eka*).

How to open up our sensibilities and recognize the universal Self? 'Selfish ego trades in knowledge for toxic stuff, and we end up consuming toxins—*manmukhu bidia bikrada bikhu khate bikhu khae*' (GGS: 938). Dualistic ego robs us of knowledge, the treasure we possess deep in our heart. If 'we crush the inflated ego, we gain the knowledge of the six schools of philosophy—*mann chure khatu darsan janu*' (GGS: 352). Guru Nanak's use of '*khat darsan*' could denote the Sankhya, Yoga, Nyaya, Vaisheshika, Mimamsa and Vedanta doxographic systems or it could be a shorthand term for all religions. Selfish and dualistic ego stands in the way of real knowledge. The Guru is therefore critical of highbrows who presume to know the mystery of creation and boast about their knowledge. He denounces any authoritarian claim by anyone from any school of thought. He reprimands the talkative show-offs, 'the babbler who presumes to know the answer is written down as the fool of fools' (Japji: 26); those who talk big are 'idiots inscribing letters in the air' (GGS: 151).

Rather than spew out pedantic answers, we must feel the glory of the Creator. This feeling inspires us to think about our role in this world, discover ways of interacting with the plurality and magnitude around us, and navigate our actions accordingly. As the Guru says, 'You are the tablet, You are the pen, You are also the writing on it, Nanak, speak of only the One, why any another?—*apai pati kalam ap upar lekh bhi tun eko kahiai nanaka duja kahe ku'* (GGS: 1291). The writer, the written, the mode of writing are not apart, and paradoxically, the ability to read and decipher letters also comes from that One:

Gyan dhyan sabh gur te hoi
sachi rahat sacha mann soi

[The guru inspires all knowledge and contemplation
Living truthfully, the true One comes to mind]

GGS: 831

The 'guru' as we defined in the opening chapter is a mechanism by which the ever-present Being gets imprinted on our consciousness. The subject of the First Sikh's epistemology, the object of his epistemology, and the medium of his epistemology is therefore the One alone. But it is only by living truthfully that the One comes to mind. Moral life is the means to achieve knowledge. It is on the tree of our actions that flowers of righteousness bloom and the fruit of knowledge ripens (GGS: 1168). Guru Nanak identifies ignorant blind people as those 'who do blind deeds, their hearts lack the eyes that see'.[7] Like morality, the seeing eyes are set in the heart. Knowledge (*vidya*) is derived from its Sanskrit root '*vid*', meaning 'to know', which is etymologically related to the Latin '*videre*', to see, and to the Greek '*oida*', to know, and even to the English 'wit'. Knowing and seeing are thus simultaneous events. The Guru instructs us to line our eyes with knowledge so we can get rid of our blindness. He wants us to take up the sword of knowledge to fight off ignorance, he asks yogis to put on the earrings of knowledge, and the pandits to wear the sacred thread of knowledge. Knowledge builds up on righteous living, so architecturally Guru Nanak's Gyan Khand follows Dharam Khand in his Japji composition, the quintessence of his philosophical vision and artistry. The First Sikh uses several pedagogies to help us realize that One.

In Stanza 21 of the Japji he asks us about our origins: 'What was the time, what was the hour? What was the date, what was the day? What

was the season, what was the month when creation took its form?'
His questions are keen, and their pacing is quick. With such minute
distinctions of time, hour, date, day, month, season, he provokes us to
recollect our origins and really think about our place in the universe.
His stimulating questions enter contemporary debates about the origins
of our universe: When did it all begin? How did we all evolve? The
First Sikh mentions that even in his time scholars were offering their
own answers in vain. 'If pandits knew the time it would be written in
the Puranas, if qazis knew the hour it would be written in the Quran,
no yogi knows the date or day, no one knows the month or season'
(Japji, 21). He accepts no theories nor presumes any knowledge himself
but his response does not shut any doors. His is quite a progressive
pedagogy, for without giving answers, he incites us to deeply examine
creation. Devotees and scientists are equally welcome to the exhilarating
challenges that lie ahead in our quest. There is no tension between
'religion' and ' science' like the one we encounter between the Biblical
account of creation in Genesis and Darwin's theory of evolution—so
volatile in the West today.

The First Sikh's interrogative technique at the heart of his teaching
instils freedom and creativity in the minds of his readers and listeners.
While opening up possibilities for us to think about, the questioning
process draws upon new emotional, spiritual and intellectual reservoirs.
His questions are a wonderful literary device that engages manifold human
talents. Our imagination is stirred to envision the glory of this universe.
He even asks, 'So dar kheha so ghar keha jitu bhai sarab samale—what kind
of gate is it, what kind of a house is it, where everyone is harmoniously
contained?' (Japji: 27). Clearly the universe exhibits order. But the Guru
does not impose any teleological arguments; rather, he poetically inspires
us to think about That One. This perfectly designed world has to have
a supreme creator! Who is the Architect? The Builder? The Mechanic?
The Engineer? Our universe constitutes the magnificent dwelling of that
singular One; the grandeur of secular scientific discoveries would only
reveal that One's absolute magnificence and power. The passage continues
on to describe the place resounding with manifold musical melodies
and overflowing with visual splendour. Indras upon Indras, sages, gods,
beautiful women, water, wind, fire, heroes, ascetics, and so on and on

accompanied by various instruments sing the glory of the glorious One. This stanza from the Japji (the morning hymn) also appears in the daily evening hymn, 'Rahiras'. So not only are daily hectic schedules prefaced with glimpses into our world, they are also repeated at the end of the day, reminding us to assess: Did we really think about those wondrous elements surrounding us during the course of the day? Guru Nanak's epistemic stimulates individuals to go beyond the motions of the day and realize the immense spiritual beauty, music and joy in the world we inhabit.

The finale of Gyan Khand:

Gyan khand mahi gyan parchand
tithai nad binod kod anand

[In the realm of knowledge
   Knowledge blazes forth
Here is music, feasting, cheering, and joy]

In this scene, knowledge is the intellectual energy blazing forth. It burns off mental, physical and spiritual inertia; it turns myopic stereotypes and prejudices into ash. All the faculties are fired up. In the realm of knowledge, we go beyond the subject–object structure, the individual goes beyond his/her self and experiences ecstasy (anand). There is nothing irrational or antirational about the infinity we see: we hear music, we feast, we cheer, we take pleasure. This is Gyan Khand.

Aesthetics

Most often, religion and aesthetics are pitted against each other. Whereas religion is considered a 'spiritual' enterprise, the aesthetic is denigrated as something merely 'sensuous'. Scholars tend to divide philosophy into logic, ethics and aesthetics, the goals of which are, separately, the true, the good and the beautiful. A person's thinking is then determined by the truth, his or her character and behaviour by the good, and his or her feelings by the beautiful. The influential religious philosopher Kierkegaard categorized three realms—that of aesthetics, ethics and religions, with the aesthetic at the bottom rung. But for the First Sikh, the aesthetic experience of an individual is neither antithetical to the knowledge of the Divine nor antithetical to moral behaviour; rather, it is absolutely crucial for self-cultivation. By honing their senses, beings acquire knowledge and spirituality; they grow ethically, intellectually. In fact, the finale to the Gyan Khand (cited above) forms a prelude to the Saram Khand, and in turn the culmination of Saram Khand is to gain heightened awareness—that of gods and mystics. The artistic design of the aesthetic realm itself illustrates Guru Nanak's poetic craft, a stunning union of content and form.

The First Sikh enunciates aesthetics integral to the development of consciousness. It is in the aesthetic realm (Saram Khand) that 'we sharpen consciousness, wisdom, mind and discrimination—*tithai ghariai surati mat mani buddhi*' (Japji: 36). All exegetical expositions start out stating how the term Saram is 'unclear', 'cryptic' or 'disputed.' Scholars provide three possible origins for the word: the Sanskrit *sharma*, meaning effort; the Sanskrit *sharman* meaning joy or bliss; and the Persian *sharm* meaning shame, with connotations of humility and surrender. Hew McLeod discusses their polemics effectively and opts for the term 'effort' in his translation.[8] In the same vein, G.S. Talib utilizes 'spiritual endeavor' in his translation, but Gopal Singh goes for the Persian 'surrender'. M.A. Macauliffe in his notes firmly states, '*Sharm* here is not the Persian *sharm*, shame, nor the Sanskrit *sharam*, toil. It is the Sanskrit *sharman*, happiness'.[9]

If we look at the original '*saram khand ki bani roop*' where beautifying is going on (*bani roop*), we are immediately in the realm of aesthetics (Saram Khand). In this verse, bani is derived from the term *banavat*, meaning creation, formation, art; it does not mean 'word' or 'verse'. In his condensed passage the First Sikh brings together topics typically associated with aesthetics: art, beauty, joy, ineffability. He does not specify any particular medium for art. Whatever it be—colour, sound, word, fabric, stone or wood—the constructed objects are beautified. Macauliffe's translation, 'Beauty is the attribute of the realm of happiness', aptly relays the joyous spirit of the third Japji realm. Beauty is not a static noun; beauty is a vigorous verb releasing symmetry, clarity, harmony, balance, radiance. Guru Nanak's Saram Khand is the realm where things are chiselled and made beautiful. Their exquisiteness is beyond description:

Ta kia galla kathia na jahi
je ko kahe pichhai pachhutae

[Its praise cannot be put into words
Whosoever tries must regret their inadequacy]

GGS: 8

Although nothing can be said, it is in the aesthetic sphere that wisdom (mat) along with consciousness (surat), mind (mann) and the power of discrimination (*buddh*) are refined. *Ghariai*, from the infinitive *gharana*, literally means to sharpen or chisel. However blunt our mental, psychological, intellectual and reasoning faculties, all of them are developed and keenly chiselled in this realm of art and beauty. The honing that takes place in Saram Khand leads to mystical and divine knowledge '*Tithai ghariai sura siddha ki suddh*—here consciousness is sharpened to that of gods and mystics' (last line of the stanza). All thinking is spurred by an aesthetic sensibility. The artistic Guru knows the device that chisels: 'The blade is Truth, its steel is wholly Truth—*sach ki kati sach sabh sar*' and therefore 'Its finesse is infinitely superb—*gharat tis ki apar apar*' (GGS: 956). The opposite of anaesthesia is aesthetics, literally the heightening of our faculties. This vital experience so refines the epistemic quartet (surat, mat, mann and buddh) that the individual realizes union with the infinite plurality of subjects acknowledged in Gyan Khand. All distances and divisions between what is to be known and the knower, what is seen and the seer, are erased.

By refining our physical sensibilities we cultivate our spirituality and moral sensitivity. The First Sikh does not negate or reject the body, as was generally the case of holy men seeking the Divine in his milieu. To conquer the body was the starting point of religiosity for many of his Hindu, Muslim, Jain and Buddhist contemporaries. At some level their anxiety is a manifestation of what the feminist philosopher Elizabeth Grosz diagnoses as 'somatophobia,' that which only exacerbates the binary between body/spirit, mind/body, material/transcendent, temporality/eternity.[10] It is with and through our senses that we grow morally, intellectually and spiritually. As the American philosopher John Dewey says, they 'serve as sentinels of immediate thought and outposts of action'.[11] By savouring the fragrance of a flower, Guru Nanak recognizes (*pachhanai*) the essential nature of that particular flower and therewith the infinite One permeating our entire universe and beyond. In contrast to somatophobic views, 'only the person who enjoys the fragrance can know the flower—*rasia hovai musk ka tab phul pachhanai*', asserts the First Sikh (GGS: 725). Since the complex process of recognition (*pachhanai*) requires a physical act, he invariably exalts the body with its sensuous experience as the conduit for divine knowledge. For him, the five senses are the 'five birds' that peck the ambrosial fruit (GGS: 1033). These five—hearing, seeing, smelling, tasting and touching—must be intensified so that they do not fly astray but synchronize to receive the full succulence of the divine fruit. Rather than overcoming it, the First Sikh projects the deepening of a multi-sensual experience. We also find aesthetic sensibility at the heart of Confucian philosophy; in *Analects*, Master Confucius repeatedly emphasizes art as the avenue to moral cultivation and political sensibility.

The First Sikh artistically expresses the beauty of the divine One and Its artistic creation. In *Concerning the Spiritual in Art*, painter and art theorist Wassily Kandinsky writes, 'Art is not vague production, transitory and isolated, but a power which must be directed to the improvement and refinement of the human soul—to, in fact, the raising of the spiritual triangle.'[12] The imagery, the meaning, the sound, the beat, the rhythm and the rhyme of Guru Nanak's compositions captivate his readers and listeners. They hit us viscerally and ignite us to imagine the infinite One in unprecedented ways. Our shair/dhadhi brilliantly succeeds in heightening our senses. The spiritual anaesthesia wears off; we see the glorious Divine ever fresh and beautiful right before us: 'You are Truth, You are Beauty, You are joy forever—*sat suhan sada mann chao*' (Japji 21). 'Beautiful, beautiful we say my people, beautiful passionate crimson—*ruro ruro akhiai bhai rurau lal chalul*' (GGS: 637). A 'precious unique jewel—*ratanu anupu amolo*' (GGS 1010), 'our supreme Owner is beautiful—*rurau thakur mahro*' (GGS: 421). An enchanted Guru exclaims, 'My Beloved is coloured in most passionate crimson—*mera prabhu rangi ghanau ati rurau*' (GGS: 1331), 'Your eyes are exquisite, Your teeth are sparkling, Your nose is lovely along with Your long hair' (GGS: 567). Yet immediately these palpable images are juxtaposed to the utter transcendence of the divine One: 'not male, not female, not any bird, how wise and lovely You are my true One—*nar na purakh na pankhnu sachao chatur sarup*' (GGS: 1010). The brilliant, crimson, passionate, dazzling Beloved never ever takes on any form or shape! Infinite and unfathomable It ever remains. This perpetual dialectic between the physical and the metaphysical does something to the reader/listener. The First Sikh's aesthetic ontology awakens the experiential, affective and sensory dimensions; how we desire to embrace the supremely beautiful One! Beauty is holy; beauty is moral; it is a doorway to the infinite Transcendent.

He makes us acutely conscious that the One is seeing us too. For the letter P in his acrostic: 'Our emperor, the Supreme Ruler **P**aramesar designed this world for the delight of seeing—*pappai patisahu parmesar vekhan kao parpanch kia*;' this One 'sees, recognizes, knows everything, dwelling inside and out—*dekhai bujhai sabh kichh janai antar bahar rav rahia*' (GGS: 433). The One is not an omnipotent figure far apart. Our Creator is an artist who lovingly designs everyone and intimately watches too: 'You designed each thing, You recognize Yourself in each—*apinhai ap saj ap pachhania*' GGS: 1279). The First Sikh brings home the proximity of the divine One. We can literally feel the Divine eyes on us, and we rejoice in the pleasure that the One is taking in us. It also evokes a moral responsibility that we be conscious of how we behave and what we say. Moreover, his tiny phrase 'ap pachhania' invests us with enormous confidence, for that One recognizes Itself in us! Reading/hearing the First Sikh's verse we glow, and to use his simile, 'like earth bejewelled by the rain everything we see is lush green'. The presence of the One in this world endows every bit with beauty; the day is beautiful, the night drenched in rain is beautiful, the season is beautiful, the bumblebee is beautiful, the she-snake is beautiful, the Name is beautiful, language is beautiful, lovers of the divine One are beautiful, and 'most beautiful is the woman who wears the jewel of love on her forehead'.

The First Sikh's surging spiritual lyrics reveal our common matrix. Set in musical measures, they extend and strengthen our bonds. Verbal language can limit human communication, but the musical setting reaches across words, infecting listeners with sonorous beauty. Tolstoy rightly said:

> Art is not, as the metaphysicians say, the manifestation of some mysterious idea of beauty or God; it is not, as the aesthetical physiologists say, a game in which man lets off his excess of stored-up energy; it is not the expression of man's emotions by external signs; it is not the production of pleasing objects; and, above all, it is not pleasure; but it is a means of union among men, joining them together in the same feelings, and indispensable for the life and progress toward well-being of individuals and of humanity.[13]

Guru Nanak valued aesthetics, and his own aesthetic radiates spiritual efficacy, it raises the spiritual triangle. The First Sikh generated the religion on the aesthetic premise so it would not be some abstract reified system. He wanted people to take off their conventional lenses and see anew the wondrous beauty. When we activate our human sensibilities, they reveal our common heritage and we revel in collective joy. His interlacing poetic arabesques make us creative and innovative; they build mental and spiritual links amongst us across religions and cultures. Enjoying the fragrance of a flower leads to the realization— unconscious and conscious—that we are but one species in an intricate and mysterious web. The realm of aesthetics thus resists the usual pattern of becoming deleteriously divorced from the artistic, the religious and the ethical. Art is not merely for art's sake; it serves cultural, political, psychological, spiritual and environmental needs. The Sikh Guru shares Adrienne Rich's call to the power of poetry: 'Poetic imagination or intuition is never merely unto-itself, free-floating, or self-enclosed. It's radical, meaning, root-tangled in the grit of human arrangements and relationships: how we are with each other.'[14]

Ethics

Ethics for the First Sikh is a 'doing'—the fourth Japji sphere is karam (actions). How can we interact more closely and more strongly amongst ourselves and with the divine One? What can we do to promote our collective well-being? The very thought of the beautiful One present in and around us is invigorating, and it gets us doing actions in harmony with the expansive beauty all around. The dynamics of 'doing' (karam) is vital to all the khands: each action we do has an impact, so the term karam denotes both the action and its fruit, and except for Saram Khand where it acquires the act of sharpening (*gharia*), it appears distinctly in each of the khands. Typically, philosophers are concerned with meta-ethical origins of moral principles, their semantics and ethical judgements. The First Sikh instead is focused on the doing of right and wrong actions; more than the 'what' of ethics, he is concerned with the 'how'. Orthopraxy thus takes precedence over orthodoxy. He deems a truthful mode of existence higher than the conception of Truth, 'Higher than everything is Truth but higher still is True living,' he said (GGS: 62). We can infer that his parallel to the Descartian premise 'I think therefore I am' would be 'I do therefore I am'. Actions impact the mind and the body: 'Blind actions turn the mind blind, and the blind mind turns the body blind—*andhi kami andhu manu andhai tanu andhu*' (GGS: 1287). In Raga Prabhati he says, 'Do not ask about caste or clan . . . Caste and status are the actions we do.' Our status, name, success, our very being—mental and physical—are contingent on the actions we perform. The First Sikh discarded conventional, biologically stipulated actions by 'caste' or gender or stage of life, so he is referring to the general activities we choose to do, which depend on our personal values, proclivities and aspirations.

The meaning of the term 'karam' for the fourth Japji sphere has also been contested by scholars and translators. McLeod notes that the majority opinion derives 'karam' from the Persian word meaning grace.[15] Sikh exegete Kartar Singh interprets karam as divine grace through which one achieves *kapra*, literally cloth or garment—the garment of 'God's love'.[16] Gopal Singh and G.S. Talib both render it as the 'realm of grace', which I admit I also went by in an earlier work.[17] On the other hand, Macauliffe discerns karam as the equivalent of the Sanskrit karma and translates Karam Khand as the 'Realm of Action'. Sikh scholars Teja Singh and Khushwant Singh retain this view.[18] McLeod, however, strongly argues against it and translates Karam Khand as the Realm of Fulfillment.[19] Revisiting my own translation from twenty years ago, I realize how I had succumbed to the authority of mainstream scholars, for I translated 'karam' by the Christian term 'grace'. I give credit to Macauliffe because his translation 'Realm of Action' is in tune with Guru Nanak's ethical philosophy in which actions are the defining factor.

It is indeed a fitting designation for the realm that begins with 'full of force' (*karam khand ki bani jor*), where dwell 'mighty warriors and heroes' (*tithai jodh mahabal sur*), and inhabitants who perform joyous actions' (*karahi anandu*). Guru Nanak's visual camera captures heroes, both male and female, and devotees from different worlds working joyously in this sphere of actions. These ethical exemplars are together, they are all equal, and they are united because their bodies are saturated with the divine One. Rather than an individual achievement, theirs is a collective experience. The finale of this wide-ranging, inclusive and egalitarian sphere:

> *Tithai sito sita mahima mahi*
> *ta ke rup na kathne jahi*
> *na uhi marahi na thage jahi*
> *jin kai ramu vasai mann mahi*
> *tithai bhagat vasai ke loa*
> *karahi anandu sacha mani soe*

> [Here abide many heroines like Sita of surpassing praise
> Their beauty beyond words
> They do not die, they are not beguiled
> For Ram is in their mind
> Here live devotees of many worlds
> Joyous their actions for the true One beats in their heart]

The First Sikh uses multiple names for the divine One that were commonly used by his contemporaries. Ram in the above passage is one such instance. In the Hindu world Lord Ram is the incarnation of Vishnu, but Guru Nanak uses it invariably to designate the transcendent One; the Divine is never incarnated in any form. Occasionally, though, he refers to Ram as the protagonist of the Ramayana—husband of Sita, son of Dashratha of Ayodhya, who defeated the ten-headed demon Ravana. This double use of Ram's name in the GGS is clarified by Bhagat Kabir when he says it is used both for the son of Dashratha and for the universal One: both for 'the particular one' (*ek samana ek*) and 'the one merged into the infinite' (*ek anekeh mil gaia*, GGS: 1374). In the Karam Khand it is clearly the non-incarnate Divine, while Sita in the plural (*sito sita*) recalls the popular ancient Indian paradigm of virtue.

Guru Nanak's usage of '*sitas*' not only increases the figures numerically, it also takes away the distant 'goddess' stature of the epic queen of Ayodhya, Rama's wife, and makes women like Sita accessible and realistic members of society and models of ethical behaviour. Sita is not deified by any means; she is not a goddess incarnated, because that would only make her into some non-physical abstract ideal divorced from reality. In her classic text, *The Second Sex*, Simone de Beauvoir warned us that the goddess can be a dehumanization of women rather than their genuine exaltation, as she ends up being largely a male urge to have women 'smooth, hard, and changeless as a pebble'.[20] In his film *Devi* (1960) the legendary film director Satyajit Ray unveils the heart-wrenching metamorphosis of a healthy young Bengali woman into a deathlike figure once she is worshipped as an incarnation of the Hindu goddess in her dual epiphany of Durga–Kali.[21] The First Sikh admires Sita and women like her not as goddesses but as beautiful heroic women. He admits that 'words fail to describe their beauty—*ta ke rup na kathne jae*' (Japji: 37). The progressive and broad-minded First Sikh reproduces and magnifies the traditional Indian figure as he gives equal place to heroes and heroines.

Unfortunately, intellectuals who wear androcentric lenses miss out on the First Sikh's inclusive vision. So they end up either completely eliding the First Sikh's innovative configuration of Sita—in the case of the highly popular and respected UNESCO volume[22]—or they marginalize and misinterpret the ancient Indic female paradigm. G.S. Talib, for instance, shrugs her aside: 'It would be superfluous to dilate on the symbolic character of Sita as representative of all that is noblest and purest in human nature.'[23] Others congeal the lively Sita and her companions into solid ice (deriving the term *sita* from *sheeta*, meaning 'cold').[24] Ernest Trumpp follows this hermeneutic axis, and in his

English adaptation we find 'there Sita is cool (happy) in greatness'.[25] Still other writers reduce the life-blooded woman to being 'stitched', misappropriating Guru Nanak's usage of *sito-sita* into a man 'stitched' in devotion: '*puran taur te seeta hoia*' (perfectly stitched).[26] By distorting or excising such female mythological figures from the First Sikh's compositions, we fail to utilize his broad-mindedness. Without being deified, the mythic and literary protagonist Sita and other women like her are cherished as strong, compassionate, intelligent and creative personalities. Their comprehensive imagery in Guru Nanak's repertoire broadens our mental landscapes and affects our attitudes and actions towards one another. As we shall explore in the next chapter, the Guru rejected notions of female pollution and made the realization of the divine One as the highest Dharma for men and women at every stage of their life.

Men and women alike are warriors and heroes of Karam Khand. The Third Guru defines warrior heroes in the measure Sri: '*Nanak so sura variam jini vichu dustu ahankarau maria*—the true hero, Nanak, is one who kills the evil of egoity within' (GGS: 86). Herculean muscle and power is not the ideal. Real might and strength lie in smashing the vicious arrogance within. Inherent selfishness and pride (*ahamkara/I-do; haumai/I-me*) motivate wrong actions. By constantly centring on the 'I', 'me' and 'mine', the individual is wrenched from his/her universal root and reduced to a narrow self-centred personality. It is courageous warriors who fight off their psychological propensities.

These warriors conquer death. The citizens of Kharam Khand 'do not die, they are not beguiled—*na uhi marahi na thage jahi*'. The doctrine of transmigration central to Hindus, Buddhists and Jains is also a part of the First Sikh's worldview. In Raga Gauri we hear his haunting intimations:

> How many trees and shrubs did we appear as?[27]
> How many animals were we born as?
> How many families of snakes did we join in?
> How many types of birds did we fly as?
>
> GGS: 156

Unlike Hindu, Buddhist or Jain texts, the Guru does not elaborate on what happens after death. For instance, the Gita explains the paths of light (*devayana*) and darkness (*pitriyana*) that the atman can take upon death: if it takes the path of daylight, the bright fortnight, and the northward course of the sun, it merges with Brahman and does not return; if on the other hand it goes through night, the dark fortnight, and the six months of the southward course of the sun, the individual returns to the mortal world (Bhagavad Gita, Chapter 8: 24–25). The First Sikh claims no such knowledge. He expresses the utter enigma of the divine One's doing: 'When Yama seizes and drags us away, nobody knows Hari's secret.' Tellingly, he discloses the thin line between life and death: 'in an instant we turn strangers' (GGS: 74–75). Instead of death and reincarnation, the Guru impinges on us to think about the actions we must do in this brief span we have. The above passage estimating the countless possibilities of our past births—as trees, animals, birds—is actually prefaced by his quintessential question: What is the purpose of life? Why are we born? What are the actions we came to perform in this world—*kahe kam upae*? These are directed towards personality development. Bad actions keep us bound, and the ideal is to free ourselves from the circle of 'come and go—*ava gavan*', to use the typical Nanakian phrase for reincarnation.

In Raga Gauri, he identifies forces 'two' and 'three' as the cause. By 'two' he means dualistic actions done by the blind egocentric; 'the ignorant dualists talk of two, they come and go in death and divisions' (GGS: 223). Likewise, the numeral 'three' represents the three '*gunas*' of Samkhya philosophy: *sattva*, *rajas* and *tamas*—truth, passion and inertia. Everything in this world, be it physical, emotional, social or religious, is composed of different ratios of these three basic strands, and the ignorant blind do not recognize the universal Reality in its myriad appearances. The king of death, Yamaraja, hovers over these deluded egomaniacs. Seduced by the dazzling illusion of the three strands, they commit error after error. The First Sikh gives a graphic description of how our sentinels of thought and action get caught: 'Death in its net catches tongues and eyes, and our ears as we hear toxic lies' (GGS: 227).

But heroes do not fall prey to the 'two' and 'three'. They are not beguiled by kam, krodha, lobh, moh or ahankar—lust, anger, greed, attachment and arrogance (GGS: 600). These thieves take away the precious moral singular divine endowment of beings. They put us out of joint; each of these emotions hurts a person psychologically and physiologically. These are the toxins that put social cohesion and cosmic integration into jeopardy. They rob individuals of the underlying unity of humanity, and brutally destroy social relations and cosmic wholeness. Obsessed with pride and arrogance, the individual is divided from the One Reality. Duality (*dubida*) comes into play. The selfish ego asserts itself in opposition to others. Individuals become oblivious of the Divine within. The singular harmony is not experienced. Such an existence is measured through competition, malice, ill-will towards others, and a craving for power. It is subject to illusion. Unable to see the singular Truth, life is false, the individual lives for himself or herself alone. The selfish person (manmukh) acts immorally turned towards the I-me, in contrast with the enlightened one who works for the good of humanity and the world at large (gurmukh). A selfish (dualized), deluded (by the three *gunas*) body piles up pain, and it is slain by death.

Heroism involves virtue, but rather than formulate deontological rules and theories, Guru Nanak depicts the mighty inhabitants of the Karam Khand cherishing the transcendent One: 'The Divine is abundantly present in them—*tinu mahi ram rahia bharpur.*' This is the crux of the realm of action as the image of the infinite One within the individual is repeated three times in his short passage. Moral heroes are not lured by the false qualities of the world; they discern the Truth in the ever-changing and moving phenomena. And so '*Karahi anandu sacha mani soe*—joyous their actions, the true One beats in their heart'. The antidote to death and transmigration is to remember the One. In a superb analogy from Raga Malar, the First Sikh gives his ethical philosophy:

Pain is the poison, Hari's Name its antidote
Grind it in the mortar of contentment
    With a pestle that gives out gifts
Take this daily, keep your body strong
At the end you'll kick Yama hard against the floor (1)
Ingest this medicine, fools
It will flush out all your vices

GGS: 1256–57

Even cognitive remembering of the divine Name is rendered as grinding (*pisan*)—a very physical activity which is continuous, rhythmic, cyclical. The grinding implies a deep pressing; it's no mere recitation or parroting of the divine Name. The mortar is a balanced and content receptacle (*sila santokh*), reminiscent of Buddhist moral precepts), a mind not deluded by the 'three', not chasing after the 'two'. The pestle in the hand (*hath*), the prime organ of dexterity and actions, is the doing of pious deeds (*dan*). This is what must be done daily; it is not reserved for any particular day or place or any coordinate of the planetary movement. The First Sikh discarded traditional belief in horoscopes and astrological charts specifying special hours and days. Once this body absorbs the pulverized Name it gains such strength that Yama, the king of death, is easily beaten to death hard against the floor (*jam marai theh*). 'When we're rapt in You, Truth,' Nanak says, 'no death, no Yama's net touches us.' Hearts soak up the divine Name, and lust, anger, lies, illusionary poisons rinse off. Guru Nanak's usage of 'dan' in the above passage is literally 'gifts of charity'. With the universal One ground into the receptacle of our mind, we naturally do actions oriented towards the good of humanity and our cosmos.

Other than doing each deed overflowing with the infinite One, the First Sikh prescribes no particular way to act, he gives no dos or don'ts whatsoever. In fact, the first Sikh was vehemently against dominant normative deontological rules which he found segregated society and cut off our intrinsic bond with the universe around. Across his hymns we hear him criticize religious leaders and elites for advocating external rules and regulations. He found their prescriptions of so-called 'purity' and 'pollution' split the wholeness of an individual and set people apart on the basis of religion, caste, race, class and gender. Guided by their experience of the one Reality, moral heroes in Karam Khand live an adventurous life; they do not follow narrow conventional paths but confidently chart out new liberating ways for themselves and for their fellow beings.

Individuals have free will. The First Sikh explicitly says so: 'Actions are in our hand, let's embellish our tasks ourselves.' Our hand holds the pestle. The transcendent Assessor 'considers each and every action we perform—*karami karami hoe vichar*'. Depending on the fruit of our actions, we are either reborn or escape the cycle of transmigration and unite with the True One. Guru Nanak's life-affirming philosophy does not dwell on any heaven or hell. In this fourth sphere of actions, the lovers of Truth, whoever and from whatever corner of the Earth they may be, are together actively engaged in performing joyous deeds (*karahe anand*). The First Sikh's ethical philosophy erases male and female exclusionary scripts, it dissolves religious and ideological divisions amongst people. The ethical code is the same for everyone. His whole emphasis is to cultivate natural internal tendencies so we live blissfully while engaged in domestic, social and economic affairs. The mighty heroes kill their ego so they do not die, they are not cheated, they are liberated from all divisive and oppressive 'isms' of racism, sexism, classism, religious fanaticism. The realm of Action carries forward the opening Dharam Khand into the final—Sach Khand, the realm of Truth.

Soteriology

The fifth and final sphere, that of Truth (Sach Khand), expresses Guru Nanak's soteriological goal: union with the One named Truth. There is no rupture between life and the hereafter, for there is no mention of death or termination of any sort; he gives no description of what happens after death. With its animated trajectory, the sphere of Truth seems to be the entry point of heroic men and women. Engaged in joyous actions, they are free from the cycle of transmigration, and make their way into this infinite sphere. Compositionally, the realm of Truth and the realm of Action are set together, as the two constitute Stanza 37 of the Japji. Philosopher Nanak describes it as the home of the formless One, writing it like 'a poem' as Wittgenstein purports:

> *Sach khand vasai nirankar*
> *kari kari vehkhai nadari nihal*
> *tithai khand mandal varbhand*
> *je ko kathai ta ant na ant*
> *tithai loa loa akar*
> *jiv jiv hukam tivai tiv kar*
> *vekhai vigasai kari vichar*
> *nanak kathna karara sar*

[In the realm of Truth dwells the formless One
Ever creating, watches creation with the gaze of love
Here are continents, constellations, and universes,
Whose limits can never be told
Here are living beings of manifold forms
All acting to the Will
The One watches, rejoices, and reflects on creation
Nanak, to describe this is as hard as iron]

This penultimate segment of the Japji conveys Guru Nanak's soteriology: a truthful existence across a vast space teeming with an endless variety of living beings—all under the tender, joyous gaze of their Creator. The Guru does not introduce unusual otherworldly doctrines; he reiterates infinity, activity, rejoicing and ineffability, and thus projects the identity between the individual and the true One.

Here, finite beings experience utter infinity; their beautifully shaped bodies by the Creator are *with* the formless One. In this state there is total freedom because individuals have broken out of their insular selves and freed themselves from the circle of life and death. There are no boundaries, no demarcations of any sort as the dwelling place never ends—'here are continents, constellations, and universes, their counting never ending, never . . .' This sphere where dwells the formless One (*nrinkar*) is no different from the world upon worlds of shapes and forms (*loa loa akar*).

Here, beings do their actions in keeping with the Divine Will (*hukam*). Guru Nanak extensively uses the Arabic term 'hukam' to denote the constant principle by which the transcendent One governs the physical, psychological and moral aspects of this multiverse of ours. The second stanza of his Japji elaborates:

By the Will all forms are created
    What the Will is no one can say
By that Will all life is formed, all are made great
The Will determines the high and the low
    The Will writes out joy and suffering
Some are blessed by the Will, others wander from birth to birth
All are within the Will, none stand apart
    Nanak, one who recognizes the Will, will not say I or me

The Guru admits its utter ineffability. Nobody can say what the Will is, and yet everything follows its course. People who recognize its power overcome their dualistic arrogance. Once the 'I' or 'me' is gone, what is there to circle in death and rebirth? The liberated know and experience everything and everyone as a part of infinite oneness, and they perform their actions accordingly. In Raga Suhi the Guru explains, 'If we absorb in the true One, we are not born a second time—*sache seti ratia janam na duji var jio*' (GGS: 751).

Closely connected with Divine Will (hukam) is the writing. For Guru Nanak 'written' (*likhia*) or 'writ' (*lekha*) or 'to write' (*likhi*) is likewise an all-embracing principle governing the existence and movement of the universe. The written was the agent of creation at the very beginning of time, for everything created was 'written in a single stroke of the pen' (Japji: 16). The written is also human destiny penned on our forehead (Pahare: 1). But we beings also have free will to write our own future. The actions we perform in life are written down, and depending on this written account of our actions, we are either reborn or escape the cycle of transmigration and unite with the infinite One. So the Divine and humans are both engaged in the process of 'writing'. Ultimately, however, Guru Nanak proclaims that the whole process belongs to the divine One: 'You are the writing board, You are the pen, You are the writing on the board' (GGS: 1291).

In the realm of Truth we find an exciting reciprocity between the actions of living beings and that of the transcendent One: 'Ever creating, the Divine watches over creation with the gaze of love.' In Guru Nanak's philosophy, the formless Truth is actively engaged. Creation did not take place once upon a time, it is an ongoing process taken up by the Creator. Ever creating, the One simultaneously beholds beings doing their activities with the gaze of love (*nadar*). From the Persian *nazar*, meaning sight or vision, nadar is also a comprehensive principle governing the ontological, ethical, psychological and soteriological dimensions of life. As we noted before, the impersonal One (Ikk) is a theistic person who watches creation with love.

Fused in Guru Nanak's visuality is the Arabic term '*insan*', meaning both 'human being' and 'pupil of the eye'. Widespread amongst Sufi masters and philosophers, 'insan' is eminently used by the medieval Andalusian Ibn 'Arabi. For Ibn 'Arabi, the archetypal 'man', Adam, is God's *insan al-'ayn* (pupil of the eye): 'It is by him that the Reality looks on His creation and bestows Mercy [of existence] on them.'[28] Guru Nanak uses the sense of 'seeing' as the common denominator between the creator and the created, the two being relational and interdependent. But rather than limit it to the figure of Adam or the Prophet known as *insan al-kamil*, the Perfect Man, Guru Nanak's ultimate reality functions in and through the faculty of vision common to the whole of creation. Everything in this multiverse mirrors the divine creator 'seen in nature' all around (*qudrat disai*, GGS: 464). The First Sikh birthed a whole new philosophy. The image of the Divine is not confined to humans, the One is reflected in all beings and things. And as discussed before, 'Man' for Guru Nanak is not merely made in the image of 'God', 'God' seeks to see 'His' own image in 'Man' too—ap pachhania. Guru Nanak's creator and creation relationship bears mutual affinity. Holy is the human body; holy is this whole multiverse.

Being and becoming depend entirely on the divine glance. 'Says Nanak, without the divine gaze, no one comes into existence—*vinu nadari nanak nahi koi*' (GGS: 661). The Guru affirms a panentheistic view that everything in the world is contained in the divine gaze for nothing happens outside of it. The values of process philosophy promoted by feminist scholar Carol Christ permeate Guru Nanak's language and understanding.[29] The One is very close to us, for we are being seen constantly. But *how are we seen*? This is the question. 'Just as true One beholds so we become—*jaisi nadari kari vekhai sacha taisa hi ko hoi*' (GGS: 66). The way we are seen depends on how we present ourselves, so our becoming depends on our own personality and doing. Paradoxically, then, while each and every action is by the divine Will, performed under divine supervision, people make their own moral choices and enact accordingly. Along with the absolute primacy of the Divine, there is human freedom. Each of us follows the dictates of our individual volition and is assessed accordingly. The gaze from the infinite One is not a mechanical or automatic Divine reflex; it is an acknowledgment of individual merit. It is through actions that we win the Divine gaze and free ourselves from the cycle of birth and death.

In Sach Khand, the self and the One become a unity, an indescribable juncture wherein the seeing by the individual becomes the seeing by the Transcendent. In the concluding verse of Stanza 37, the One 'watches, rejoices, and reflects on creation, says Nanak, to describe this is as hard as iron'. We picture a mother watching over her child lovingly, being happy and reflecting upon her or him, being concerned about her or his future. Elsewhere, Guru Nanak says, 'You bless us with Your love— *ape bakhse dei piar*' (GGS: 1278). We are snuggled by Divine love. A continuous and unconditional love pours forth from the Transcendent, and in this harmony, there is no sense of conflict between the individual and That One. The reflection by the One evidences a real concern for what exists rather than taking existence to be a random play. Being and becoming are jointly validated. What this unity actually means is hard to describe—as hard as iron is the simile he employs. So the world here and the beyond are no different. The five spheres (khands) coalesce here and now. Planet Earth, Dharam Khand, is our spatial and temporal location and its perpetual motions give us opportunity to expand our knowledge (Gyan Khand), refine ourselves aesthetically (Saram Khand), engage in ethical action heroically (Karam Khand), and live freely with and in Truth (Sach Khand). This is liberation. This is moksha, a distinct condition of those who live truthfully. For Nanak the philosopher, *doing* true actions is no different from *being* Truth. His focus is not on heavenly and hellish regions beyond death, but on living fruitfully with fellow beings, ever alive to the touch of the one formless Truth—Ikk Oan Kar Sat Nam.

The Mystic

Admitting his verbal hardship to describe Sach Khand, Guru Nanak immediately offers a step-by-step manual of his philosophy through a jeweller working in his/her smithy. A mystic performance, the scene in this final stanza of the Japji (#38) both summarizes and vividly showcases the Guru's ontological, epistemological, aesthetic, ethical and soteriological framework. While the metallic resonance of his iron simile continues to ring, the imagery shifts from the expansive multiverse of Stanza 37 to a rather 'confined' space. The limitless continents, constellations and universes of Sach Khand turn into a small smithy in Stanza 38, driving us into our deepest self. The familiar and ordinary workshop with its anvil and hammer, bellows and fire, is a heart that beats sonically and forges the divine word on the crucible of love. This final stanza of the Japji strongly proves the mystical grounding of the first Sikh's philosophical worldview. It could well be the mystical experience Guru Nanak underwent himself but could not quite express.[30]

> Make discipline your smithy, and patience the goldsmith
> Make wisdom your anvil, and knowledge your hammer
> With awe as your bellows blaze the fire within
> In the vat of love pour the ambrosia
> So the word is forged in the true mint.
> This fulfillment of action comes to those blessed with the gaze;
> Says Nanak free are they who are gazed upon
>
> Japji, Stanza 38

We could also read the goldsmith describing the role of moral heroes. Each verse in this stanza appears as a parallel to the preceding five Khands. By exploring this stanza microscopically, we recover the sonic, semantic and existential aspects of Guru Nanak's mystical philosophy.

The Mystical Locus

Jatu pahara dhiraj suniaru

[Make discipline your smithy, and patience the goldsmith]

Corresponding with Dharam Khand, the opening verse of Stanza 38 underscores each particular temporal and spatial locus as the ontological base. It introduces us to an ordinary person engaged in everyday affairs taking his or her time to create their work of art as a means of unlocking the timeless mystery. Guru Nanak's jeweller illustrates the foremost rule spelt out by the expert on Christian mysticism, Evelyn Underhill. According to Underhill, 'True mysticism is active and practical, not passive and theoretical. It is an organic life-process, a something which the whole self does; not something as to which its intellect holds an opinion.'[31]

Guru Nanak's mystical locus of the smithy evokes a secular landscape. Clearly it is not any particular religious site, nor some spot in nature far from home and society. If anything, the jeweller's workshop transports us to a narrow lane in the hustle and bustle of a bazaar, putting us in close proximity with fellow beings. Furthermore, Guru Nanak's choice of the goldsmith as the paradigmatic mystic defies the elitism of an upper-class Brahmin or that of Plato's philosopher-king. The goldsmith would be at par with Guru Nanak's self-identification as a dhadhi—a group of bards who were classified at the lower rung of society. We also do not hear Guru Nanak addressing anybody particular. His extended analogies (like that of the smithy) are typically used to urge religious leaders from different traditions—Pandit, Mullah, Yogi—to be authentic practitioners in their respective traditions. In this case, the absence of a specific interlocutor conveys mysticism's universal application. The agent working away in a smithy transcends gender, class and religious boundaries, and opens up the mystical experience for everyone. Since our being is rooted in the intersection of each temporal and spatial movement, worldly orientation is the premise of Guru Nanak's mysticism.

The smithy (*pahara*) is specified as self-discipline (*jatu*). Our attention is immediately drawn to the body, the corporeal and sensory aspects of the self. Human faculties need to be developed so they get to feel the universal reality. Ascetic practices, breath control, pilgrimages to holy sites, purification rites, rituals or fasting have no effect. Several preceding stanzas of the Japji categorically reject external measures for they merely enfeeble the body. Actually, we find Guru Nanak's ideal articulated in the journal of David Henry Thoreau:

> Every man is the builder of a temple, called his body, to the god he worships, after a style purely his own, nor can he get off by hammering marble instead. We are all sculptors and painters, and our material is our own flesh and blood and bones. Any nobleness begins at once to refine a man's features, any meanness or sensuality to imbrute them.[32]

The body (*kaia*) as the temple (*mandir*) of the divine (*hari*) is prefigured in the GGS (*kaia hari mandir*, GGS: 1059). Guru Nanak's goldsmith is an artist, creatively fashioning the ontological self. By making themselves aesthetically attractive in a style purely their own, the jeweller but spiritualizes his/her sensuous faculties. The First Sikh does not prescribe any ceremonial injunctions. Balance and equipoise practised in the natural rhythm of daily routine would be the way to build up their 'own flesh and blood and bones'. Both Guru Nanak and the American Transcendentalist share a melioristic goal to transform the self, so there is full reciprocity between the inner and the outer self. In the prelude of the Japji, the ontological reality is named truth (Sat Nam), and for truth to manifest itself in a person, all mean and false impediments must be chiselled away. The 'nobleness' of truthful life radiates in the features, facial expressions and bodily bearing of the sculpted self: 'Truth is in the heart, truth is on the lips, truth is in the eyes, truth is the physique . . .' (GGS: 283).

The corporeal is conjoined with the mental, for the goldsmith (*suniar*) is patience (*dhiraj*), proclaims Guru Nanak. When Herman Hesse's young Siddhartha embarked on his spiritual journey, one of the virtues he pronounced was his patience, 'I can think. I can wait.' Besides being a Buddhist ideal, the goldsmith's attitude of dhiraj recalls *sabr*, embodied by the Prophets Job and Jacob, and cherished as an important milestone on the Sufi Path.[33] In Sufism it is a correlative of gratitude (*sukr*), and comes after the stages of repentance, abstinence, renunciation, remembrance and poverty. In Guru Nanak's mysticism, though, it is a correlative of self-discipline (*jatu*), and appears as the foremost 'station'.

His goldsmith strikingly represents patience as an active and positive cognitive state developed through the cultivation of the body. Some translators render dhiraj as 'resignation',[34] which misses out on the active and deliberate engagement with temporality, the starting point for Guru Nanak's jeweller. His is a mental space devoid of the feelings of hostility, anger, resentment or anxiety, for all restlessness has been arrested. The 'five birds' do not take off. The goldsmith using their familiar 'five teleceptors'[35] in the workshop take their time to make the jewel. Their whole self is *actively and practically* engaged.

The Mystical Preparation

Ahran mat ved hathiar

[Make wisdom your anvil and knowledge the hammer]

Preparation involves the anvil of wisdom and the knowledge of hammer. These two utilitarian objects bring out both critical epistemic distinctions as well as a dynamic unity. The anvil of wisdom (*mat*) implies a firm grounding, an innate sense that does not move or shake when struck by any sort of hammer. We hear of rocks utilized as anvils by chimpanzees to crack the nuts they eat, by birds to crack the shells of snails they feed on, by otters to break open the shellfish and clams they consume.[36] This instinctive 'proto-tool' shared by the species is the goldsmith's matrix on which the gold is placed. Guru Nanak's image illuminates wisdom as our primal substrate—the taste of universal values that make up our very being. Just as an anvil supports the metal placed on it, so does that primal wisdom ground each of us. He even calls it 'mother' (*mata mat*, GGS: 304), evoking a maternal matrix, also regarded as a rich treasury brimming with jewels, gems and pearls (Japji, Stanza 6). Thus, the bedrock of mysticism is the visceral wisdom each of us is born with, strong like a boulder, and precious and beautiful like a jewel. The First Sikh's epistemological perspective emerges vividly.

The hammer (*hathiar*) is the *veda*, specifies the First Sikh. For him the term 'veda' denotes the whole body of knowledge, not just the four traditional Hindu texts Rig, Yajur, Sama and Atharva. So veda is a cognitive perception. The image of the hammer in hand suggests this knowledge is something that belongs to the world and is consciously accrued. It would be the knowledge of the cosmic, social, political, cultural and religious currents all around us. If the anvil is the 'proto' tool, the hammer could be an 'associative', 'secondary' or 'sequential' tool.[37] But it would not entail mastery over any traditional language or grammar or scripture or philosophy or logical expertise. The First Sikh repeatedly criticizes traditional scholars for their pedantic preaching, exclusivist claims and intellectual arrogance. The hammer in the goldsmith's hand is a working-class symbol.

Knowledge is all around us, and everyone can avail of it and apply it (again not limited to the privileged Brahmin class or the philosopher-king). A technical device, it amplifies the force that is already within every being.

These distinct epistemic faculties—the anvil and the hammer—conjoin to shape and design the gold. Two features for mystical preparation come to the fore. First of all, by striking the hammer, the metal on the anvil spreads out and becomes smooth; its imperfections and indentations start to disappear. Likewise, knowledge expands the self, and as the egotistical self stuffed with dualities deflates, scratches and stereotypes in the mind begin to iron out. The lingering trope in Guru Nanak's realm of knowledge (Gyan Khand, Stanza 35) *kete* ('how many') recounts the sheer ecological, political, economic, linguistic, cultural, religious diversity. 'Hammered' by such a wondrous expanse, individuals realize their own infinitesimalness; their pride, arrogance and prejudices disappear; their confining dualistic constructs break open. The hammering, secondly, prepares the workpiece for imprinting designs. Not only do the designs on the surface of the anvil get transferred on to the gold, the metal is also ready to take on new and novel patterns that the jeweller would imagine. Knowledge of the diversity in the external world thus reinforces what is primal in us, and simultaneously gives birth to unexpected ideas and visions, to new attitudes and modes of being in the world, to exciting literary, visual, aural and philosophical works.

The hammering produces vibrations, and so Guru Nanak replays the importance of sonics in awakening the mystic sensibility. After all, the incus and the malleus are laterally connected in each body. The hammer-shaped small bone (malleus or hammer) of our middle ear transmits the sound vibrations from the eardrum to the anvil-shaped incus. Like the primal wisdom shared by the cosmos at large, there is for the First Sikh the soundless sound (anahad) existing through the ages. The transcendent sound is each heartbeat. In the Japji scene, the goldsmith is not performing any extraordinary activity. Rather, engaged in his artwork, his hammer of knowledge rings audibly as it strikes the gold on the anvil. The soundless sound is heard when the consciously heard sound(s) of this multiverse hit the primal sound within. The regular auditory canal with its malleus and incus is deemed important. In the opening chapter, we discussed how the Japji devotes four full stanzas to the importance of hearing. Our innate wisdom has all the jewels, gems and pearls, as the Guru already told us, but their sparkle is felt only when we become physically conscious. Hearing enables comprehension of what lies outside and thus serves as a connector of the exterior with the interior self. This spontaneous resonance hearkens the unstruck sound and all the sounds of the world; all the languages used by the various species are heard as reverberations of that singular primal sound. His hammer of knowledge striking the metal on the anvil of wisdom prepares the goldsmith to hear the primordial sound permeating his lane, village, province, country, continents, planets, constellations, universes.

The Mystical Ignition

Bhau khala agan tap tau

[With awe as your bellows blaze the fire within]

Art, like life, is contingent on fire (*agni*). Fire sustains the smithy; fire in the womb sustains the foetus. In an unforgettable verse, the Guru says, '*Vismad agni khedeh vidani*—wondrous fire plays out wonders' (GGS: 464). 'Each of us has the flame, and the flame is that One—*sabh mai joti joti hai soi*' (GGS: 663). But how do we discern it? The fire in the smithy is useless until it is flared up. How to ignite (*tap tau*) it? To do so, we must use the bellows (*khala*) of fear/awe (*bhau*), says Guru Nanak.[38] By using bellows, the dreary dead habits of daily routine surge into fiery passion.

The term 'awe', I suggest, is a better translation of 'bhau' than ordinary 'fear'. The bellows furnishes a strong blast, raising the rate of combustion and the heat output—a blast of excitement that increases a person's heart rate and fires up their imagination. To some extent, Otto Rank's familiar phrase '*Mysterium tremendum et fascinans*' is effective in grasping Guru Nanak's intricate analogy. The bellows fans the inner energy for the jeweller to get a sense of the One permeating the multiverse (*Wholly This!*),[39] and their response is not fear and trembling, but rather a compelling attraction for Its wondrous infinity.

Just as knowledge expands the mind, so does awe. In his description of the realm of knowledge, the First Sikh resorted to the image of a fiery blast: 'In the sphere of knowledge, knowledge blazes forth—*gyan khand mahi gyan parchand*' (Japji, Stanza 36). The heat is what melts the gold. Guru Nanak's smithy scene is reproduced by the Third Guru: 'The heated-up gold is purified of all pollution' (GGS: 666). Guru Nanak himself replays it in Raga Gauri where he contrasts the Japji jeweller with jewellers who lack divine awe: 'All that is shaped by them is flimsy, an amorphous mold hammered by the blind' (GGS: 151). In order to produce fresh designs, the goldsmith must ignite the creative fire with the bellows of awe.

Ironically, this awesome fear fuels a state of fearlessness. For Guru Nanak, ordinary fears and anxieties are mental inventions that inhibit union with the Divine. Only the egoistic self fears, fearing the loss of wealth, health, status or power. The bellows of awe snuff out egoism, and so

. . . Latent fears are frightened away
　　How amazing this fear
　　　　It frightens all other fears away!

GGS: 151

The jeweller then courageously turns towards new artistic directions. The heroic conquest of fear hearkens the fourth realm of action (Karam Khand). Its fearless protagonists do not rule over others, nor do they turn away from society; they live morally, harmoniously and courageously with fellow beings. The fire set ablaze with the bellows of awe generates self-empowerment. The jeweller confidently begins to compose the unfathomable One.

Guru Nanak's bellows conjure up the Kantian aesthetic of the sublime as well. Its blast kindles our supersensible nature, stretching us towards absolute totality. In Kant's distinction of the beautiful from the sublime, the beautiful objects appeal to us because of their form—a flower, for example. But the sublime is a sense of being overwhelmed by the formlessness—like that of a stormy ocean. Painful though the experience may be, it still brings us pleasure, for akin to Otto's 'Mysterium tremendum et fascinans', the sublime has an aura of mystery and ineffability. Kant's critics do take him to task for polluting his 'pure' aesthetic judgements of the sublime with moral feelings![40] In the Japji context, the synthesis is just perfect, for the goldsmith using the bellows becomes exquisitely alive aesthetically, cognitively, spiritually—and ethically. Confronting the grandeur of the infinite One sparks off the mystical potential lying dormant within.

The Mystic Pour

Bhanda bhaau amrit titu dhali

[In the vat of love pour the ambrosia]

The integral relationship between the emotions of awe (bhau) and love (*bhaau*) is a constant theme in Guru Nanak's oeuvre, and it dynamically plays out in this packed Japji stanza. The arteries have to be cleared of toxic fear (bhau) before the nourishing love can circulate in the body. Once the expansive emotion of bhaau takes over, we have the setting on of the mystical experience enunciated by the First Sikh. Solid gold becomes molten, ready to be designed.

The gold melted by the jeweller is ambrosia (*amrit*). This traditional Indian drink of immortality (*a+mrta*), the food of the gods, is for Guru Nanak the precious metal belonging to everyone equally in this world of ours. The molten sap is necessary for physical survival, for emotional sustenance and for spiritual renewal. The First Sikh sipped it during his own mystical experience. What was churned up by the gods at the beginning of creation in Hindu mythology is poured out by the jeweller—*after* s/he cultivate their senses, build up patience, synthesize knowledge with wisdom, and ignite the fire in the smithy with awe.

The pouring enacts movement, becoming, creativity. The mesmerizing pour of the ambrosial elixir is a popular image in the GGS, '*Jhim jhim amrit varsada*—the elixir rains ever so softly' (GGS: 74). The tender ambrosial shower generates feelings very different from that of being submerged into an ocean or consumed by a tornado. The jeweller retains his/her corporeality, sense of selfhood. Being and becoming are represented by the two states of gold: 'While the heated-up gold moves about intoxicated, the solid stays static' (GGS: 1203). Pouring the molten gold evokes a condition of reality pregnant with movement, plenitude and mystery. The temporal and sensuous experience of the mystic is consistently maintained.

The vat (*bhanda*) is love (bhaau). Metonymically linked with the body, nothing is polluted or impure about the vessel. 'Whatever is the transcendent beyond, that itself is the body—*jo brahmandai soi pinde*,' said the First Sikh unambiguously (GGS: 695). But it must be morally upright because 'nothing stays in an upturned vat; look, the ambrosia pours only into an upright one—*undai bhande kachhu na samavai siddhai amrit parai nihar*', he cautions (GGS: 504). The vat is purposively styled by the jeweller. Morality, sincerity, trust and strength of character make it stand upright (*siddhai*).

And of course it has to be empty of the vicious ego for it to be filled. Guru Nanak warns that the precious molten gold can be stolen by the five terrible thieves—lust, anger, greed, attachment and pride. The jeweller destroys this quintet of psychological and inner propensities by the intense heat fanned by awe and pours the precious liquid into the vessel of love. Love for the infinite One is the essential ingredient of Nanakian mysticism, a synonym for the molten amrit itself. As it flows through the veins and fills up the vessel, it takes the jeweller to those depths of richness and fullness where there is freedom from every limitation and barrier—extending the pores of the skin so wide that s/he savours the One in Its absolute unity and vibrant plurality. The Japji utensil corresponds with Underhill's mystic heart:

> ... not merely the 'seat of the affections,' 'the organ of tender emotion,' and the like: but rather the inmost sanctuary of personal being, the deep root of its love and will, the very source of its energy and life.[41]

Guru Nanak would only amplify Underhill's definition by saying that the heart is identical with the precious jewel being shaped by the jeweller: '*Rid manak mol amol*—the priceless jewel is the heart' (GGS: 22), the absolute One. Guru Nanak also regards 'liver' (*kaleja*), an organ crucial to bodily functions, as the biological, emotional, moral and spiritual sanctuary of personal being. The vat (vessel/heart/liver/body) is indeed the individual self, made of material and transcendent textures. Being and becoming are synergistically experienced by the mystic. The chemical golden elixir suffusing her is the universal One. Guru Nanak admits, 'Sipping ambrosia, we are inebriated with truth—*amrita pia sache mata*' (GGS: 945). Just like liquid gold moves about intoxicated, so does a person who ingests it. His successor Guru echoes how both mind and body are enraptured: 'Sipping ambrosia, the treasure of treasures, mind and body are in bliss—*nidh nidhan amrit pia mann tan anand*' (GGS: 814). As s/he works on the jewel s/he intrinsically *is*, Guru Nanak's goldsmith creatively fashions their own self. The mystic experience is an ardent realization of the ontological being—Ikk Oan Kar—prefaced in the Japji.

The Mystic Achievement

Ghariai sabad sachi taksal

[So the word is forged in the true mint]

What is unique to Guru Nanak's mysticism is the crafting of the jewel—a solid, material object is produced. The goldsmith's endeavour does not end with the infusion of the golden passion; s/he actually forges (*ghariai*) the word (sabad) in the true (sachi) mint (*taksal*). The monetary term 'taksal' denotes both 'coin' and the 'place' where it is minted. The agent and the product are authentic for the First Sikh—like the formless Truth he described dwelling in the final khand. In another verse he enumerates the holy word being forged joyously from eight metals of the Sovereign (GGS: 61). Of course, the metals belong to the Divine, but it is the artist who designs them for their secular consumption. The One is all space and time, present everywhere, and it is the mystic who shapes it for the good of society. The goldsmith is not an elite artist sitting in his or her private studio, but labouring in the smithy. Their work has a practical and functional import. The coins are bought and sold. They exchange many hands. Social conventions and financial networks hinge on these metallic commodities. The mystic experience for the First Sikh vibrantly contributes to the enrichment of the collective social, political, economic and spiritual life.

The 'coin' image is an essential component of the First Sikh's poetics. He extensively utilizes business terminology to validate a world-affirming, action-oriented philosophy. Religiosity is not separated from the material, the practical or the public; there is nothing pejorative about making business deals, trading and earning profit. Commercial language, with its 'principle', 'profit', 'loss', 'stock', 'coins', 'weights', 'scales', 'trading', 'deal', 'merchant', 'treasury', 'peddlers', 'price' and 'priceless', is widespread in his canon. Having worked in granaries, he was familiar with it and used its lexicon with an innate force. Importantly, the First Sikh opens up the commercial infrastructure equally for all members of his society: 'We are all peddlers of our merchant, a heavy-weight Owner—*sahu hamara thakur bhara ham tis ke vanjare,*' he declares (GGS: 155) The stratified caste system is upended; Vaishyas are not the only ones to be involved in business. Commercial employment proves to be a potentially useful activity for the individual and the larger community. Guru Nanak knew that the winds and waters of business and trade carried opportunities for the economic and social welfare of everyone. And so axiomatically 'unpoetic' terms employed by him acquire exquisite tenderness:

> *Ape kanda tol taraji ape tolanhara*
> *ape dekhai ape bujhai ape hai vanjara*

> [You are the indicator, the weights, the scales
> You are the appraiser
> You observe, You recognize
> You Yourself are the dealer]

GGS: 731

Indeed, the third and fifth spiritual spheres converge in the jeweller's commercial product. Saram Khand (Japji 36) is the realm of beauty, where wisdom (mat) along with consciousness (surat), mind (mann) and power of discrimination (buddh), are sharpened. What the jeweller 'sharpens' is the intangible holy word (sabad)! In their extraordinary performance, the jeweller *materially* designs the *word* that is usually heard, read, recited, spoken or written. For Guru Nanak 'the Word is the divine Itself—*hari ape sabad*' (GGS: 165). The goldsmith's 'sharpening', therefore, is giving form to the formless One—shaping the absolute solid gold into a dynamic verb, fashioning the unfathomable intelligibly, evoking the infinite in the imagination, imprinting the transcendent on the consciousness, pulling the timeless reality into seconds and minutes, holding the imperceptible palpably in the hand, projecting the infinite in palpable social spheres. The shaping is not imaging of the Divine in any sort of form; to reiterate, in Stanza 5 of the Japji Guru Nanak loudly declares that the formless One 'cannot be moulded—*thapia na jae*'. Rather than into physical imagery or icons, the infinite is sculpted in the consciousness in such a way that the individual somnolence is transmuted into keen rapture. Relationships, ventures and undertakings in this world are important to the First Sikh because they function as reproductions of the formless One. The goldsmith's work is the consubstantiation of the sacred and the secular, the metallic and the metaphysical, the aural and the visual.

The fifth mystic realm of the Japji where dwells the formless One (*vasai nrinkar*) is that of Truth (Sach Khand), and the mint (taksal) where the word is sharpened is true (sach) too. Thus, Guru Nanak reinforces the relationship between the ontological Truth and the practice of Truth in all spheres of daily life. The coin crafted by the jeweller is identical with Truth itself. The product is an integral expression of the transcendent that can be touched and seen and passed around. The Nanakian verse 'Truth is higher than everything but higher still is true living' circulates in the jeweller's coin as it serves the economic needs of society. The mystical experience is the transforming of the logos into ethos, so that when the coins and jewels move from the smithy to the wider community they advance a style of living with the realization, 'Every complexion, dress, and form is the One, the One Itself is the wondrous Word' (GGS: 946).

The Sikh Guru thus veers from the mainstream view that the aims of mysticism 'are wholly transcendental and spiritual. It is no way concerned with adding to, exploring, re-arranging, or improving anything in the visible world' (Underhill, *Mysticism*, p. 81). The term 'mysticism' comes from the Greek *muo*, meaning to shut the eyes or the mouth, and 'mute' is derived from the same root. In Guru Nanak's instance, the songster bursts into sublime verse on the 'isness' of the One Being—a reflex that shakes off any privacy, withdrawal or esotericism commonly associated with 'mysticism'. He stages the goldsmith precisely as a model to be emulated. Step by step, the audience is distinctly guided, so they imbibe the goldsmith's sensibilities and practices, and awaken to the radiance of the jewel they hold in their very hands. For Guru Nanak, the approach is an epiphany, a realization, a recognition, a discernment, a passionate experience of the ineffable One, sharpened, shaped, designed, imprinted, forged, lived out in the nitty-gritties of life—*with the aim to ameliorate the self and others*. Like the moral heroes, the First Sikh, an innovative goldsmith, promotes moral progress. He did not intend for philosophers or mystics to conform to any external codes, but to conform with the inner harmony evoked by the realization of the singular Infinite.

~

The symmetric weaving of philosophical and mystical dimensions highlights the First Sikh's socio-ontological matrix, one on which he developed his entire teaching, and his core institutions of sangat (togetherness), langar (community meal) and seva (selfless service). Dharam Khand to Sach Khand, the spheres are mapped on the longitudes and latitudes of our space and time. With the universal One as the premise, men and women equally live morally, reaching out horizontally towards family, society and the cosmos at large. Love for wisdom is an ineffable mystical experience; it is an embodied experience celebrated in the secular world.

The work in the smithy metonymically extends to all the professions on Earth: from the dyer dyeing fabrics, to the tailor stitching them, and to the acts of dressing up, applying make-up, trading goods, shopping sundries, squeezing sugarcane, selling and buying bangles, churning butter, gardening, farming, drawing water from the well, etc. Guru Nanak treasures each of these worldly activities. As the golden liquid flows through the body, all daily routines, tasks and sources of income are performed vigorously. There is no antithesis between spirituality and economic or political success. There is no suppression of the senses either, no extinction of the self; the sacred and the secular, corporeality and divinity, time and timeless, synchronize in the philosopher's mystic vision. It was on his socio-ontological premise that the First Sikh affirmed marriage and family; liberation is found 'midst sons, wife, and family' (GGS: 139); morality and spirituality develop in the company of saints. Guru Nanak himself makes use of an alchemical simile akin to Plato's: 'The company of the saints does marvels, like the touch of a philosopher's stone turns metal to gold' (GGS: 505).

The ontological, epistemological, aesthetic, ethical and soteriological facets converge in the individual experience of the singular universal Truth overflowing in each and every being in the now of the moment— the bliss of unbounded wholeness. Plato's magnetic stone moving iron rings serves as a useful simile to decipher the First Sikh's mystic philosophy. The ontological One is the prime magnet attracting the patient, disciplined and innovative goldsmith. As Socrates goes on to say in *Ion*, 'This stone not only pulls those rings, if they're iron, it also puts power *in* the rings, so they in turn can do just what the stone does—pull other rings—so that there's sometimes a very long chain of iron pieces and rings hanging from one another.'[42] Likewise, this divinely inspired Guru continues to impart his magnetic force across the generations. The First Sikh, a philosopher mystic, indeed is the goldsmith himself who in medieval India set forth a powerful spiritual momentum which only gets stronger with the passage of time.

4

The Revolutionary Thinker

Though we have been getting intimations of the First Sikh's progressive outlook, our focus thus far has been on the dynamics of the founder Guru, mapped on his mystic philosophy in the poetic mode. Admittedly, the Janamsakhis introduced us to his revolutionary spirit in various scenarios. We saw an eight-year-old Nanak disrupt his family's tradition of the sacred thread ceremony. His household is ready for this important rite of passage, a privilege of upper-caste (twice-born) Hindu boys. The kitchen is plastered for the ceremony, relatives and friends have gathered, the priest arrives to invest him, but little Nanak refuses to wear the sacred thread. How audacious of him to defy such a haloed rite in such an elaborate set-up! We also saw him in Kurukshetra (where the famous Mahabharata was fought), in another episode from the Janamsakhis, during a solar eclipse with meat being cooked in a pot beside him. From the conventional perspective, the landscape is intensely sacred, both spatially and temporally, and a host of perturbed ascetics approach the Guru, pointing their fingers at him for his sacrilegious act of cooking meat in such a holy site. The First Sikh, again, boldly challenges the rigidity with which vegetarianism was upheld by the orthodox. In another narrative, he meets priests offering waters to the rising sun, and he starts to sprinkle palmfuls of waters in the opposite direction: if theirs could reach such faraway entities, his sprinkling could surely water the fields down the road. The Janamsakhis sharply bring out Guru Nanak's radical views and behaviour, but since they are considered stories, they are dismissed by historians and the academy overall.

Generally, Guru Nanak is seen as an exalted figure, removed from everyday concerns. Even his iconic image depicts him as an ethereal, otherworldly person wearing a patched cloak, rapt in contemplation, with his eyes closed. His poetic, mystic and philosophical genius can sidetrack us from discerning his revolutionary impulse. The emphasis on his theology has deterred scholars from examining his courageous engagement with the structures of injustice and violence infecting his society. He actually fits in the phenomenon Salman Rushdie defines as 'revolution', for Guru Nanak 'challenges, questions, overturns assumptions, unsettles moral codes and disrespects sacred . . . entities'.[1] He lived in medieval India, centuries before the Universal Declaration of Human Rights drafted under the chairwomanship of Eleanor Roosevelt was adopted by the United Nations General Assembly on 10 December 1948; he lived centuries before the feminist movement officially got started; he lived centuries before issues of environmentalism or gay rights or pluralism came to the fore. And yet, as a twenty-first-century Sikh American woman teaching at a liberal arts college in New England, I am completely taken by his revolutionary spirit. I feel that this revered person from five and a half centuries ago has enormous resonance for our twenty-first century.

So we welcome his literary oeuvre as 'engaged literature', a term formulated by the French existentialist philosopher Jean-Paul Sartre.[2] Guru Nanak's verse imparts Sartre's hope that literature can serve as an instrument of social and political action. As noted before, the Guru's works are not 'art for art's sake'; they are not meant to entertain. His timeless melodies intersect with concrete historical moments, and in today's global, rapidly evolving society, they can meaningfully serve our cultural, political, psychological, social, spiritual and environmental needs. As they cement relationships between and among humans, nature and the universal Divine, the First Sikh's melodies disclose the two poles of the moral axis: the selfish manmukhs who face their ego, and the expansive gurmukhs who face the universal Reality. For the oppressive leaders, dictators, greedy exploiters and religious elites, they are a mirror reflecting the wrongs they perpetuate; for the weak and the oppressed, the underprivileged and the marginalized, they are a call to action. They fill us with confidence and energy. They motivate us to challenge the so-called 'sacred' codes, fight for justice, and live authentically in our common home.

In this chapter, we will focus on his two central and interdependent values of human rights and feminism, and in the next on his environmentalism. The First Sikh's revolutionary thoughts in his melodious lyrics have the potential to change the attitudes and behaviour of our polarized society festering with xenophobia, bigotry and violence.

Champion of Human Rights

Guru Nanak happens to be the founder of one of the five world religions, but he valued the 'human' above any religious category. In the Sikh collective memory, he expressed his revelation in a simple sentence: 'There is no Hindu, there is no Muslim.' The Guru here is not making a pronouncement on the quality of the religious life of the Hindus and Muslims of his day, nor was he refuting these, or, by implication, any other religious designations such as Jain, Buddhist, Jew and Christian. He was, in his revolutionary way, pointing towards the indivisibility of people: the oneness of the Divine embodied in the oneness of humanity. Neither does his statement aim at a uniform unity or a reduction of the pluralistic variety of Hindus, Muslims and others into a single religion. The First Sikh does not ask people to abandon their faith and adopt another. His words underscore the fundamental, common truth he perceived underlying the faith of diverse people; universal Reality was the lens through which he saw the commonness and unity amongst his fellow beings. The equality of humanity was to become the ethical paradigm for Guru Nanak and his followers. To cite Professor Harbans Singh, 'This was a simple announcement, and yet a significant one in the context of India of his day. To a society torn by conflict, he brought a vision of common humanity—a vision which transcended all barriers of creed and caste, race and country.'[3]

Guru Nanak's ideal was to go beyond the external categories of religion—Hindu or Muslim or any other. For him, 'religions' were institutionalized by the custodians of the respective traditions into systems for their own control and power, taking away the most essential aspect of life—the humanity of each person. Being human meant we realize the universal Reality we equally share, and therefore treat each person with dignity, relate with one another intimately, and work for the common benefit and joy of humanity and for the larger home of ours. And if one lived their humanity, they would automatically be a good

Hindu and a good Muslim, and a good Buddhist, and so on. The First Sikh underscored pluralism. All of us with our external differences need to go beyond diversity, relate with one another with all our differences from that fundamental human core that we unequivocally share.

As discussed earlier, Guru Nanak's ethics are grounded in '*eko dharam*' (one dharam). This was a radical overturning of the ancient codified system of *varnashramadharma*. Dharma in the Indic world denotes specific injunctions to specific classes (varna) at specific stages of life (*ashrama*). The rights and rites of people varied according to their biological birth in the four social classes: Brahmins (priests and teachers), Kshatriyas (administrators and warriors), Vaishyas (merchants and farmers) and Shudras (labourers). A Rig Vedic hymn (I: 10) unfolds this four-tiered system created from the different parts of the cosmic person as he is being sacrificed: from the mouth emerge the Brahmins at the apex of society for they chant the sacred hymns, from the muscular arms the Kshatriyas who protect and administer, from the thighs the Vaishyas who move about in their professions, and from the feet come the Shudras who do menial tasks for the upkeep of society. Furthermore, the four *ashramas* mandated different roles for different stages of life—student life, household life, retirement and renunciation. For the women, though, these stages were divided into three main phases: maidenhood (*kaumarya*), marriage (*vivaha*) and widowhood (*vaidhavya*). Like the Shudras, women were classified below the 'twice-born' upper-caste males. Guru Nanak protested against the ancient caste system, untouchability, religious divisions and basic human degradation. Against all divisions and categories, he stipulated the same moral obligations for each caste, class, religion, gender and age. In Guru Nanak's 'eko dharam' we read Article 1 of the United Nations' Universal Declaration of Human Rights: All human beings are born free and equal in dignity and rights. The First Sikh emphasized over and again that we are born from the same parent, we share the same creator, we have no biological or hereditary differences, and he made the divine One listen as well, '*Karta tun sabhna ka soi*—You Creator belong to all of us equally' (GGS: 360).

In times of uncertainty and fear we become unsure of ourselves and act in ways that alienate us from ourselves and others. Our xenophobic policies, rising economic inequities, religious conflicts, anti-immigration laws, and the wall(s) we are building are a symptom of our fears and phobias. The First Sikh helps us diagnose our state of mind and offers us guidelines that can be useful for us. His relatively peaceful milieu ended with the Mughal invasion of India. The pressure to please the new Mughal rulers and their officials made indigenous people insecure. Instead of becoming more diverse and accepting of the varied expressions of religious experience, some became more orthodox and fanatic. Others like the upper-caste Brahmins and elite Hindus, who sought positions in the Mughal court, were caught between the faith of the 'foreigners' and their own, between their public persona and their personal lives. Guru Nanak points out the tension:

> They levy taxes on cows and on Brahmans, and yet they expect
> Plastering kitchens with cow-dung will release them[4]
> They wear loin-cloth, holy dot, and carry a rosary
> While they eat the offerings made by foreigners[5]
> At home they perform Hindu worship
> In public they read Muslim scriptures
> They behave like brother Turks[6]
> Get rid of such hypocrisy

> GGS: 471

As we face our own conflicts today, the Guru forces us to examine ourselves. What is our vision of the world? What are our political and social attitudes? How are we acting? Are we being manipulated by the powers that are officiating? What can we do to remove the inequities of our present-day systems?

He boldly opposed the ethnic and social superiority of the Muslim rulers and their strict policy of Islamization. In spite of the brotherhood of Islam, segregation between the *ashraf* (honourable)— those of immigrant descent—and the *ajlaf* (ignoble)—those of convert descent—kept the Muslims in India stratified. Subgroups of the ashraf were the Sayyids, Sheikhs, Mughals and Pathans. The Indian converts were treated as inferior. Even the upper-class Indians lost their political, economic and social status. Another's religion, language, culture, aesthetic ideal and power structure were imposed on the Indian masses. Indians under pressure or suffering from an inferiority complex and a false consciousness imbibed the culture of their sultans and emperors. Guru Nanak challenges the aggressiveness and exclusivity of the 'foreign' rulers towards their Indian subjects:

Adi purakh kau allahu kahiai sekhan ai vari
deval devatian karu laga aisi kirati chali
kuja bang nivaj musala nil rup banvari
ghari ghari mia sabhna jian boli avar tumari

[The Timeless Person is called Allah
    The turn of the Sheikhs has come
Temples and deities are taxed, such has the practice become
The ablution bowl, prayer, prayer-mat are Muslim,
    Even the Preserver is dressed in blue
Each and every home resounds with Muslim greetings,
    Another language has taken over]

GGS: 1191

The worldview and the language of the rulers begin to supersede the prevalent mode of communication. The Hindu population, with its magnificent plurality of millions of gods and goddesses, is forced to accept a monotheistic Allah. The colour blue, symbolic of Muslim royalty, both sacred and secular, predominates. The Muslim god begins to hold sway over the imagination and language of the Hindus, Buddhists and Jains. In the second line, Guru Nanak alludes to the taxation on Hindu gods and their sacred spots. He may be citing the Jizya tax which all non-Muslims living in Muslim territories had to pay annually as the price of their protection by the state.

It is also the period of the Sheikhs, says Guru Nanak, which is most likely a strike against the built-in hierarchy of the Sufi orders like the Chisti, Suhrawardi, Naqshbandi and Qadariya. Often, the founders of these orders were perceived as the head of a spiritual hierarchy, parallel to the secular kingdom: 'The great Sufi leaders held a court that rivaled that of temporal Sultans; the patched cloak, the prayer carpet, the wooden sandals and the rosary were the mystics' insignias of chieftainship.'[7] The hereditary descendants of shaikhs (*shaikhzadas*), pirs (*pirzadas*) and the Prophet (Sayyids) received especial patronage. As Professor J.S. Grewal observes, Guru Nanak disapproved their identification with the regime, and their dependence upon the madad-i-ma'ash grants of land given by the government: 'Guru Nanak's denunciation of the contemporary government and administration is quite unequivocal.'[8] Any identification with and subsistence on the government was unacceptable. The First Sikh serves as the voice of the people, challenging the country's controlling elite and their authoritarian structures. The enduring power of his poetry empowers us too to resist the rising authoritarianism confronting us.

We must keep in mind that the Sufi approach to god through love had great appeal for the First Sikh, and across his vast literary repertoire, he expresses enormous respect for Islam. We hear him use the Islamic theological terms Allah, Khuda, Rahim, Parvardgar, Sahib, Meharvan, Haqq, Kabir, Karim, Maula, Rabb and Sahib with utmost respect. The preceding chapters illustrated his attraction for Sufi imagery, and the musical measures and styles popular with the Sufis. The First Sikh exalts 'Sufis who receive the Truth, live in the divine Court' (GGS: 15). What our revolutionary thinker adamantly opposed was the discriminatory attitude of the foreigners. He spoke against the wrongs of his day. Poetically, he protested against the political and cultural hegemony of the rulers, their unfair levying of taxes, and their suppression of the freedom of religion. He was sad to see the Indian masses being deferential to Muslim rulers, and adopting the cultural norms and style of the reigning elite. Guru Nanak was not against the Sheikhs as such, he was only critical of the way in which their 'ablution bowl, call to prayer, and prayer mat' were imposed bureaucratically. His overarching principle was to respect the rights of all. In a balanced tone he says in Var Majh, 'Violating another's rights is as bad as eating pork for some, eating beef for others.' Since pork is forbidden to Muslims and beef is forbidden to Hindus, the First Sikh uses the prevalent idiom to speak against the violation of human rights: 'We must not devour another's due' (GGS: 140-141). He guides us. He inspires us. He compels us to own up to the injustices infesting our society.

At times we do hear Guru Nanak pungently disrespect 'sacred' entities. He challenged reductionistic notions that lead to false pride. He clashed with those who obsessed about ritual practices and dietary restrictions. He drew no lines between the sacred and the profane, or the pure and the impure; everything that permeated with the divine One was sacred for him, and anything devoid of the One utterly impure. Pollution for him was all in the mind, it did not reside in objects. He therefore condemned external acts like bathing, going on pilgrimages, smearing the body with ash, eating purified food, reciting chants, drawing lines in the kitchen to demarcate sacred areas, etc. Here is an example of his sharp satirical critique:

> First the priest purifies himself
> > Then he seats himself in a pure spot
> Dishes yet to be tasted or served
> > Are placed before him.
> He eats his pure food, and purified still more
> > He begins to read his sacred verse
> Soon his purities turn into waste
> > Now who's to be blamed for this?
> Grain is holy, water is holy, fire is holy
> > Salt too, and by adding ghee, the fifth
> Our food is purer still . . .

GGS: 473

Guru Nanak's visual camera captures all the fuss about the rules of purity and pollution that are very much in practice even today. Just the other day, for the inauguration of their new house in my Maine neighbourhood, an Indian family invited a priest from New York City. These elaborate rules of purity we read in Guru Nanak's work were exactly observed for the priest's meal. The Guru wittily relays the fact that all that pure food turns into foul waste! His pithy comment is transformative. Instead of stressing about rigid purification rites, we learn to celebrate the sacredness of every bit of grain, water, fire, salt, ghee. He tellingly asks, 'What is meat? What is mustard leaf? In which of these does vice reside?' (GGS: 1289) Differentiations of vegetarian and non-vegetarian were for him mere external rigidities that pulled people away from their human nucleus. In contemporary times, Pope Francis offers a valuable diagnosis of why we humans get carried away by external formalities: It is insecurity that makes us tense, and to give the appearance of security we hide behind easy answers, ready formulas, rules and regulations.[9]

Since insecure times breed insularity, each religious group in Guru Nanak's milieu aimed to outdo the other. His society was rife with religious prescriptions, external performances and orthodox viewpoints. Reflecting on the moral twilight of his society, the First Sikh appeals to his contemporaries, Hindus, Muslims, Buddhists, Jains, Yogis and Siddhas alike, to get rid of external paraphernalia and feel the palpitations of the universal Infinite. He was critical of exclusivist claims, that one's own tradition was the only valid one; he was critical of all who usurped basic human values and exploited fellow beings in the name of religion. Religion was to be a moral guide and a fundamental human right. He wanted people to freely practise it—to be who they were. So neither to emulate anybody else nor to put down another. That they match their beliefs with their praxis is what he relayed to the diverse religious groups he conversed with on his long journeys.

Wherever he went and whomever he met, Guru Nanak championed freedom of thought. He wanted people to break their old habits and think anew for themselves. He urged them to be authentically who they were. To the Brahmins, he says:

> Brahmins see the ultimate being Brahmu[10]
> They earn their actions by meditation, austerity, and morality
> They abide by the religion of peace and contentment
> They break all fetters, they live free
> Such Brahmans indeed are worthy of worship

GGS: 1411

To the Muslims:

> It is tough to be called a Muslim
>   We can only be so called if we are one

We first cherish the sweet faith of the Prophet
    And scrape off all rusty layers of pride
A Muslim must follow the religion of the Prophet
    Remove doubts about life and death
Trust the Will of Rabb, hold the creator supreme
    And dispel the egoistic self
One who has loving kindness for all beings, Nanak
    Is called a Muslim

GGS: 141

To the Yogis:

Real yogis recognize the way,
By the guru's grace they know the One

GGS: 662

He could harshly criticize a Brahmin priest obsessed about purity, but here the Guru praises Brahmins, finds them worthy of worship—so long as they discern the infinite Being in all the parts and particularities of this world. His verse is a terse reminder of the etymology of their name—*brh*, to grow, flourish, expand. A Brahmin, therefore, must abide by recognizing Brahm, the single cosmic ever-flourishing Reality. Likewise, an authentic Muslim holds 'loving kindness for all beings— *sarab jia miharamati hoi*', and the real yogis too practise their way of life, yoked to the knowledge of the One. His leitmotif: to remain cognizant of the ultimate One, and not operate in dualistic, discriminating and divisive ways. Fellowship of humanity is Guru Nanak's supreme goal, one that we find desperately lacking in our contemporary life.

The Guru championed justice for all people—across religion, class, caste and gender. His institution of seva (selfless service) extended to one and all. When Babar invaded India, the First Sikh empathized with the defeated Lodi Sultans and their subjects. He suffered the anguish of the victims, male and female, Hindus, Muslims, Bhatts, Thakurs, alike. Importantly, he even questioned god: 'Don't You feel their pain? *Tain ki darad na aia?*' This is radically courageous of him. The revolutionary First Sikh goes on to say, 'If the powerful were to duel with the powerful that would be bearable, but when a ferocious lion pounces on cattle, then the Owner has to be taken into account for not protecting it.' The destruction of the weak and innocent torments him. He describes the destroyed city as '*Mas puri*', literally, the city of flesh. It is from the city of corpses that he sings hymns of Divine praise:

Sahib ke gun nanaku gavai
mas puri vichu akhu masola . . .

[Nanak sings the glory of the Sovereign
In the city of flesh he proclaims . . .]

GGS: 722

Guru Nanak's proclamation is that 'the One who started the flashy sport watches sitting afar alone—*jini upai rangi ravai baitha vekhai vakh ikela*' (GGS, p. 723). For him the creator and progenitor of this historic devastation is of course the universal One. Especially in the context of the stark scenario where it is being sung, Guru Nanak's praise does bear a harsh reprimand: How could the divine One sit afar detached watching this destructive sport? The First Sikh demands god to account for the horrible events. That divine One has to be actively engaged in the linear progression of humanity. That One cannot sit isolated—*vakh ikela*. The Guru raises important ethical issues. In Guru Nanak's mind there is a standard of justice to which god can and must be held. That One is not just the source of justice but is also under the jurisdiction of justice. His depiction of a historical event contains a passionate plea for involvement and change, so much so that he even urges the divine One to be engaged in the plight of the victims and not remain aloof. The supreme Judge has to be actively involved to protect the weak and innocent. The First Sikh's is a loud call, an ardent plea to uphold and guarantee human rights.

Though written centuries ago, the Babarvani hymns possess the sensitivity of contemporary scholars. Columbia University anthropologist Lila Abu-Lughod urges us to 'examine our own responsibilities for the situations in which others in distant places have found themselves . . . We do not stand outside the world, looking out to this sea of poor benighted people . . . we are part of that world'.[11] Arising out of his deep reflection and immediacy of experience, Guru Nanak prepares us for our own cause of social justice and equality today.

Women are at the centre of Babarvani. The marginalized objects of medieval Indian society become very significant subjects of Guru Nanak's thought. It is intriguing that a discourse on war would give so much narrative space to the women's condition. We hear his nuanced critique of regressive customs of purdah (veiling of women), sati (self-immolation) and widowhood from a woman-centred perspective. With a profoundly feminist consciousness, Guru Nanak describes the gruesome ripping off of the veils of Muslim women from head to foot ('*kina peran sir khur pate*', GGS, p. 418). Many women continue to wear the veil, and those who do not still live as though they were encaged—excluded from the public sphere, and from political and economic processes and interactions. The First Sikh makes us revisit the cloistered and claustrophobic life women continue to lead across religions and ethnicities with enormous empathy. He incites us to see through the physical, psychological and social coverings imposed on girls and women all over the world.

He also reports on the tragedy of Hindu women who 'make their homes a crematorium—*ikkna vasu masani*'. This most likely is a reference to the upper-caste women who were obligated to immolate themselves. Battling against foreign invaders, Hindu men were killed, so their widowed wives gave themselves up to the lapping flames. Through sati, which literally means 'good wife', a woman performed her morality by consummating her life of devotion to her husband. This self-sacrifice was renowned throughout the world, and in 30 CE, a Roman author extolled the Indian wife for her exemplary bravery: 'She flings herself on top of her husband's funeral pyre, and she is burned alive on it beside her husband's body, as if she were the happiest of women.'[12] Widowhood was an expression of *adharma* (immorality), a wife's failure in her supreme duty to her husband (pativrata).

Despite the fact that the practice of sati has been illegal since the early nineteenth century, violence against widows is still rampant. The Women's Media Center, Delhi, reports an estimated 40 million widows living in a state of 'social death.' The First Sikh graphically reports:

Jin sir sohan patian mangi pai sindhur
se sir kati munian gal vich avai dhuri

[Those who once had luxuriant braids lined with auspicious vermilion
Their heads are shaved off, their throats choke with ash]

GGS: 417

Having lost their husbands to Babar's men, the wives lose their basic
human rights. When we hear the First Sikh in medieval India voice
the shame inflicted on widows, we today are put to shame. How could
we remain so negligent? How could we allow any culture or religion
to sanction such inhumanity towards women? A common abuse I
heard growing up in the Punjab, 'husband-eater' (*khasama nun khani*),
for the reason that Indian women from time immemorial have been
accused of being responsible for their husband's death. It is *her* bad
karma that brings death to the husband and bad luck to *his* family is the
stereotypical thinking. Deepa Mehta's 2005 film *Water* exposes how
widows are forced to have their heads shaved; every ornament, colourful
outfit and tasty food is usurped from them. However young they may
be, they cannot remarry. Viewed as inauspicious, widows are shunned
by society. Even their shadow is considered bad luck. In the making of
her film, Mehta faced many challenges. Her movie set was ransacked
and Mehta's effigy was burned. She ended up making the film in Sri
Lanka and has been successful in raising global awareness. On 5 July
2007, CNN reported:

> Ostracized by society, thousands of India's widows flock to the holy
> city of Vrindavan waiting to die. They are found on side streets,
> hunched over with walking canes, their heads shaved and their pain
> etched by hundreds of deep wrinkles in their faces.

In their haunting tone, the First Sikh's two short lines (cited above) report
an awful lot. Their tiny syntactic units, perfectly structured parallels,
are amazingly powerful. Each reading generates a new insight. They
show us the rapidity of the grisly transformation brought on the wives
of Indian warriors who died fighting against Babar. Psychologically,

the women can barely digest the tragic news, and they are physically stripped. Gone is the crimson in the parting of their hair (*mangi pae sindhur*). Invested at her wedding by her husband, sindhur is a marker of women's sacredness, auspiciousness, joy and sexuality. The Guru's visual camera reveals the suddenness of the widows' heart-wrenching condition: those beautiful braids (*sohan patian*) are sheared off (*se sir kati*), their heads are shaved (*munian*). Their bodies are violated, their physicality taken away. Furthermore, the First Sikh movingly recounts 'their throats being choked with dust—*gal vich avai dhuri*'. We know that renunciates smear themselves with ash as a mark of giving up their sexuality and worldly aspirations, so the Guru here is recounting the tragic circumstance of widows being coerced into an ash-smeared, 'de-sexed' condition. His diction compellingly divulges the widow's utter voicelessness as well. Their throats are choked, what can they utter? How much burning can they bear? Reduced to cinders, widows have no voice, no identity, no social status, no life. Such Nanakian verses hit us viscerally and make us question the complex norms involving the patriarchal control of female sexuality from a global perspective.

With the Guru as our model, we must keep our eyes open to the socio-political-economic situation. We cannot shirk our human responsibility and remain apathetic. We must respond to the circumstances around us. He raises the consciousness of his contemporaries by acutely depicting the historical and social conditions of the Mughal invasion. Guru Nanak's verses, notes Professor Harbans Singh, significantly, 'are unexcelled for their power of expression and moral keenness. His poetry has important social meaning. Nowhere else in contemporary literature are the issues of the medieval Indian situation comprehended with such clarity or presented in tones of greater urgency'.[13] The First Sikh makes us feel our humanity, and so he compels us to think about the problems facing our global society: religious wars, gender justice, poverty, disease, climate change, xenophobia.

But we need to figure out what is the cause of each problem. We must think through our conflicts: Is it religion or is it human lust, anger, attachment, greed, pride—*kama, krodha, moha, lobh, ahankar*? Very often, religion is exploited for the sake of economic, political and social gain. We transfer our psychological conflicts on to external differences, and religious difference is an easy target. So instead of facing our issues, we easily misplace and dislocate our propensities and our psychological sicknesses as 'religious' conflicts. Guru Nanak offers an incisive analysis of Babar's aggressive conquest of India, *'Jaru vandi devai bhai*—it's wealth that divides brother from brother' (GGS: 417). During Babar's invasion, Guru Nanak did not see him as a 'Muslim' conqueror of a 'Hindu' India. A descendant of the Mongol conqueror Genghis Khan and also of the Turkish conqueror Timur the Great, Babar had territorial and financial aspirations; failing in his westward operations, he invaded India. Babar did not intend to pit one religion against another; in fact, the rulers of north India at that time were the Muslim Lodis. Clearly, his was not a religious conflict; a 'Muslim' was not invading 'Hindu' India.[14] It was purely Babar's greed for the wealth of India which divided the Muslim Babar from his Muslim Lodi brothers. Guru Nanak did not get stuck on superficial differences; he saw through their basic humanity.

How often we transfer our own phobias and deep psychological conflicts on to external differences, and we blame religion as the root cause. Actually, we fabricate individual desires and demands into a dangerous rhetoric for arousing exclusivism and communalism. The Hindu–Muslim conflict confronting Guru Nanak's society is carried over into modern times—between Israelis and Palestinians, Sikhs and Hindus, Catholics and Protestants, Sunnis and Shi'as. But what we are really doing is avoiding facing up to the root causes of conflict: human lust, anger, greed, attachment and pride. The First Sikh impels us to be self-critical and sort out our political and economic motivations. We must look into our own selves, and discern the root of our maladies, our sibling rivalries and jealousies, our desire for control and power.

Furthermore, we learn to advocate human rights with empathy. Guru Nanak's is not a patronizing rhetoric of 'saving' others, but a painful ache for the victims of Hindustan. The anguished Guru questions the supreme One: 'Don't You feel their pain? *Tain ki darad na aia?*' With enormous pathos he describes the devastation of the Lodi Sultans: 'Where are the sports, the stables and horses? Where are the drums and clarions? Where are the shining sword-belts, where are the chariots and the soldiers in red?' (GGS: 417). His haunting questions disclose the chilling speed with which the rich and powerful Sultans vanished. Deeply empathetic, he describes the abuse inflicted on women: on *her* body, *her* rituals, *her* religion, *her* daily tasks, *her* loved ones. The tragedy of Muslim and Hindu women is the same; the tragedy of an upper-caste and lower-caste Hindu woman is the same. The straight horizontal sequence of his verse bridges any chasms that may segregate women, 'Turks, Hindus, Bhatts or Thakurs'. The way women are ravaged manifests the suffering of the country perpetrated by the invaders. War sucks away the rich resources of India, her strength and her vitality, depleting her of herself. The rape of the women is not just a symbol for the conquest of Hindustan, both of them are real and simultaneous events. A distraught Guru says, '*Ratan vigar vigoe kuttin muia sar na kai*—this jewel of a country is now a ravaged bitch, no one cares for her dead' (GGS: 360). Empathy, not anger or hostility, should be our motivation to fight for justice.

Furthermore, the Guru teaches us to respect particular cultures and histories of people. He is neither Muslim nor Hindu, yet he is devastated by the loss of the daily pattern and rhythm of life in wartime north India: 'Some have lost their time for Namaz, some their Puja—*ikkna vakht khuaiahi ikkna puja jai*' (GGS: 417). Both Muslim and Hindu forms of worship are honoured by the Sikh Guru. Much as he was anti-ritual, in a heart-wrenching tone he asks, 'How can the Hindu women without cleaning their kitchen square anoint themselves with saffron marks?' (GGS:417). Though he was against women's segregation, he is pained by the way the veils of Muslim women were ripped from head to toe. Guru Nanak fully realizes that people have different histories, and therefore different customs, and has enormous respect towards all of them equally. It is a great lesson. In our quest for equality and freedom, we must not impose our values; we must put ourselves in the other's shoes and analyse the situation from *their* perspective. The drive for justice emerges from an authentic acceptance of others with all their difference and diversity.

And our agendas today? Utterly clueless about people far away, we justify going into war to impose our values on them. The 'democracy' we proclaim to fight for, is it not a cover up for our greed? In the prevailing hazardous Islamophobic atmosphere, we confuse extremism with Islam, and discriminate against the entire Muslim community. We need to inquire into the root cause of our discontent: What is the source of our phobias? Is it Islam or the lingering consequences of Western colonial history? Is it disguised greed for oil or territorial expansion or status, power, racial superiority, or a tactic to win votes and elections? Is it an exploitive devise to get public consent for disastrous wars?

Following the First Sikh, we must build life around the values of human rights; we cannot take them for granted. It involves actively creating a world where everyone is equal and free. In this egalitarian community, no one ought to be subject to the superiority of another—based on either class, caste, race, religion or sex. Although the Guru does not directly address the LGBTQ issues that have come to the forefront today, we must draw upon his fundamental values and work for the equal rights of the lesbian, gay, bisexual, transgender and queer community. He voices no discrimination against anybody for their sexual preference anywhere in his corpus. As we analysed in Chapter 2, the B-40 Janamsakhi (dated 1733) captures the pluralistic First Sikh conversing most naturally with the cross-dressed Sheikh Sharaf. This is not a scene of mere tolerance; rather, the Guru is shown to have great respect for the musical talents of the black-bearded saint decked up in female accoutrements. Nobody could ever be excluded from sangat, his ideal of us coming together in and with all our differences.

We find Guru Nanak's essential ethics of selfless service (seva) articulated in the words of liberation theologian James Cone: 'No one can be truly liberated until *all* are liberated.' This quest for liberation is not simply the end of war or the end of bloodshed, but a space and time where *everyone* has equal opportunities for material, moral and spiritual growth. The characteristics *nir bhau* (without fear) and *nir vair* (without enmity) that Guru Nanak attributed to the Divine in his prelude to the Japji define human character as well. When falsehood, injustice and tyranny take over, we cannot remain complacent. We are to fight fearlessly, but with empathy, with respect for the cultures in which they evolved, and with a keen understanding of the broader historical, political and economic circumstances. A just cause must be the motive for battle, not revenge or greed or enmity towards anyone.

The Feminist

As a graduate student, I attended the annual meeting of the American Academy of Religion in 1984. Hearing Jewish and Christian feminists like Mary Daly, Judith Plaskow, Rosemary Ruether, Carol Christ, Rita Gross and Naomi Goldenberg was an epiphanic moment for me. Whatever these thinkers said, and how they said it, changed me. I dropped off the androcentric lenses I was accustomed to wearing and started to explore my Sikh heritage from my 'female' perspective. For several years now I have been studying, interpreting and translating the First Sikh's works from my feminist subjectivity, and I loudly and proudly proclaim him a revolutionary 'feminist'. He never ceases to amaze me! How did this male figure, living in patriarchal north India midst doubly layered androcentric Indic and Islamic attitudes, possess such a feminist consciousness? Was it his closeness with his older sister, Nanaki? Was there any particular incident he witnessed?

The term 'feminist' generally has negative associations. Mainstream Sikhs reject 'feminism' as a Western gimmick, and in scholarly circles it is reduced to a tangential lexicon. In reality, though, it basically entails understanding the First Sikh's verse in its expansive and inclusive imagery and using that understanding in everyday practices to empower both Sikh men and women in their private and public lives. For me, then, Guru Nanak is a feminist because he championed equality and justice for both men *and women*, just as he did for Brahmins and Shudras, Hindus and Muslims; no one to be treated any more *or any less* than the other. It is an issue of human rights. We recognize the First Sikh's revolutionary feminism in his (a) gender-inclusive theology and (b) female-centred spirituality, but we need a feminist interpretation of his verse.

Gender-inclusive Theology

The basic ingredient of human thought and action is language, and language, generally spoken or written, is constrained by gender. As the sociolinguist Robin Lakoff remarks, 'Language uses us as much as we use language.' Constructed by humans and for us humans, our use of language, says Lakoff, embodies attitudes as well as referential meanings.[15]

Like gender, language is not a natural construct; socially and culturally programmed, it also tends to be sexist and androcentric. The binary opposition between men and women and the language they use signifies the different genders and the different roles the sexes play in society. Implicitly and explicitly, language maintains the superiority of men over women and reinforces various social and political structures of patriarchy.

Guru Nanak's fundamental theological doctrine, Ikk Oan Kar, is expressed in gender-inclusive language. This unique and expansive configuration spells out the infinity of the singular Divine, without gender specifications. The inclusive numeral 'One' shatters the dominance of male imagery and creates a space for the Divine to be experienced in other new and important ways. Logically, it does not matter how the Divine is understood in human terms; the One is infinite, transcendent and beyond all categories. But in Guru Nanak's horizon, both female and male dimensions run parallel. He identifies the Divine in both genders: 'Ape purakhu ape hai nari—Itself male, Itself is female' (GGS: 1020), and goes on to describe infinite forms of the infinite One. His sense of plenitude strips off patriarchal stratifications and blots out masculine identity as the norm for imaging the Divine. We feel new emotions. We see new vistas. We experience joy in so many different ways. Overall, Guru Nanak gives us a balanced perspective of ultimate reality, which is crucial for mental and spiritual health.

I find it revolutionary that he would affirm women's biological processes, the very processes on which society erects its gender categories and justifies women's subordination and oppression. To date our society is horrified at the sight of women's blood—whether it is her monthly period or the blood that accompanies every birth. 'Polluted' because of their monthly period, women are barred from religious services. In India, violence has erupted as recently as 2 January 2019, because two women aged forty-two defied a traditional ban on women of menstruating age (between ten and fifty) by entering the Sabarimala temple, one of the largest Hindu pilgrimage sites (as per a BBC report). Across cultures, menstruation is considered a private, shameful process and equated with being ill or weak. The fear of the gaze, touch and speech of a menstruating woman has been internalized by Indian society for centuries. These deeply rooted negative attitudes to women have seeped into all of India's religious traditions. In the Hindu tradition, for example, they are expressed in the Laws of Manu (2nd century BCE–2nd century CE): Any touch of the 'Untouchable, a menstruating woman, anyone who has fallen (from his caste), a woman who has just given birth, a corpse, or anyone who has touched any of these objects' is deemed polluted.[16] Food touched by a menstruating woman is forbidden.[17] Likewise, the blood of parturition is also stereotyped by society as impure and dangerous, and it is ritually avoided. Giving birth is a biologically natural mode of creation, yet it is deemed dirty, with all sorts of lingering fears of pollution attached to it. In medieval India, any home with a new birth was feared toxic for forty days, and only the performance of elaborate rituals would bring it back to normality. In Japan, parturition huts were built away from the home in order to contain birth-related pollution.[18] These misogynistic views transcend religious boundaries; they prevail through space and time, and they were prevalent in Guru Nanak's society.

The First Sikh empathized with the situation of women, and he tried to create a window of opportunity through which they could achieve liberty, equality and sorority. Women became equal partners in the earliest Sikh community he established in Kartarpur. Together, they formed a democratic congregation without priests or ordained ministers. Single, married or widowed, no woman was barred. What we remember of his life and his enlightening lyrics overturn the age-old taboos against women's bodies. In Var Majh, he jolts us out from our placid acceptance:

> If the outfit is stained with blood we call it polluted,
>   And those who suck the blood of humans we call them pure-
>   minded?

GGS: 140

Do we ever question the rules of purity and pollution sanctified by society? Through his pungent juxtaposition of images, Guru Nanak exposes the deceptiveness of patriarchal assumptions. His witty and brilliant style has an echo in 'Anaya's Anthropology', a modern short story by Professor A.K. Ramanujan. It is about a young Indian Brahmin who comes to Chicago and discovers, ironically, his Hindu tradition through Western scholars. Like Guru Nanak's verse, the short story is a critique of time-honoured rites and practices. Guru Nanak subtly mandates what Ramanujan's protagonist explicitly states:

> Silk, which is the bodily secretion of silkworm, is nonetheless pure for human beings. Think of that! . . . A dead human being is unclean. But the urine and dung of a living cow are purifying. Think of that!'
>
> 'Annaya's Anthropology', 45–48

'Think of that!' is the refrain of our modern and medieval authors. They challenge us to question our ingrained assumptions. Indeed, the revolutionary Guru Nanak 'challenges, questions, overturns assumptions, unsettles moral codes and disrespects sacred . . . entities'. According to him, pollution is not in blood-stained garments, nor in the home where a mother gives birth. If pollution attaches to birth, then pollution is everywhere (for birth is universal).

> Cow-dung [used as fuel] and firewood breed maggots;
> Not one grain of corn is without life;
> Water itself is a living substance, imparting life to all vegetation.
> How can we then believe in pollution
>   When pollution inheres within staples?
> Nanak, pollution is not washed away by purification rituals
> Pollution is removed by true knowledge alone
>
> GGS: 472

Pollution is a state of mind, pollution is not the product of any natural bodily process.

The First Sikh further questions the legitimacy and purpose of devaluing women on the basis of their reproductive energy: 'How can we call her polluted from whom the great ones are born?' (GGS: 473), He often praises insightful people, while he praises their mothers even more lavishly: '*Dhan janedi maia*—blessed are the mothers who gave them birth' (GGS: 138). The maternal exaltation must be on his lips for it slips out frequently: 'Nanak, blessed are the mothers who give birth—*Nanak janani dhanni mae*' (GGS: 1257), and yet again in Var Malar: 'Blessed are the mothers—*dhan janedi maia*' GGS: 1286). His repetitions seep into the reader's psyche and fill us with honour for mothers devalued by patriarchy. The Guru challenges us to rethink our negative attitudes to the female body. Do we ever question the rules of purity and pollution sanctified by society?

His interrogative strategy can bring about a seismic mental shift. His questions put a brake on our usual attitudes and behaviour. From our rear-view mirror we can see the status quo we have been taking for granted over the centuries. Why have we allowed the subjugation of women? How could something so magical as birth be polluted? In a recent BBC report, pregnant women in the Ghanaian village of Mafi Dove are not allowed to deliver in the village because it's believed that it will offend the gods. Expectant mothers are forced to make last-minute journeys in excruciating pain to avoid breaking the tradition.[19] Why such inhumanity towards the female sex? It is neither natural nor correct to subordinate women. From the front-view mirror we see directions for turning around from these discriminatory conventions.

The seriousness with which Guru Nanak takes women's genealogy is quite remarkable. He celebrates the various natural female processes, menstruation, gestation and lactation. The maternal space where the foetus is lodged is spiritually exalted as the divine One is fully rooted here: 'The One performs wonders in the colourful body—*ape coj kare rang mahali*'; that One has not made the entry from the outside or above but constitutes an essential part of her creative physiology: '*Antari udar majhara he*—inside the womb flourishes the One' (GGS: 1026). Not only does she feed her foetus with her nutrients, she also suckles the newborn with her life-giving milk. The Guru recognizes mother's milk full of biological and spiritual nutrients, and experiences the recitation of the divine Name as succulent milk in the mouth. His language joins in with the words of contemporary French feminist scholar Hélène Cixous, 'Voice: milk that could go on forever. Found again. The lost mother/bitter-lost. Eternity: is voice mixed with milk.'[20] Her milk is a biological necessity, keeping us from dying. So is the divine word (bani). By pouring the two together, Guru Nanak makes knowledge essential for everybody, upper class and lower, Brahmin and Shudra. The textuality of his verse lies in its physical sensuousness, in drinking the words as though they were the mother's life-giving milk.

His maternal imaginary is palpably accessed; it is not a matter of religious deification, because 'she' is not idolized into some distant goddess as an object of worship. It is when the Divine is genuinely imagined as Mother that her positive characteristics begin to filter the mind, and ignite respect for mothers, sisters, daughters and wives. An authentic subjectivity is born only if women are perceived as life-and-blood individuals partaking the qualities and powers of the divine One. Guru Nanak thanks women for their creating and nurturing: 'Blessed are the mothers!' (GGS: 138) he exalts. This respect for the mother is extended to all the mothers from all the species, and so his feminist imaginary fills humans with pride in their own bodies, and charges everybody, men and women, to respect all bodies and relish the Divine in the daily rhythms of life.

It is critical, however, that the 'mother' not be viewed as the only female symbol for the Divine. Guru Nanak offers countless ways of imagining and experiencing the infinite One. Even in one short hymn, he imagines the Divine as the bride in her wedding dress, as the groom on the nuptial bed . . . as the fisherman and the fish, as the waters and the trap, as the weight holding the net, as well as the lost ruby swallowed by the fish! (GGS: 23). In a speedy tempo, his similes and paradoxes free the mind from narrow walls. Male is not the only way to imagine the Divine. Motherhood also is one aspect of womanhood, and surely all women are not mothers, and may choose not to be mothers. With the singular stress on the maternal paradigm, a woman's creative powers can be misconstrued as an automatic and mandatory process.

The First Sikh's 'mother' symbol must not be abused to make women into reproductory machines to beget sons! It is important that we do not equate the maternal potential with physical conception or limit the maternal to the domestic world. French philosopher Luce Irigaray rightly says, it is not necessary that women give birth to children; they can give birth to many other things such as 'love, desire, language, art, social things, political things, religious things'.[21] The 'mother' as a Nanakian theological principle reveals the potential to create, physically, intellectually, emotionally, politically and spiritually. It shatters the gender roles that assign production to men and reproduction to women; conferring a sense of reality on women's creativity, it enables everybody to cultivate meaningful relationships with their past and future generations, and with their geological and cosmic community.

Female-centred Spirituality

Guru Nanak was male, but he connected with the woman at a very deep level. A woman is not a 'body' below the spirit, a hindrance in the spiritual goal; rather, she is regarded as physically and spiritually refined, so it is in her tone, her mood, her image, her dressing up that the First Sikh expresses his longing for the Divine. She opens the way to the transcendent. He envisions the One as a handsome Groom, and takes on the personality of a bride, totally merging with her feminine feelings and thoughts in his desire for spiritual union. The male–female duality which violates the wholeness of human nature and deprives each person of the other half is overcome, undergirding in turn, the significance of being human. Men and women are united and share their human angst and human hope. Language is truly gender-inclusive, for the male Guru experiences the Divine from *her* female presence.

In his epistemology, feelings and passions are totally fused in with the mind and ideas, and the female body is spiritually exalted. We hear him express the indivisible unity of mind and body in unmatched beauty and profundity:

Mann mandir je deepak jale kaia sej karei
gyan rao jab sejai avai ta nanak bhogu karei

[If she prepares the bed of her body, lights up the lamp in her mind's temple
The Ruler of knowledge gets in bed with her and revels, Nanak!]

GGS: 359

The sphere of knowledge in Guru Nanak's *weltanschauung* does not parallel the concept of 'pure' knowledge that we find in Greek philosophy, for instance. In the writings of Plato and Aristotle, the transcendent mind remains far above feelings and passions. Feminist theologians have condemned this harmful division which has remained the basis of Western philosophy. Referring to Aristotle's *Politics* and Plato's *Timaeus*, Rosemary Ruether disagreed with Greek philosophers for subjugating matter or the body to be ruled or shunned by the transcendent mind.[22] Guru Nanak's epistemological experience, embodied by the intellectually refined woman, is an expansion of human faculties, at once cognitive and sensuous, physical and metaphysical, ethical and intellectual. She makes her bed and lights up her mental lamp, and the Ruler of knowledge (*gyan rao*) begins to enjoy revelling with her. Her Lover is coherently and tightly integrated into her daily activities.

A profound human–divine intimacy is at the heart of his verse:

Dhan sachi sanguti
hari sang suti

[The woman abides in Truth,
Intimately locked in the divine embrace]

GGS: 843

Evidently, female sexuality is healthy and wholesome. The Guru's paradigm incarnates physical beauty and spiritual awakening, and she rapturously makes love with her divine Lover. Many scriptural verses follow his imaginary and offer powerful images that overturn the fears of intimacy prevalent in our culture and inspire us to enter exciting new horizons with all of our human faculties. In the context of the translation process, Gayatri Spivak has suggested a surrendering to the original text that is 'more erotic than ethical',[23] and interestingly in the First Sikh's verse, we have a woman who, morally refined, is erotically locked in the arms of her divine Lover, her surrender at once erotic and ethical.

His pervasive bridal symbol continuously evokes a sensuous and palpable union with the Infinite One. The Groom (*sahu*) is known as *agam* (infinite), *agocaru* (unfathomable) and *ajoni* (unborn); He is utterly metaphysical and beyond all sense perception. The bride perceives and proclaims the infinity of her Groom: 'O my Beloved, your limits I cannot fathom.' She is perplexed and wonders how she is going to 'see' her True Groom who has no colour, no garb, no form'. Ultimately, it is the bride who succeeds in creating proximity to the distant Groom. She is the one to chart out the way that will make the Transcendent accessible to human experience. She addresses the impersonal Being in most personal terms: 'O my handsome, unfathomable Beloved'; 'My Beloved is the most delicious inebriation.' For her, 'my loved Groom isn't far at all' (GGS: 1197). She praises him lavishly:

> My Beloved is utterly glorious, brilliantly crimson
> Compassionate, beneficent, beloved, enticer of the hearts
> Overflowing with *rasa*, like the *lala* flower
>
> GGS: 1331

Some feminists may of course object to the longing bride as a model. They might see an inherent dualism in the relation between the bride and her Groom, and the role of the bride seeking her Beloved may be viewed as restrictive and stifling. In this case we must remember that it emerges at a point in time and space when the Indian woman was humiliatingly subjugated, so to see *her* as the paragon of physical and spiritual refinement, and hear *her* desire being expressed, is significant. The symbol has to be fully understood and not simplistically read as though women must be dependent on their husbands. That would be a grave distortion. Guru Nanak's bride is dependent only upon the divine One, and men, women and the entire cosmos share this dependence. The First Sikh's message is not the subjugation of the female to the male, for her Groom is beyond gender; rather, it is the rising of the individual spirit towards the Absolute. The rich variety of his images reveals the complexity and dignity of the female experience and loosens the grip of masculine symbols upon contemporary imagination.

In fact, women in the roles of sister, mother and sister-in-law are quintessential to his epistemology and spirituality. Guru Nanak identifies the mother with wisdom: '*Mat mata pita santokh*—mother is wisdom; father is contentment' (GGS: 151) which is later repeated by his successors: '*Mat mata*' (GGS: 172), '*Mata mat santokhu pita*' (GGS: 1397). Socially engaged, the sister-in-law is regarded as 'the most admirable member of her entire family—*sabh parvari mahi sreset*' for 'she guides her brothers-in-law, both younger and older—*mat devai devar jeset*' (GGS: 371). Guru Nanak regards women as vital subjects. They possess knowledge, they are morally and spiritually refined, they are beautiful, and they exist as palpable models for the human–divine nexus. As friends, companions, lovers and wives, they are embedded in a web of intimate relationships. They have a high status in daily spheres of life.

For our gender-biased society, he offers a revolutionary motto: '*Laj maranti mar gai ghungat khol chali*—deadly honor died; I walk free, my face unveiled' (GGS: 931). Against the veil that enshrouds physically, mentally and emotionally, the First Sikh strongly calls for the death of deadly androcentric honour codes. In a recent interview, Nawal El Saadawi, the leading feminist of the Arab world, exposes the manifold violence behind the veil: 'Everybody is very much interested in the physical veil—the religious Islamic veil. But what we don't see is the veil of the mind. We are all exposed to the veil of the mind, by education, by religion, by patriarchy, by fear, by marriage, by the moral code. As women, we are always pushed to be hidden, to be veiled, even if we are not aware of that.'[24] A medical doctor in an Egyptian village, Saadawi witnessed honour killings, sexual abuse and female circumcision, which she documented in her influential book *The Hidden Face of Eve* (1977). Honor (laj or izzat) continues to be the most cherished value for Muslims, Hindus and Sikhs across classes and regions. This ancient patriarchal code of conduct (laj/izzat) safeguards male honour by controlling women—wives, daughters, sisters and nieces. The so-called 'honour' resides in the woman's body, and the man is its regulator. Therefore, women's bodies are to be veiled and kept pure; young girls are circumcised, their sexuality is tightly supervised. Widows are de-sexed. Threatened by modernity and affluence, misogynistic honour codes are becoming more rigid. Crimes of honour killing in Pakistan, India and Bangladesh are common news reports. Half a millennium ago, the First Sikh unambiguously condemned such abusive customs and honour codes. His paradigmatic image of the young woman walking out of her veiled circumscriptions and confidently voicing her newfound autonomy could prove to be hugely liberating.

Need for a Feminist Hermeneutics

Guru Nanak's lyrics have untapped potential to bring about a new future, but to make us effective agents of change requires engagement with and reflection (*vichar*) of his verse. Regrettably, commentators of Sikh scripture simply deem it unnecessary to remember *her* body or our origins. I doubt his emancipatory citation above ('*laj maranti mar gai ghungat khol chali*') has ever received much attention either from the community or the academy. The First Sikh's distinctive emphasis on the divine constitution of female physiology, spirituality and theological imaginary is missed out, and its impact on our integrated subjectivity is lost. For instance, he explicitly affirms that the Divine permeates both the heart and the womb: '*Ghati ghati vartai udari majhare*—it pervades every heart and flourishes in the womb' (GGS: 1026). But modern scholars like G.S. Talib and Gopal Singh register the heart (*ghat*) and utterly ignore the womb *(udar)* in Guru Nanak's feminist sensibility.[25] The particular female organ even gets altered into a generic 'stomach'[26] or 'belly'.[27] The radical vision of the First Sikh and his invigorating overtures remain unseen, unheard. His womb-respecting, birth-oriented glimpses and melodies need to be remembered so that their lingering can make each of us more wholesome and our world a better place.

It is ironic that modern scholars are unable to access the First Sikh's feminist sensibility. Indeed, he has been far too revolutionary for his ideas and values to be fully realized over the generations. Early on, we hear exegetes and commentators reversing his progressive message. Chaupa Singh—a tutor and aide of the Tenth Guru—dictates in his ethical manual a Sikh woman's primary mode of religiosity as her worship of her husband: she is to 'know her husband as god—*apne bharte nu karta janai*'; she is to 'keep fasts for the sake of her husband' (*patibratu rakhe*).[28] The 'eko dharam' advocated by Guru Nanak is discarded. The ritual fasting denounced by him is brought right back. The ideals and practices he launched in his Kartarpur community where men and women recited enchanting sacred verse, cooked and ate together were soon overturned. Instead, segregation and discrimination were stipulated: women may listen to but are prohibited from reading the Guru Granth Sahib in public (*The Chaupa Singh Rahit-Nama*, #538).

The glamorous regime of Maharaja Ranjit Singh (1799–1839) brought great splendour to the Sikhs, but it was also accompanied by old patriarchal norms. With the elaboration of pomp and ceremony at his royal court, the formal rituals and ceremonials discarded by the First Guru and his successors were ushered back into the Sikh way of life. The customs of purdah and sati performed by women from elite Muslim and Hindu families respectively began to be emulated by the upper echelons of Sikh society. In a shocking scene depicting Maharaja Ranjit Singh's funeral at the British Museum in London we see four queens and seven slave girls heroically prepared to commit sati.[29] W.G. Archer's comment 'The picture lacks the majesty of a great painting' not only trivializes the colossal tragedy of these women but also condones the horrific brutality of the sati ritual.[30] Memories of a feisty Maharani Jindan—who refused to go into purdah and did not perform sati—are reassuring, but this symbol of Sikh sovereignty too was reduced to a caricature by the Raj.[31]

We reread Guru Nanak's poignant poetry and question the past, we question present-day assumptions. What are our values and attitudes towards women? The practice of sati has been illegal since the early nineteenth century, yet tragically, its lethal flames continue to char the psyche of Indian women. Yes, the widow lives, but can her dreary dead existence be called *living*? These liminal figures learn to shun entertainment and are forced to swallow all sorts of emotional and physical abuse. Alas, do daughters, sisters, nieces and wives live as fully or freely as their male counterparts—at *any* stage of life?

British colonialism provided yet another oppressive layer, which produced a 'hyper-masculine' Sikh culture. The Punjab came under the Raj in 1849, and the imperial masters so admired the 'martial' character and strong physique of Sikh men that they recruited them in disproportionately large numbers to serve in the British army. A vigorous new patriarchal discourse with its patriotism and paternalism was thereby attached to the 'Brotherhood of the Khalsa'.

That drive continues on. With the Green Revolution and the enterprising spirit of its people, postcolonial Punjab became the bread basket of India. Today, it is in the ferment of globalization. Contemporary economic and technological priorities have made the patriarchal compulsion for sons even stronger. Parents regard sons as their social security and financial insurance and as religious functionaries who will eventually perform their funeral rites. Sons are deemed essential for carrying on the family name, property and land. With the combination of ancient patriarchal values and new globalization, gender disparity is deteriorating at an alarming rate. Thus, despite the recent economic boom and better laws to protect women and girls, the proportion of baby girls is declining rapidly. The selective abortion of females (through technological means such as amniocentesis) has only reinforced the devaluation of girls and further entrenched gender prejudices. Women are held responsible to preserve the honour of their fathers and brothers. Parents with daughters are severely pressurized by dowry demands—be it cash, jewellery, furniture, cars or property.

The post-9/11 era has produced new complications. Valerie Kaur, a third-generation Sikh American activist, captures the gravity of the contemporary situation in this extract from the Huffington Post:

[I]t took me nearly a decade after 9/11 even to begin talking about women again. After the terrorist attacks, we women tacitly agreed to put our issues on hold. We needed to protect our men first—our brothers and husbands and sons whose turbans and dark skin marked them as primary targets for hate in the years after 9/11. This was a mistake. As we waited (and are still waiting) for the discrimination to pass over us, some of the cultural dysfunctions in our community worsened. Women and girls are always the first casualties within minority communities under siege. . . . When riots and massacre swept Punjab during the 1947 Partition of India, some Sikh men poisoned their daughters before letting them fall into the hands of Muslim rioters. Today in America, while many Sikh families champion education and freedom for sons and daughters alike, others have tightened control over women and girls in the 9/11 decade. In the worst anecdotes, domestic violence is an outlet for men who bear racism on the street, intermarriage an act of betrayal, and honor killings an actual threat.[32]

In her book *Sikhism Today*, Dr Jagbir Jhutti-Johal gives a snapshot of women's exclusion in religious service at the central place of Sikh worship—the Golden Temple:

> Here Sikh women are not allowed to read from the Guru Granth Sahib, play *kirtan* or perform any *sewa* in the sanctum sanctorum (main prayer room). These *sewas* are 'reserved' for men only.[33]

Jhutti-Johal also cites the widely publicized discriminatory case from 2003, when two Sikh women were not allowed to even touch the palanquin carrying the GGS during its evening ritual. Likewise, Dr Opinderjit Tkahar, director of the Centre for Sikh and Punjabi Studies at the University of Wolverhampton, describes taboos preventing women from cooking meals and preparing *karah prashad* during their menstrual period at gurdwaras in the United Kingdom.[34]

The Sikh community is recognizing the gravity of the situation. Men and women are taking steps towards gender justice. Campaigns geared specifically against female foeticide are being initiated by the Shiromani Gurdwara Prabhandak Committee (SGPC), and political leaders and NGOs are forging important infrastructures for the protection, welfare, education and employment of girls and women. Women writers, artists, poets and film directors are trying to raise social awareness. Along with these important steps, I strongly feel that there must be the disclosure of feminist possibilities permeating the GGS. The sacred verse so central to Sikh life has the power to reach the deeply unconscious self—the template of real change. The transcendent lyrics have the potential to open up a vast egalitarian horizon free from sexism, classism and racism. But they need to be retrieved through feminist interpretations and gender-inclusive translations.

The existing English translations of the sacred verse end up being androcentric. In fact, they betray a colonized mentality. Whereas the

Divine is the transcendent, metaphysical One, it is invariably translated into a Western monotheistic 'god' and given a male identity. Another tendency of translators is to reduce the robust and authentic presence of female scriptural models into a mere figure of speech.[35] Somehow or the other, 'soul' gets latched on to powerful females, killing their vibrant bodies. Guru Nanak's simple 'suhagan', for example, in translation becomes 'bride-soul'. Laden with Jewish–Christian connotations, the soul imposes the mind–body dualism, shifting attention from the present situation to an afterlife and heaven. Feminist scholars have warned us about the terrible consequences of the bipartite 'body–soul' framework on the devaluing of bodies, of life on earth, and of female gender and sexuality. Despite the fact that the original verse does not mention the soul, it is lavishly present in English translations. Its usage dichotomizes the fullness of the Guru's experience and vision. New gender-inclusive, female-sensitive translations would provide access and help promote the liberal vision of the First Sikh.

His works need to go beyond the Sikh community and reach wide-ranging audiences. Every society in the world to date remains a patriarchy. Despite the progress women have made in the USA over the last several decades, 'they are still treated like second-class citizens in all the ways that matter', observes Samantha Paige Rosen.[36] This systemic characteristic 'combines dynamics at the level of the family, the economy, the culture and the political arena'.[37] Guru Nanak did not specify 'women's issues' as such either, which Rosen perceives operate as discriminating and insulting categories. She incisively says:

> It's time America stops referring to issues that affect women as 'women's issues.' Almost a century since women's suffrage, it's insulting to address equal pay, reproductive rights and topics surrounding the home and children as issues solely relating to women, when they have consequences for men as well.[38]

Guru Nanak rightly and wisely championed 'human' issues. He deemed each individual—male, female or queer—as an equal and important part of the fabric of society. His verse chimes significantly with men, women and transgender persons. In my classes at Colby, my Western students from different religious backgrounds find Guru Nanak's 'engaged literature' empowering. Male, female, gay, lesbian and transgender youngsters can intimately relate with his impassioned verse; it speaks to them. In turn, they bring fresh interpretations from their respective orientations to his universal and timeless words. If we collectively understand, interpret and apply the First Sikh's lyrics, we can make this world a better place for all of us.

Ultimately, it is love that propels the First Sikh's revolution. His vast oeuvre is calligraphed 'in the language of infinite love—*bhakhia bhaau apar*'. He explains the antithetical emotions of fear (bhau) and love (bhaau) which lead people in different directions. While fear pulls us back from life, love opens us up with acceptance and excitement. Unfortunately, in our quickly shrinking digitalized globe, our humanity is shutting down. Fear is taking over love. Prejudices and stereotypes are getting fiercer, the fear of immigrants is making us paranoid, public policies are getting harsher, governments are discriminating against religious groups more so than ever. Anti-Semitic attacks, Islamist assaults on churches and Buddhist agitation against Muslims are on the rise; hate crimes are rampant. We are, as Diana Eck warns, becoming 'afraid of ourselves'.[39] We must clear our arteries of toxic fear so that nourishing love can circulate in our bodies. A positive energy, love is passion that reaches out as compassion from one body to the other to everything around. Love involves hearing each other in humility, beholding each other's faces, seeing through each other's eyes, welcoming the other into ourselves. Thus, we go beyond semantic categories like Sikh or Christian, Hindu or Muslim, Black or White, Brahmin or Shudra, male or female, rich or poor, host or immigrant to that point of ultimate unicity, the 'Ikk' articulated by Guru Nanak. Empowered by our togetherness, we will work hard for the well-being of our collective community. The First Sikh's inclusive verse can substantially promote the work of social activists, human rights organizations, politicians and legal advocates.

5

The Environmentalist

With Earth's climate changing faster than ever and the oceans getting hotter and more acidic, we face the gravest environmental challenges today. The First Sikh would not have been privy to our daily news reports about unprecedented hurricanes, floods, wildfires, health threats, depletion of agriculture, extinction of plant and animal species, and other such hazards. The Janamsakhi narratives primarily stage him in harmonious rural landscapes in medieval north India, and his own lyrics form serene arabesques with the natural world. Nevertheless, we discover in them some vital cures for our contemporary ecological crisis. As Rachel Oliver from CNN says:

> Whether we are actively religious or not, religious belief permeates the very fabric of our existence. Namely, it influences—if not directly shapes—our legal systems; and therefore our constitutions; and therefore our nations' policy choices, both at home and abroad.[1]

I wholeheartedly think sacred texts make it to that visceral hub where external policies and rules do not quite reach.

Without prescribing any rules or policies, Guru Nanak's open-ended melodies move us out from our narrow selves towards appreciating nature's rhythms, Earth's abundant gifts and the cosmic beauty surrounding us. His reverence for our planet is infectious. The more we read and hear him, the more we question our economic, profit-making, capitalist attitude. But in order to tap into his literary reservoir, we must hear him attentively, and we must hear him intentionally with our twenty-first-century ears sensitive to ecological warnings. In this section, we will try to retrieve the interlinking elements of Guru Nanak's ecological theology, non-anthropomorphism, aesthetic-ontology and biophilia. By mobilizing our sensibilities in a concerted way, we could forge a meaningful relationship with nature that should help us devise and implement sustainable environmental solutions, and reverse what we have made of our planet—in Pope Francis's words, a 'wasteland full of debris, desolation, and filth'.

Ecological Theology

The few biographical facts we have about Guru Nanak's life underscore his consanguineous relationship with nature. Apparently, as a youngster, he did not like the confines of school, and opted to commune with nature. The Janamsakhis repeatedly illustrate his at-homeness in nature. We even see young Nanak grazing cows, and when he falls asleep, a cobra shades him while the sun smiles from above; in another narrative, the shade of the tree stands still while he is asleep. The terrestrial and the celestial, the spheres human, animal and vegetation, are all integrated into a harmonious whole. The Guru travelled to many different places and acquired a deep knowledge of and appreciation for the abundant diversity of flora and fauna. As we know, the first Sikh community developed in Kartarpur, the village he founded by the rippling river Ravi. Men and women who gathered around the First Sikh to hear and recite his hymns were in sync with the soil and spirit of its natural landscape. Planting, irrigating, ploughing, harvesting, rotating crops, cooking and cleaning—all with their own hands—were their daily practices. This fundamental nature orientation subsequently led to the Sikh institutions of seva (service for the larger community), langar (eating together without social segregations) and sangat (sense of fellowship).

An enchanting plurality of trees, plants, flowers, animals, birds and elements forms the script of Guru Nanak's sublime verse. It is very much with them, in them, that Guru Nanak envisions the transcendent One. His hymns like 'Barah Mah', 'Pahare' and 'Thiti' manifest the correlation between cosmic and human rhythms, physical and spiritual currents. Guru Nanak's theology does not posit 'god' above or different from the cosmos: the sole Creator creates everything, is in everything, and watches over each and all with care and joy. All of natural phenomena is the Divine's household (*eco* from the Greek word for household: *ekos*).

Here we get a very different feel from that of a monotheistic notion of a Creator apart from His creation that was detected a while back by scholars in the West: 'The emphasis in Judaism and Christianity on the transcendence of god above nature and the dominion of humans over nature has led to a devaluation of the natural world and depletion of its resources for utilitarian ends.'[2] Guru Nanak reveals this very cosmos as the dwelling place of the divine One and our life together with fellow beings, biotic or abiotic, in an interlinking web. He approves of neither Western anthropocentricism nor an instrumentalist attitude to nature. We must absorb his lyrics so we value the natural world and work together to sustain its precious wealth for future generations.

Nature is not a romantic reverie. In heartwarming ways, the First Sikh establishes a familial relationship with the environment:

Air is our guru, water is known as our father
The unifying womb, our Mother Earth
Night and day are the two male and female nurses
This is how You keep the play of the world playing

GGS: 1021[3]

Guru Angad reiterates this warm kinship, and so the First Sikh's imaginary reappears twice more—as an epilogue to the Japji, and in Var Majh. Indeed, this wholistic scenario holds enormous import in Sikh scripture. The elements are our parents, without whom we would not even be here. Earth is the mother, the matrix from which we all originate, and the father is water which is approximately 80 per cent of our bodies. The air we breathe every second is our teacher from whom we learn about our utter reliance on the infinite One, who keeps up the momentum of worldly play. Night and day are our male and female nurses who look after us. Thus, all planetary beings are children belonging to the same family. The verb 'playing' (*khelai*) intimates our delightful movements in the rhythmic lap of night and day—with the awareness of the infinite One each moment as we breathe (air is our guru!).

Today, our horizon darkened by the tragedies of pollution, global waste and alienation from our environment, both natural and social, the task of *recognizing* Guru Nanak's consanguineous relationship with nature is more urgent than ever. How can we drown our rivers, seas and lakes in chemicals, plastic, waste and other pollutants? How can we poison the air with pollutants from cars, planes, factories, power plants, refrigerants? How can we destroy fields and jungles to set up our lucrative industries and towering gated communities? We are a close-knit family. Earth is the matrix from which we are born, from which we are created, and from which we grow, evolve and thrive. We cannot degrade *her* or any of our siblings. Guru Nanak shares the feminist emphasis that the mother *bodies* forth her child. For, in the process of giving birth, the most intimate and organic connection between mother and offspring is expressed. It is an organic relationship. Though malestream scholars may dismiss it hastily,[4] we desperately need to *recognize* the image of Mother Earth as our primal womb. As eco-theologian Sallie McFague compellingly argues:

> There is simply no other imagery available to us that has this power for expressing the interdependence and interrelatedness of all life with its ground. All of us, female and male, have the womb as our first home, all of us are born from the bodies of our mothers, all of us are fed by our mothers. What better imagery could there be for expressing the most basic reality of existence: that we live and move and have our being in God?[5]

Guru Nanak opens us up to a relational, ecological horizon of being in the world.

He is captivated by the cosmos, a spontaneous unfolding and blooming of the Infinite. The various cosmic phenomena are created by and in turn manifest the divine One. As we discussed in Chapter 2, Guru Nanak uses the Arabic term 'qudrat' for the Creator's vibrancy. There is no hypothetical or contingent relation between the Creator and Its creation (qudrat). They are one and the same, totally non-dualistic. The life energy circulating amongst beings in the world is communicated by each to all within the comprehensive Oneness of the Divine. Like the thunderous sound of the dazzling lightning flash in the night skies is plainly seen and heard by all of us, he urges us to see the same divine light present in each of us without any distinctions: 'Like we see the lightning flash in the night sky, discern the light in all without distinctions—*nis daman jio chamak chandain dekhai ahinis jot nirantar pekhai*' (GGS: 1041). His social imaginary of the equality of all beings is effectively conveyed through natural phenomena.

The cosmos is not created in any particular sequence, therefore, there are no hierarchies or segregations:

> People, trees, sacred sites, river-banks, clouds, fields
> Islands, continents, constellations, planets, universes
> Species born of egg, womb, earth, and sweat
> Oceans, mountains, beings, Nanak
> > Only the one knows the limits
> Nanak, that One gives birth to beings and treasures each one
> The Creator who creates also cares for us
> The Creator who creates this world
> > Does worry about it . . .
>
> GGS: 467

Guru Nanak refers to the four species as *andaj, jeraj, utbhuj* and *setaj*—born of egg, womb, earth and sweat. There is an equivalence of all beings and things, as well as a simultaneity and infinity about them. All share the chemical, biological, material and spiritual reality. The First Sikh foreshadows scientists and biologists who inform us that DNA processes are the same across life forms. 'The DNA molecule specifies the characteristics of all living organisms, from bacteria through human beings . . . the same genes, the same parts, turn up again and again, from one species to another . . . We [all life forms] emerged from an ancient single-celled being.'[6] Guru Nanak's awareness of the intricate web of relationships, endorsed by science, promotes socio-ecological action. In addition, the Creator's caring for and treasuring creation, poetically described above, are some traits we humans could imbibe ourselves for a praxis-based life and service to the cosmos.

In a host of images the First Sikh solidly situates the divine One in *this* world. He exuberantly says, 'All that exists exists in You—*jeti hai teti tudh andar*' (GGS: 1034). A short passage celebrates the immediacy of the One in nature and its elements. It connects and affirms human architectural, domestic and economic activities as well.

> Your room above in four directions
> Has land on one side, water on the other[7]
> This whole world is a coin
> Minted with Your face alone

GGS: 596

The architectural construction (*caubara*) indicates an airy space on the roof of a double-storey house. Its location between the land and the waters evokes the traditional hand mill that women used to grind corn and grains till very recent times. Guru Nanak's Punjabi term for 'side,' *pur*, refers to the two sides of a *chakki* (hand mill), which brings to mind Sufi devotional songs (*chakki-namahs*) sung by mothers as their hand spun around grinding flour while their babies slept in their laps. And the whole universe (*sagal bhavan*) for the Sikh Guru is a single coin imprinted with the face of the transcendent One. If only our society would see the world through the First Sikh's eyes! Would we be so money-centric? Would we be so self-indulgent? Economic wealth belongs to all of us equally. How can we have such massive disparities in our global world? How can billions of our siblings be denied access to basic food, health, education and sanitation standards?

Guru Nanak's successor redesigns his caubara as a *kothari* (hamlet): 'This world is a hamlet of the True One, the true One lives in it—*ihu jagu sachai ki hai kothari sachai ka vichi vasu*' (GGS: 463). This whole universe is a cozy home of the divine One. Twentieth-century leaders like Mahatma Gandhi and Rev. Martin Luther King used the idea of home as a popular image for our world community. All beings are equally a part of this construction. Over and over the First Sikh brings home the point that 'the One dwells in each shape, complexion, and mind, says Nanak praise the One—*sagal rup varan mann mahi kahu nanak eko salahi*' (GGS: 223). The noumenon is the phenomenon. He restores the integral value of all things physical and mental. Every bit has an intrinsic value for it is Divine. Nothing in this world is a commodity to belittle or exploit. Who are we to destroy the home of the ultimate One who created it all and lives in it? We must partner with fellow beings and work to sustain the balance and diversity of our variegated community, the home of the divine One. In the words of Martin Luther King Jr, 'We have inherited a big house, a great "world house" in which we have to live together—black and white, Easterners and Westerners, Gentiles and Jews, Catholics and Protestants, Moslem and Hindu, a family unduly separated in ideas, culture, and interests who, because we can never again live without each other, must learn, somehow, in this one big world, to live with each other.'[8]

Guru Nanak uses several names for the divine One that have immense ecological import. Maula, Jagjivan, Banvari and Sriranga appear across his verse. Each time, they remind us of the Divine presence in myriad forms of nature. We open our eyes to buds smiling into blossoms, to stars twinkling joyously. They invite us to celebrate the abounding presence of the One in every colour, shape, sound and movement. Maula makes the world bloom, Maula makes the world lush green, Maula keeps waters and land in balance (GGS: 28). Countless shades of green, yellow, red, blue, black, white, orange, brown, purple and others reflect the resplendent colours of Sriranga. This rich biodiversity is but a burst of Sriranga. Each heart, says Guru Nanak in Raga Sorath, 'blooms with the Forest-Owner Banvari, hidden in the waters, on land and in space'. He warns us too that that this wonderful diversity belongs to Jagjivan, the life of the world. In pre-modern, pre-industrial society, he cautions us as we are not owners of nature. It is not ours to consume, destroy or degrade the colourful beauty and wondrous animation. And in the passage of time, in the life cycles of flora and fauna, we must constantly remember our singular Banvari, Jagjivan, Sriranga and Maula. Thus, we respect our biosphere and keep it vibrant. 'As the months and seasons keep moving on, keep an eye on what you do, Nanak, the guru-centred do not wither; drenched in the One, they're green forever' (GGS: 1168). The guru-centred live and act and relate to natural phenomena by holding the universal reality in their consciousness, so they stay evergreen (*hare*) and keep the larger cosmos vibrant and thriving.

Non-anthropomorphism

The divine, humanity and nature are linked together rather than tiered into hierarchical levels with humans in the middle distorting and oppressing the life-support system. The First Sikh gives us a profound lesson in relativity which serves as an antidote to the ecological crisis caused by homo sapiens. We hear in his verse instructions given by modern theologians, poets and leaders. The current president of Berkeley, Carol Christ, makes us realize 'we are no more valuable to the life of the universe than a field flowering in the colour purple, than rivers flowing, than a crab picking its way across the sand—and no less'. The Guru too usurps the arrogant superiority of humans and praises even the tiniest creatures. In his Japji we hear him say, 'Kings and sultans may rule over kingdoms vast as oceans, possess wealth piled high as mountains, yet none can match an ant whose heart does not forget' (Stanza 23).

Various species are admired by the First Sikh. He envies the doe, fish and female serpent for being close to their lover. His spontaneous utterances splendidly illustrate his eco-centrism, his non-anthropomorphism. With matchless beauty he says:

> I wish I were a fish living in waters
>> Seeing the reality of all beings
> To my lover living across the shore
>> I'd dash off with arms wide open

GGS: 157

He appreciates a bumblebee's refined sense of smell: 'It inhales such fragrance that trees blossom, woods become green' (GGS: 1190). The bumblebee also gets inebriated on the scent of the lotus and hums praise as it flies high. Likewise, the lotus-lily senses the distant moon, and elated she bows her head (GGS: 990). The Chatrik bird calls out 'beloved, beloved', and looking for her raindrop, she cries her heart out. For the First Sikh all these beings have refined sensibilities. Humans are not at the apex. He regards them as models who could teach us humans to see Reality, aspire for It, and enjoy It fully. We could even learn from them how to praise, be humble and work enthusiastically.

The simplicity and immediacy of Nanakian lyrics fill us with respect for the environment we live in. Guru Nanak's intimacy with nature inspires us to embrace all that is around us so we too immerse ourselves in sensuous resplendence right here and now.

He is also acutely pained by the way we treat vegetation, the way we treat the elements. In contrast with those who view natural phenomena as lifeless, the First Sikh feels with and for every material thing. He regards natural phenomena as individual organisms, quite like the eco-ethicists championing today. We assume the vegetative state is to be without mind, write Hitchings and Jones, 'Yet the root meaning of the word vegetative is associated with activity and enlivened animation . . . which suggests a closer, more intimate, connection with the active concerns of the organic in past societies.'[9] Guru Nanak fully understands the animation, dynamism, and I would even add 'humanity' of all non-humans. He gives nature a poignant voice. When we hear nature from nature's perspective and not ours, we begin to think with nature, like nature, for nature. For instance, in his passages from Var Majh and Asa di Var we hear the heartbreaking cries of the voiceless:

> Look how the sugarcane is being sheared
> Chopped up, beaten, tied in bundles
> Shoved between rollers, muscular men crush it
> As if in punishment
> Its juice squeezed out, boiling in the cauldron
> Fills the air with agonizing wails . . .

GGS: 142–43

> The clay from a Muslim's grave
> Ends up in the potter's wheel
> It is moulded into clay jars and brick, and when
> Heated up in the furnace it cries out
> Louder and louder the poor clay wails
> As the crackling sparks lash out more and more . . .

GGS: 466

The sensitive Guru hears the wailing of the sugarcane! He shows us exactly how the greed of our consumer culture operates: shears the sugarcane crop, chops it up, bundles it tightly, shoves it between rollers, crushes it, squeezes out the juice, boils it up. The Guru hears the wailing of the poor clay too. His empathy knows no bounds. The crescendo of sounds from the victim and the victor acutely articulate the horrific plight: the more the potter's fiery sparks lash out, the louder the poor clay wails. And her ardent pleas hit us in the twenty-first century, forcing us to assess our greed and our painful, oppressive and exploitive mechanisms. Hearing these pitiful cries evokes sympathy; they compel us to change our behaviour.

The Guru often utilizes self-references from the animal world. His identification with 'dog' is rather curious, but importantly, it discloses his innermost perception of non-humans. The Guru does not hold to any stereotype; rather, he showcases the affinity between humans and animals. Prone to doing good and bad actions, both humans and dogs are equally capable social agents. At times the Guru expresses his ignorance and obtuseness: 'Listen, my blind dog of a mind, without being told the truthful One knows it all' (GGS: 662). Another time his greedy materialist self: 'There are so many dogs, and I am a stray one, I bark to appease this body' (GGS: 785). But then in an entirely contrasting tone, 'Nanak, the dog intoxicated at the divine Court, constantly gets higher and higher' (GGS: 1291). The Guru projects not only his ignorance and greed but also his spiritual exaltation in partnership with a dog.

In the final Raga Prabhati we hear the First Sikh perform a duet with a calf:

> A cow bearing mercy and patience
>   I, a calf, serenely suckling her milk
> Beg to be dressed up in Your praise and beauty
> Nanak sings rapt in the song of the divine One
>
> GGS: 1329

The Guru's intense spiritual desire harmoniously joins with the pleas of a calf as he begs to be dressed in the outfit of divine praise and beauty suckling his merciful and patient Parent. Earlier, he imagines the divine One simultaneously as the calf, the cow and the sweet milk— '*Ape backhara, gau kheer*' (GGS: 1190). His successor Guru Ram Das utters his heartfelt wish: '*Jiu bachara dekh gau sukh manai tiu nanak hari gali laviai re*—like the cow rejoices seeing her calf, says Nanak, take me in your arms, O divine One!' (GGS: 1118). How different these tender loving scenes from the cruelty we wreak on our livestock today. In the push for increasing profits, bodies of female dairy cows are terribly abused. Genetic manipulation, artificial insemination, milking regimens and hormones are forced upon them to produce more milk. Their male calves are immediately torn away from them to be processed into veal while their female calves are sentenced to the same tragic cycle—for human exploitation of their milk and flesh. Rather than live their natural life span of about twenty years, they turn miserably weak by the age of five and are driven to slaughterhouses.

The Guru's poignant lyrics reveal the absolute One as the giver and the sustainer of everything that exists; that One is the light, the voice, the sound, the taste and the touch of the whole cosmos. He radically shifts the view of human dominion over nature in terms of partnership and kinship with nature; and a commitment to justice for all creatures, not just humans. We learn to be self-critical: we humans are one species in the system, a part of nature, so how did we get to be the 'owners'? Is it not time we shake off our arrogance and dominance?

Aesthetico-ontology

Early in my academic career, I advanced 'aesthetico-ontology' for the synergy between aesthetics and ontology in Guru Nanak's worldview. While 'aesthetic' provides the immediacy and directness of Guru Nanak's experience, ontology reveals the is-ness, the divine substance of it, and ethics is its natural corollary. The aesthetico-ontological process is also useful in discerning the import of Guru Nanak's eco-theology. The Guru is struck by the wonder and brilliance of the insubstantial and formless composition of the divine One in every particular entity: '*Jahi jahi dekha tah joti tumari tera rupu kaneha*—wherever I turn, I see Your light, how wondrous Your form!', 'My Sahib, Your wonders enchant us. You flow in the waters, on land, across space You're in everyone' (GGS: 596).The Guru's enchantment with the Divine overflowing all over creation awakens our sensibilities to rejoice in Its presence. We are inspired to look more keenly and discover more of the magic around us. We also read in them the implication that we continue to make scientific discoveries—the infinite One has no boundaries and we must keep on exploring to the farthest edges of interstellar space. Simultaneously, these Nanakian lyrics make us question our negative assumptions and derogatory attitudes toward natural phenomena, and their beauty and force instil in us a sense of responsibility to strive for the welfare of our intricate universe. The realm of aesthetics resists the usual pattern of becoming deleteriously divorced from the religious, the ethical and the scientific.

Since everything permeates with the Divine, nothing in this world could be inferior or polluted. Everything is sacred: 'Grain is holy, water is holy, fire is holy, salt too, and by adding ghee, the fifth, our food is purer still . . .' (GGS: 473). As they cast a sacred halo on our everyday consumption, these Nanakian verses cast a radically fresh angle on eco-theology as well. They connect what is on our plate with the larger world, they make us cognizant of the ethical problems in the processes of global food production, consumption and distribution. To cite a recent thesis:

> It has become clear to me that the concept of food itself is key to the transformation of our ecological crisis. Unless human species can open itself to the contemplation of food as a holy mystery through which we eat ourselves into existence, then the meaning of existence will continue to elude us. Our present cultural experience of food has degenerated into food as fuel, for supplying the energy for our insatiable search for that which will fill the hungers of our soul. When we understand that food is not a metaphor for spiritual nourishment, but is itself spiritual, then we eat food with a spiritual attitude and taste that are nourished by the Divine directly.[10]

Indeed, for the First Sikh, every grain of food is holy *itself* as long as we taste its holy ingredient. The universal Divine has to be tasted.

'The elixir, the taste, and the enjoyer is the One Itself—*ape rasia ape rasu ape ravanhar*' (GGS: 23). With the First Sikh, we cultivate an attitude of gratitude and mindfulness towards food. We can also free ourselves from the surveillance cameras of our culture which coerce women (and men) to hate their bodies and the food they take in. Letting go of our obsession with control and power, we crusade against hunger and famine, we work to end environmental suffering from pesticides and fertilizers. (It is hard to believe that the soil Guru Nanak tilled was chemicalized with toxins during the Green Revolution.) Each morsel we eat we remember the One, we taste the complex interplay of land, air, water, plants, animals and people that make up that morsel. No wonder Guru Nanak stipulated langar as the central institution, a hub for ameliorating the physical, social, moral and spiritual aspects of his community.

However, in our approach to the web of life, we must keep alive the exciting dialectic of the particular and the universal, the physical and the metaphysical, the secular and the Divine. Each and every phenomenal form is informed by the formless One. In Plato, ideas and pure forms are divorced and distanced from the particular as well as from everyday phenomena. For example, only the is-ness, the essence, the formlessness of the rose is real; the particular roses, those that can be seen, smelled and touched in this material world, are but mutable, temporary and unreal. From Guru Nanak's eco-centric perspective, each particular rose we smell here and now gives us the awareness of reality (*rasia hovai musk ka tab phul pachhane*). In the particular we recognize the universal; the universal in turn highlights the particular; form is formless and vice versa. It is important that this dialectic never cease; otherwise, Guru Nanak's eco-theology would be misperceived. If and when the Divine is understood as actually residing within or encapsulated inside a form, then it becomes substantialized, reified, reduced to finitude. We are to respect each bit as divine potential—and not make it into a static entity. 'It cannot be moulded—*thapia na jae*,' he cautioned us in his Japji.

Therefore, the Divine exists everywhere without being contained in anything as such. Guru Nanak's is not a pantheistic vision; the Ultimate never becomes immanent; it is transcendent and remains so. The particular is constantly thrust into the beyond, towards the universal.

Guru Nanak's aesthetico-ontology is a dynamic and joyous process whereby a fluid connection between the particulars and the universal is maintained, and the entire multiverse pulsates with divine potentiality, every atom vibrating with ultimate possibility. An ever-fresh presence empowers us—'*Sahib mera nit navan*—my Sahib is perpetually new,' sings the First Sikh (GGS: 660). The perpetual dialectic frees us from constricting dead old habits of thought and action. We become alive to the spiritual in the material. We begin to question. How could multinational companies single-mindedly invade remote areas in search of delicate rose petals, alas, to bottle them up into expensive perfumes? How could human greed set fiery infernos across the Amazon rainforest? How could we destroy the home of more than half the world's species of plants and animals? Aren't we committing suicide by destroying the 'lungs of our planet'? Why are we bent on destroying the web of life for our consumption?

It is critical we keep our sight on the constant dialectic between unity and diversity; for sure, the cosmic and human oneness and equality does *not* denote uniformity. The First Sikh's magical paradox resounds across the 1430 pages of the GGS: the same divine One is in everyone and everything, and yet no two beings or things are the same! In his words: '*Jah jah dekha tah jot tumari tera rup kineha ikat rup fireh parchhanna koe na kis hi jeha*—wherever I turn I see Your light, what a form You possess! Your one form is everywhere but no two forms are alike' (GGS: 596). Here the difference and uniqueness of every single phenomenon is celebrated—*koe na kis hi jaisa* (none is like any other)!

This is an important lesson for our contemporary world wherein the trend is to homogenize society and nature. Journalists Montenegro and Glavin warn us about the 'global epidemic of sameness' which is speedily eradicating human languages, destroying a domesticated food-crop variety, and killing off entire species.[11] In reality, globalization is 'Westernization'; more specifically, an American-Anglo domination. Rather than all of us assimilate into a 'melting pot', we need to respect and engage with other cultures, races, genders, religions and species. We heard Guru Nanak marvel at the sheer diversity surrounding us: 'How many species, how many languages, and how many rulers and kings/ How many mystics, how many devotees, O Nanak there's no end to their end' (GGS: 6). Until we authentically accept *others* with all their difference, appreciate *their* individuality and diversity, feel an affinity with *them*, we cannot work for people or species that are different from us. And this acceptance, appreciation and kinship come with the realization that all particularities palpitate with the same One. 'All species and languages come together in You,' proclaimed the First Sikh (GGS: 1021).

Biophilia

So essential is 'biophilia' in Guru Nanak's metaphysics that we have come across it in almost every chapter. Biologist E.O. Wilson defines it as an 'innately emotional affiliation of human beings to other living organisms'.[12] Feminist thinkers have appropriated 'biophilial' as a psychological and philosophical category. Literally a love for life, biophilia counters the patriarchal order with its preoccupation with death and the other world central in most religions and shifts, explains feminist philosopher and theologian Grace Jantzen, the necrophilic fixation to life and living here on Earth.[13] Pursuing the goal of personal salvation, religious people from most traditions emphasize heaven and the world beyond, and they end up repudiating this world. Even Guru Nanak's contemporaries from various schools of the Yogis, Naths, Siddhs and Jains rejected this world as corrupting. His was a revolutionary voice that turned the focus from death and the afterlife to life and living sensuously here on Earth. His focus on life in this world inspires environmentalist commitment to the social justice and ecological integrity of our planet. The First Sikh embraces earthly ethics that value temporality, historicity, change and passage.

Temporality as an integral feature of the divine Reality was noted at the outset of this work. In the very opening of the Japji (the first hymn in the Sikh scripture) the Guru presents the Timeless One involved in the passage of time, past, present and future. Eco-theologically speaking, the Divine is intimately and constantly related with the material universe with its growth and transitions. Unequivocally, he says, 'Our months and seasons are You, each auspicious moment is to think of You.' In Raga Asa, the Guru marvels at the single Creator in myriad forms. Paradoxically, his eco-theological lens brilliantly catches the many forms through invisible time: 'Moments turn into seconds, minutes into hours, days, dates, and months, many seasons, but there is only the one sun; O Nanak, our one Creator with so many forms!' (GGS: 12). The movement of the stars and planets, the whirl of electrons and protons, the ebb and tide of life, the flow of the Infinite into the finite are choreographed throughout the First Sikh's oeuvre.

It is most significant that the raga organization of the sacred text itself is based on the time theory of the Indian musical tradition. Each raga has its season prescribed for its singing, time of day, and a particular cultural climate. The raga framework harmonizes the verses with the natural rhythm of the day, season, region and emotions. Connecting humans with space and time, they bring out the intrinsic force of the verses. Several of Guru Nanak's compositions like the Barah Mah (Twelve Months), Thitin (The Dates) and Pahare (The Hours) voice his reverence for the dynamic intersection of each second with the Timeless One. Altogether they project an organic and authentic mode of existence in the here and now. We don't need to aspire for eternity out there. The Barah Mah depicts the lunar and solar days through the movement of the twelve months, and their impact not only on the young woman desiring her Beloved but also on the diverse species— andaj, jeraj, utbhuj and setaj, born of egg, womb, earth and sweat. Humans, vegetation, animals, birds, light, temperature, water—*alike*— participate in the changing reality of the twelve months. The hymn establishes a strong human–nature nexus. In his finale we noted that Guru Nanak acknowledges all units of time as 'blessed' (*bhale*): 'The twelve months, the seasons, the lunar and the solar days, the hours, the minutes, the seconds are blessed, for they are naturally ticking towards union with the true One—*be das mah ruti thiti var bhale ghari murat pal sache ae sahaji mile*' (GGS, 1109). The First Sikh's hymns saturate us with an existential appreciation for the ticking of time.

In his Pahare the first quarter is an affirmation of our primal home—the magical locus of the mother's womb where life is produced. Pulling us away from death and 'necrophilic' ideologies, the First Sikh's foetus imaginary reveals our extremely positive entry into this world. The Guru perfectly photographs the creative site of pregnancy. This is not any scopophilic or fetishistic construction, but a visual recollection of our spiritual devotion and rootedness in women's physiology:

> In the first quarter of the night, my roving friend
>> We receive the command in the womb
> Turned upside down we perform austerities
>> We beseech our Husband my roving friend
> We beseech and praise our Husband
>> Turned upside, rapt in meditation . . .

GGS: 74

The embryo lodged upside down is the Guru's paradigm for one rapt in meditation and contemplation. Lodged in the mother's body we praise our Creator. Several other scriptural verses resonate with this view of the womb as a locus for both biological and spiritual growth.[14] With the Infinite delighting inside her body, the foetus grows, drawing upon the nutrients of the physical elements that the mother herself shares with the rest of the cosmos. The male Sikh guru seems to have used the lens of modern feminists for whom natural elements 'constitute the origin of our bodies, of our life, of our environment, the flesh of our passions'.[15] But if we come out of the womb and forget our Creator, then we lose out on life and living. An alienated and selfish mode of existence is anthropomorphic. We live inauthentically by going against biophilia, aesthetic-ontology, eco-theology. Guru Nanak urges us to actualize the potential with which we enter this world. He opens us up to the possibilities of change, a key to future relatability with the cosmos.

The poetic form of his Thitin composition is based on the monthly cycle of the lunar days. The Guru goes through the motions of each day, and on the fourteenth day we enter the fourth stage of bliss:

> We go beyond time with its strands
>> Of passion, inertia, and truth
> The sun enters the house of the moon
> We learn the value of doing yoga

And in the divine One spread through
>   The fourteen worlds, the netherworlds
The galaxies, the constellations
>   We absorb in love

GGS: 84

Clearly, the spiritual progress takes place in and within the fluctuations of time, the movement of the moon around the earth. Guru Nanak's lyrics highlight the intimacy of the celestial and terrestrial worlds. His finale captures the unifying force of the multiverse—the single Divine spread through various worlds, galaxies, constellations. Absorbed in the love of the infinite One, we finite individuals are at home in the multiverse, nestled together with biotic and abiotic beings alike. Here is a moment when human consciousness is joined not only with its own body or that of the earth, but with the body of the entire multiverse. This imagery represents the vastness of the Divine and Its creation. Without taking away the significance from human existence or action it promotes the idea of a larger world which we recognize as important to our own lives and the divine world in which we function. Such a consciousness is sure to impact our global society. It has the capacity, as essayist, poet, novelist and playwright Susan Griffin would say, to 'infuse every kind of meeting between self and the universe, even in the most daily acts, with an eros, a palpable love, that is also sacred'.[16] The interrelationships demonstrate that the elements and the rest of creation are not for humankind to own; they were formed by the divine One and function for that One for the continued existence of all.

By nurturing love, we are sure to develop new modalities for the continuous existence of all beings right now. Guru Nanak's environmentalism upholds the ethical objectives of contemporary eco-theologians—their concern with justice based on care pertaining to our present lives. We cannot be waiting for the future 'kingdom' of god, caution feminist scholars. The love of life extends to our immediate families, to our primary communities, and to other species. The First Sikh's biophilial, non-anthropomorphic, aesthetic-ontological and eco-theological lyrics have the potential to generate 'a new synthesis, a new creation in which human nature and nonhuman nature become friends in the creating of a livable and sustainable cosmos'.[17]

A Perennially Fresh Tree

Nanak, the guru is tree of contentment
  Its flowers are morality, knowledge its fruit
Sap of succulent love keeps it evergreen
  Mindful actions ripen it
And as we eat each bite of this gift of gifts
  We savour glorious honors.

GGS: 147

So said the revolutionary First Sikh. We regard him as a perennially fresh tree, creating a vibrant ecosystem. Trees give us delicious fruit and comforting shade, they take away harmful gases like carbon dioxide and they give us our breath of life—oxygen. The philosopher–mystic's melodies absorb our toxic egotism; they replenish us with passion, compassion and an urgent responsibility to promote human rights, gender justice and vibrant ecosystems across the globe. Trees exclude no one, no thing; they extend their shade and fruit to each and all. The First Sikh was just that. His melodious lyrics are not just for the Sikh community. They cannot be circumscribed to religious performances or sacred spaces. Every member of our pluralistic society, anywhere, is free to draw upon the First Sikh's precious gifts.

Conclusion

The Enduring Legacy of the First Sikh

The legacy of the First Sikh is so alive in every which way. What Sikh men and women say and do and wear and write and think derives from him. Of course, his successor Gurus are vitally important in the crystallization of this major world religion, but each of them built upon the foundations of unicity envisioned and established by the First. Complete continuity between the First and the Tenth Gurus was explored in various chapters of my book *Birth of the Khalsa: A Feminist Re-memory of Sikh Identity*. Even the blueprint for Guru Gobind Singh's Khalsa initiation, I claim, goes back to the First Sikh's revelatory experience.[1] In this chapter, I'd like to look at some of the ways in which the First Sikh continues to be the epicentre of Sikh personal and public life, and is extending in many exciting scenarios on the global stage. This admittedly is a relatively cursory look, barely scraping the surface of the First Sikh's phenomenal impact on society and culture, but it will help illustrate the extent of his enduring appeal.

For the Sikhs, their everyday greeting for welcome or goodbye, 'Sat sri akal' (praise to the timeless Truth), embraces his prelude to the Japji. Guru Nanak named the infinite One as Truth (sat) and characterized It as timeless (akal), and the two together have become a part of cultural parlance. Even their reflex 'Waheguru' (before a meal, after a sneeze, or embarking on any venture or travel) surges with a sense of wonder and echoes Guru Nanak's wonder (wah) as he experienced the glory of the infinite One. Their daily routine revolves around the First Sikh's verse. Young and old may find a quiet space or be involved in their daily chores such as preparing breakfast, combing hair or cleaning house—their day invariably begins with a recitation of his Japji. Their day also ends with his hymns from his Kirtan Sohila. Their walls, desks, kitchen counters and dashboards display his iconic 'Ikk Oan Kar', a 'coincidence of sensible appearance and supersensible meaning', as Gadamer would describe.[2]

The nub of their collective being is the First Sikh. Morning public worship includes his Asa di Var. The new month commences with a reading from his Barah Mah. For all Sikh rites of passage and for any family celebration—a new house, a new job, birthdays, engagements and times of uncertainty and difficulty like sickness or death—a forty-eight hour non-stop (akhand) reading of the GGS (several readers take turns) begins with his Japji. His place of birth (Nankana Sahib, now in Pakistan) and the sites he visited have accrued great historical value. Gurdwaras have been built in commemoration, and Sikhs derive tremendous sustenance and joy revisiting them. Their calendars are marked with Gurpurabs (days of the Guru) when uninterrupted readings of scripture take place, intellectual symposiums are held and musical performances are organized. Gurpurab celebrations also include huge Sikh processions with colourful floats carrying the Guru Granth Sahib and depicting different aspects of Sikh life. They are becoming familiar scenes in metropolises, be it Los Angeles, Vancouver, London, Dublin or Paris.

The institutions started by the First Sikh have evolved in unprecedented ways, testifying to the social equality and familyhood of all people so cherished by him. In gurdwaras both at home and abroad, the community meal (langar) is voluntarily prepared and served to people irrespective of caste, class, religion or sex. At the central Sikh shrine, the Golden Temple in Amritsar, about 80,000 visitors daily eat meals prepared by enthusiastic volunteers. Over weekends, almost twice as many are served langar! The *New York Times* calls it the 'world's largest free eatery'. Along the same lines, the

Guru Singh Sabha gurdwara in Southall serves close to 5000 meals on weekdays and 10,000 meals on weekends. Rich or poor, Sikhs and non-Sikhs relish sitting together and partaking the Guru's langar. It could be a small and humble meal in a tiny village gurdwara, or it could be an abundant meal as in the larger gurdwaras (San Jose, Toronto, Southall). A group of us taking a taxi to Gurdwara Sahib in a Montreal suburb once started to give directions to the local Canadian driver who needed none: 'I go there all the time for the delicious vegetarian meal,' he said. The community members also transport langar from the gurdwara to homeless shelters, especially during Thanksgiving and the holiday season. How the tradition begun by Guru Nanak functions in our global society today is reported by BBC:

> 'We come here because we get food . . . A hot meal. It's a luxury for me.' John Davidson is 55 and homeless. He is one of 250 people who have just received a hand-out of hot soup, drinks, chocolate bars and other supplies from the Sikh Welfare and Awareness Team van parked up on the Strand in central London on a cold Sunday evening. The Swat team, as they're known, park at the same spot every week so a group of volunteers from the Sikh community can hand out vital supplies. Homeless people, who overwhelmingly are not Sikh, patiently wait in line to be served.[3]

The strong leadership, social activism, humanitarian relief and innovative advocacy of various Sikh organizations worldwide are grounded in the concept of seva (selfless action) instituted by the First Sikh. Just to name some of these organizations: the Canadian Sikh Council, Dasvandh Network, Ensaaf, the Jakara Movement, Kaur Foundation, Kaurs United, Khoj Gurbani, Sarbat LGBT Sikhs, Sikh Feminist Research Institute, Sikh American Legal Defense and Education Fund, Sikh Coalition, Sikh Family Center, Sikh Helpline Australia, Sikh Research Institute, Sikh Women, Sikh Women Now, Sikh Youth Federation, Sikhcess, Sikhlens, Surat Initiative, UN-affiliated United Sikhs and the World Sikh Organization of Canada. To commemorate Guru Nanak's 550th birth anniversary, the international environmental action group EcoSikh has pledged to plant over a million trees by creating native forests. Afforestt, the service provider for creating natural, wild, maintenance-free, native forests (based in Bangalore and Delhi) is collaborating with EcoSikh to achieve their goal. Men and women from different nationalities and religions are working together. In their own and different ways, these organizations are dedicated to the realization of civil and human rights for all people, and the guardianship of our Mother Earth. Their objectives, praxis and activism are based on the biophilial and pluralistic principles of the First Sikh. His ethics of seva is propelling Sikh humanitarianism, philanthropy and activism. In any crisis anywhere, whether a hurricane or a tsunami or a terrorist act, Sikhs reach with the speed of light to serve those in need. Seva in the form of food and shelter is being extended to Rohingya, Syrian and Iraqi refugees. For the many who died in Christchurch in New Zealand in March 2019, the Sikh community performed obsequies. The *Telegraph* reports:

> The reflexive activation of the core of their faith as enunciated by Guru Nanak in the Guru Granth Sahib had another feature: the offering of votive space to Muslims to undertake *namaz* in *gurdwaras*. For sheer originality and sublimity, this gesture was unique, redemptive.[4]

Gurdwaras everywhere provide services to the elderly and the needy. Orphanages, hospitals, dispensaries, eye centres, medical colleges and charitable trusts in Mumbai, Delhi, Ludhiana, Amritsar, Patiala, Nairobi and many other places have been set up to continue the legacy of the First Sikh. Schools, colleges and universities, even factories, industries and flights, are being named after the First Sikh! He is the heartbeat of Sikh religious, cultural, civic, political, economic, intellectual and creative activities.

Make-up of the Five Ks

I reiterate my thesis that the momentous Khalsa initiation at Anandpur on Baisakhi day in 1699 evokes the First Sikh's sipping of amrit, recorded in Raga Majh and later confirmed in the Puratan Janamsakhi. In a very meaningful way, the Tenth Sikh Guru returns to this primal moment of Sikhism and opens it up into the future through his inauguration of the Khalsa. He expands the First Sikh's personal revelatory experience into a public, social and institutional rite. In the final analysis, the historic rite of passage initiated at Anandpur is a visual re-enactment of the First Sikh's metahistoric experience. The Tenth Guru brilliantly choreographs the First Sikh's experience into a fixed and enduring ritual for the present and future of the Sikh community.

Guru Gobind Singh marked the internal transformation of his newly constructed subject with the five Ks which are patterned on the Sirpao that the First Guru received in the River Bein. It is essential to realize that Guru Nanak's Sirpao is the paradigm for the code of dress that the Khalsa wears. The Sirpao was the symbol of divine honour bestowed on the First Sikh, and the five Ks for the Tenth Guru were also a symbol of honour and respect for his Sikhs, both men and women. And these five Ks worn on the body are made out of scriptural materials.

The fusion of the devotional and the martial was the most important feature of the philosophy of Guru Gobind Singh and of his career as a spiritual leader and harbinger of a revolutionary impulse, which I firmly believe was birthed in the sublime textures of the GGS. Guru Gobind Singh gave the five items of faith to be worn by his Sikhs as a mark of their identity—(*bana*): long hair (*kesha*), comb (*kangha*), steel bracelet (*kara*), sword (*kirpan*), and underpants (*kachha*). These everyday articles from his culture—something so simple and common as a comb, a bracelet, long hair, underwear, a sword—had great personal meaning for the Tenth Guru because they were laden with spirituality in the bani (sacred text) that he grew up on. That he would endow the Granth with Guruship in the final hour of his life manifests the profound motivational significance the sacred text had for him. The metaphysical ideals cherished in his sacred text coincide with the simple items in his sociocultural context, and their 'coincidence' leads to the five Ks as the items of Sikh identity.

These five Ks ontologically draw upon the accoutrements introduced by Guru Nanak. The symbiosis of the First Guru's bani and the Tenth Guru's bana is vitally important and I very much wish the Sikh community to take note of it. The bani–bana unity heightens the psychological, physical and spiritual power of the five Ks. As an expression of the divine One and the tenacity of individual character, the five Ks cement the intimacy between the individual and the Divine while strengthening bonds amongst community members.

Long hair (kesha) is a vivid expression of the process of cultivating humility and overcoming the selfish ego. It serves in the First Sikh's verse as an external symbol of a serene interior, an interior purified from the defilements of conflict, aggression and arrogance. The long hair is an expression of the sanctification of the human personality: '*Mathi gundain pattia*—she has her hair braided,' says Guru Nanak (GGS: 558). The relationship between the individual and the Divine is tightly braided by following her example of love and tenacity. Later Sikh Gurus picture kesha as a whisk that fans their intense devotion. Guru Arjan says, 'I dust the feet of the Enlightener with my hair—*gur ke charan kes sangi jhare*' (GG: 387). 'My only objective in life is to dust the feet with my hair as your slave—*kes sangi das pag jharo ihai manorath mor*' (GG: 500). The image of the brutally shorn hair during Babar's invasion recounted by Guru Nanak in his Babarvani must have been absorbed by his ninth successor. What was violated had to be restored. Guru Gobind Singh reacts to the political repression in his own times by reconstructing tragic memories into triumphant hopes: his people evermore were to keep their hair long, untouched by any scissors.

Similarly, the comb receives religious significance in the First Sikh's melodies. We can see the comb in her hands as 'the woman patiently gets her braid knotted—*dhiraj dhari bandhavai kaman*' (GGS: 359). The poetically charged alliteration of 'Ds' in the original evokes a rhythmic application of the comb—its teeth turning and returning, smoothing and arranging the hair express her mental tenacity. Another verse from the GGS further qualifies: 'It is with Truth that she braids her hair' (GGS: 54). Profoundly captured, Truth is in human hands holding the long hair, and with the help of the comb, weaving the different strands together. The kangha (comb) is not an antithesis to the kesha (hair); there is a synchronicity, a close relationship between them. Both together release, redesign and retrieve infinite human potential. The comb is the instrument for attending to oneself, and so combing the hair becomes a self-reflective process which leads to a life of beauty, imagination and Truth for both men and women.

The third K, the kirpan (sword), is not only worn on the body of the Sikhs, it is mentally evoked in Ardas (liturgical prayer), and physiologically partaken both in the amrit sipped by the Khalsa and in the karah prashad partaken by the Sikh congregation. Amrit is prepared by churning water with a double-edged sword, accompanied by the recitation of sacred verses; karah prashad, the warm and delicious Sikh sacrament, is not distributed to the congregation until it is sanctified by the touch of the sword. The sword thus exerts tremendous influence in the daily life of the Sikh community. The prototype for this K of the Sikhs is distinctly found in the metaphysical materials where it is made up of *gur gianu*, literally 'divine wisdom' (GGS: 235, 574, 983, 1072). The paradigmatic person utilizing the sword in Guru Nanak's verse is a woman. The female subject heroically fights against her inner propensities: 'by taking up the sword of knowledge, she fights against her mind and merges with herself' (GGS: 1022). Not only does she know how to wield the powerful sword but she also triumphs over her hostile opponents. The kirpan worn on the body of the Khalsa is welded by divine knowledge; it is the instrument to annihilate the ego and any such brute force that stands in the way of an enlightened existence.

The fourth K, the steel kara (bracelet), also evokes ornaments and the mode of dressing up treasured by the First Sikh. Worn by men and women, it is but another endorsement of the scriptural expression of spirituality through everyday activities and embellishments. Like the sword, its material substance is the Divine. According to Guru Nanak, 'By wearing the bracelet created by the Creator, consciousness is held steadily—*kar kari karta kangan pahirai in bidhi chitu dharei*' (GGS: 359). The bracelet (*kangan*) is a symbol of dynamic action, and the word 'action' (*kar*) recurs constantly in this line: the bracelet is made (*kari*) by the creator (*karta*) and worn around the hand (*kar*). It is artistically set in the midst of many spiritual adornments. Essentially, all of the human articles and movements are imbued with the sacred, and morality is gained through action (kar); we must attend to the physical self. Since the texture of the bracelet is literally the Divine creatrix, by wearing it on our bodies the chasm between the material and the Divine is suspended. The bracelet around our wrist lays our consciousness still and bare—ready for an intimate experience with the transcendent One. All narrow, discriminating, self-centred, self-serving actions, and all heavy-handed hegemonic operations are discarded by the hand that wears it. The kara formulated by Guru Gobind Singh for his Sikhs is modelled on this Nanakian bracelet. It is a symbol of the equality of humans, an expression of freedom from hereditary professions and exclusionary handcuffs.

Finally, the kachha (underpants) too is modelled on the metaphysical garments important to the founder Guru. Not those 'who take off their clothes and go naked like Digambaras' (GGS: 1169), but she who 'wears the clothes of Love' (GGS: 54) is prized by the First Sikh. He denounces ascetic mortification and any denial of the body. He exalts her who 'wears the clothes of Love' (GGS: 54) and presents her as the paradigm to be emulated by both men and women. As I discussed in an earlier paper, kachha is a marker of respect for the human body.[5]

It is in the fusion of bani and bana that the full sacrality of the Sikh symbols opens up, radiating wholeness and illumination to our fragmented selves. It is not simply that the body be dressed in the five Ks (bana) and the mind think about the hymns (bani), but only when the Divine is palpably experienced do the external markers identify Sikh men and women. The five symbols are both representations and revelations of our full humanity. The synergy of the Guru's bani and bana would release new reservoirs of human potential and enchantment in *everybody*.

Musical Legacy

Guru Nanak's musical influence remains untapped in the Sikh world. His verse is found in nineteen out of the thirty-one GGS ragas, and ragas like Majh and Tukhari are even attributed to him. Musicians and exponents of musicology alert us about the general neglect of music in Sikh scriptural studies. Important steps are being taken in India, Europe and North America to fill in this gap. The Punjabi University in Patiala instituted the Gurmat Sangit department, and Hofstra University in New York established the Sardarni Harbans Kaur Chair in Sikh musicology, the first of its kind in the Western Academy. Scholars are hosting conferences, and significant publications are coming out. At the academic conference at Loyola Marymount University in California (February 2016), scholarly papers were accompanied by uplifting kirtan performances by Dr Nirinjan Khalsa, Bhai Baldeep Singh and Professor Francesca Cassio.

Kirtan, the singular religious performance in Sikh worship, is traced to Guru Nanak and his accompanist Bhai Mardana on the rabab. Bhai Mardana's sons, Bhai Banoo and Bhai Saloo, were official musicians for the Third and Fourth Gurus, and the tradition was carried on by Satta and Balvand. When the Fifth Guru was compiling the canon, these two grandsons of Bhai Mardana assisted the Fifth Guru to ensure continuity in the singing and playing style of the GGS compositions. Over the centuries, diverse performers have brought in their diverse musical styles and plurality of intonations. From Bhai Mardana's rabab or the typical twentieth-century tabla and harmonium, the musical repertoire in the modern milieu has expanded considerably. Ancient instruments are being revived, new ones are being added, and both Eastern and Western instruments and accents reverberate the First Sikh's holy words. Kirtan ensembles include instruments such as the saranda, taus, dilruba, tanpura, jori/pakhawaj, santoor, sitar, zithers, violin, cello, mandolin, piano and even the Australian didgeridoo. Ragi Jhathas from India travel widely to perform kirtan in all corners of the world; diasporic Sikhs in America, Australia, Africa and Europe are avidly training in kirtan performance. Last summer, it was sheer joy to hear little children captivatingly singing the First Sikh's hymns on the harmonium and tabla drums in Emily Reggio Gurdwara Sahib in Italy. Non-Sikhs are becoming a part of kirtan ensembles as well, and though the musicians and instrumentalists may belong to different regions and religions, they are in tune with the basic precepts of the First Sikh.

The classical style of kirtan is being devoutly performed, enthusiastically heard and rigorously studied all over. To name a few distinguished experts, Bhai Baldeep Singh of New Delhi heads the Anad Conservatory in Sultanpur Lodhi and has trained several Indian and western musicians. Dr Gurnam Singh is the founder and head of the Gurmat Sangeet Chair at Punjabi University in Patiala, and his complete recording of the GGS's thirty-one ragas is a valuable resource for kirtan studies. Dr Francesca Cassio, the Sardarni Harbans Kaur Chair in Sikh Musicology at Hofstra University, promotes kirtan in various venues: teaching, scholarship, performance and hosting conferences. A dedicated scholar, Dr Inderjit Kaur teaches musicological and performative aspects of sabad kirtan at the University of Michigan, and reaches a wide audience through her writing and presentations. Gurminder Kaur Bhogal, professor of music at Wellesley College, incorporates an innovative acousmatic approach to listening and performance practices in the Sikh tradition. Dr Nirinjan Kaur Khalsa, a student and scholar of the Gurbani Kirtan tradition, fosters an expansive experience of Guru Nanak's legacy that is dynamic, ever flourishing and resilient.

In London, the Raj academy headed by yogi professor Surinder Singh pursues Guru Nanak's musical approach to communication and inner exploration by drawing upon the melodies, tones and rhythms of the GGS ragas for holistic healing, happiness and personal growth. In the USA, young American Sikhs have formed Chardi Kala Jatha, which is adding another layer of spiritual intensity to Sikh music. These young Americans inspired by the Sikh Healthy, Happy, Holy Organization (3HO) founded by Harbhajan Singh Yogi in 1969 are fully steeped in Sikh life, and several of them have received training in classical music from Ustaad Narinder Singh Sandhu.

Incorporating a variety of musical genres, Sikh kirtan today is World Music. Sat Kartar Khalsa synthesizes Eastern and Western melodies and opens up Sikh music to a wide Western audience. A pioneer in fusion Kirtan music, Shivpreet Singh blends Indian classical music and US pop, folk and country styles. Sardar Dya Singh, who created a core musical ensemble of leading musicians in Australia, aptly describes his group's music as 'bringing Sikh music to the world and world music to the Sikhs'. The accompaniment of Eastern and/or Western musical instruments only amplifies the intrinsic enchantment of the First Sikh's hymns.

The 'light' musical genre of kirtan is also becoming popular. It is not based on the raga structure, but draws upon popular Bollywood songs, Sufi qawwali music, folk songs and ghazals—romantic love songs shared across West Asia and South Asia. In films like *Nanak Nam Jahaz Hai* hymns were sung by eminent Ragi Bhai Samund Singh, and also by major Indian film playback singers like Asha Bhosle, Mohammad Rafi, Mahendra Kapoor and Manna De. Kirtan today is performed and heard not only in gurdwaras but also in concert halls and festivals; it is relayed on the radio, TV, YouTube, Spotify, Soundcloud, iTunes and other platforms. The First Sikh's melodious hymns relayed from distant venues resound in homes across the globe. The musical legacy of our dhadhi is diversifying and expanding and reaching the hearts of listeners in all corners of the world—just what he intended: '*Dhadhi kare pasao sabadu vajaia*—this dhadhi will spread the holy word far and wide' (GGS: 150). The pluralistic contemporary kirtan performance is in consonance with the plurality of accents, regions, centuries, religions, philosophical notes, classical ragas and folk tunes enshrined in the GGS. Deeply etched in my mind are the First Sikh's melodies as they fused into the vibrations of the taus, dilruba, tabla and harmonium amidst a diverse American audience at the White House—it was the Guru's birthday celebration in November 2015. The sound of music in that White House auditorium transported me across time and space. I was listening to kirtan with my grandmother in Bathinda, with my parents at the Harmandir Sahib, with my brother in the California desert. I could imagine the first Sikh congregation seated around Guru Nanak. My inner self expanded towards a larger reality. There was something numinous in the air. In my ears hummed Guru Arjan's '*Tahan baikunth jaha kirtan tera*—it is paradise where Your kirtan is performed' (GGS: 749). The compiler editor of the sacred text here uses the pronoun '*tera*' (Your) for the universal Patron who employed the first Sikh. No voice or instrument or melody could be excluded from extolling this One— the timeless beat of music, the soundless sound, the holy word.

Artistic Legacy

Sikh art had its genesis in the Janamsakhi illustrations depicting the life of Guru Nanak (see Chapter 2). Whereas the art of the Buddhists, Jains, Hindus, Muslims and Christians from the Indian subcontinent has been an important academic subject, Sikh art is only recently beginning to gain attention. The tercentenary celebrations of the founding of the Khalsa in 1999 generated a number of exhibitions and conferences. Among them was *The Arts of the Sikh Kingdoms* curated by Susan Stronge for the Victoria and Albert Museum in London, which subsequently travelled to the Asian Arts Museum in San Francisco and the Royal Ontario Museum in Toronto. The published volume richly illustrates Sikh arts from jewellery, gemstones and textiles to intricately wrought weapons and armour, to paintings and contemporary photographs.[6] In India, B.N. Goswamy put together a comprehensive exhibition entitled 'Piety and Splendour' for the National Museum of India in New Delhi.[7] In 2003, the Satinder Kaur Kapany gallery was inaugurated at the Asian Arts Museum in San Francisco. In July 2004, with the efforts of Paul Taylor, the Smithsonian's National Museum of Natural History opened 'Sikhs: Legacy of the Punjab'. In 2006, Dr B.N. Goswamy and Caron Smith brought together materials on Sikh art and devotion for the Rubin Museum of Art in New York. The exhibition and its beautiful publication, 'I See No Stranger', appropriately carries Guru Nanak's message of the common human bond. Objects from the Toor collection of Sikh art have been exhibited at major global institutions including at the Kunsthalle der Hypo-Kulturstiftung (Munich), Art Gallery of Ontario (Toronto), Asian Art Museum (San Francisco), Virginia Museum of Fine Arts and the Brunei Gallery (London). Recent publications 'Sikh Art from the Kapany Collection' (2017) and 'In Pursuit of Empire: Treasures from the Toor Collection of Sikh Art' (2018) are valuable additions. With their illustrations of paintings, lithographs, weapons, coins, stamps and contemporary art, these volumes sumptuously showcase the culture and history initiated by the First Sikh to broad audiences.

It is heartening to see him lavishly exhibited at the Asian Art Museum in San Francisco. Its Satinder Kaur Kapany Gallery, established in 2003, is the first permanent gallery on Sikh art outside of India. An elegant volume on the Kapany Collection comprising the portraits of the Gurus, the Janamsakhi manuscripts, artwork depicting the Golden Temple, and art from the Sikh kingdoms (coins, arms, armour, textiles, paintings, sculptures) has just been published.[8] In 2017, Dr Parvinder Khanuja and his wife, Parveen, both collectors of

Sikh art, funded another permanent Sikh gallery in the Phoenix Art Museum with its inaugural exhibition entitled 'Virtue and Valor: Sikh Art and Heritage'. Art collecting is a means of safeguarding the Sikh past for the larger community, and so the Khanujas regard it as a form of religious practice, their seva. These visual sites offer diasporic Sikhs an access to their Guru's rich heritage. They not only bring their past dynamically alive, but also make their distant homeland seem close. The synergy between the 'home' and 'host' countries in the founder Guru's imagery reproduces an authentic sense of being and belonging. For those outside of the religion, the materials introduce some of the fundamental aspects of this vibrant north Indian tradition. Sikh art opens up new horizons for the Western imagination. Philosophers and theologians like Susan Langer and Margaret Miles remind us that the function of a society's art is to hone our sensibilities, expand our emotional repertoire and enhance human relationships.

Guru Nanak's life and message are being retold creatively by numerous modern artists, writers and poets. The twentieth century witnessed the traumatic division of India. On the eve of India's independence from British rule on 15 August 1947, the colonial policy of 'divide and rule' came to a horrific finale. The motherland of the Punjabis who had drunk the waters of the same five (punj) rivers (ab) and grown up together speaking the same language was territorially divided, religiously split and linguistically broken up into Pakistan and India. Poet W.H. Auden poignantly criticizes Cyril Radcliffe and the British enterprise for their utter callousness:

> Unbiased at least he was when he arrived on his mission,
> Having never set eyes on this land he was called to partition
> Between two peoples fanatically at odds,
> With their different diets and incompatible gods . . .
> The maps at his disposal were out of date
> And the Census Returns almost certainly incorrect,
> But there was no time to check them, no time to inspect
> Contested areas . . .
> But in seven weeks it was done, the frontiers decided,
> A continent for better or worse divided

With the two new national borders, millions of Sikhs and Hindus had to migrate from regions in the newly created Pakistan into India, and millions of Muslims in the opposite direction. In this violent demographic restructuring, people on both sides were seized by a mad communal frenzy. Over a million men, women and children were brutally murdered. Many twentieth-century artists and poets tried to heal the charred psyche by recalling Guru Nanak's harmonious and pluralistic currents. In this section, we explore the Guru's enduring impact on a few of the artists, and in the next we will sample a few poets writing on the First Sikh.

Sobha Singh

Born in 1901, Sobha Singh started out his career in the British army and witnessed human violence early in his life. He left the army, mastered the Western classical technique of oil painting, and dedicated himself to resurrecting prototypes of peace and love on his canvas. He painted Guru Nanak and his successor Gurus, as well as figures across religious traditions—Jesus Christ, Lord Krishna, Lord Rama, Hindu and Muslim saints like Bhagat Ravidas and Baba Farid, and national heroes Shaheed Bhagat Singh, Kartar Singh Sarabha, Mahatma Gandhi and Lal Bahadur Shastri. His artistic legacy includes images of immortal lovers from the Punjabi folk romances of Heer–Ranjha, Sassi–Punnu and Sohni–Mahival.

As early as 1934, Sobha Singh started to paint Guru Nanak's life. He depicts baby Nanak in the lap of mother Tripta flanked by sister Nanaki and the other women of the family. Like the cherubs in medieval Christian art, Hindu gods and goddesses appear in the skies above, showering flowers on baby Nanak. The art gallery of Parliament House in New Delhi showcases Sobha Singh's murals of Guru Nanak with Bhai Mardana and Bhai Bala. For Guru Nanak's fifth centennial, Sobha Singh painted a portrait of Guru Nanak which has become iconic. The Guru's face is tenderly bent, his soft flowing beard is white, his turban and robe are a delicate yellow, his eyes brim with spirituality, and his hand gestures a gift of blessings. The prints of this painting are extremely popular. A metonymic marker of a Sikh home, it is projected in movies like Gurinder Chadha's *Bend It Like Beckham*.

Arpana Caur

On Arpana's canvas we see a very differently styled Guru Nanak, though equally magnetic. Here too he is white-bearded, but dressed in sheer black, and he has an orange mala, and glows brilliantly.[9] Arpana is among the foremost contemporary Indian painters. Daughter of the renowned author Ajeet Caur, Arpana has won many prestigious awards. Her works bring us face to face with a range of themes and provoke serious reflection and critical thought. Through the play of exquisite colours, designs, spacing and impressionistic figurations, she ushers her spectators into the life of the First Sikh. Amidst vibrant trees, flying birds and inebriated peacocks, we feel Guru Nanak's luminous presence, and like him we begin to think, we question, we rejoice.

Arpana also exposes the tragic consequences of our contemporary consumer society. Five and a half centuries after the First Sikh, the champion of love and serenity, what have we done? Sexism, oppression, poverty, political violence and environmental degradation are all around. She weaves social, economic and political tragedies with the philosophical themes of time life, and death. By superimposing her modern sensibility on traditional folk drawings, Arpana creates powerful psychological and visual tensions. Her works appear surrealist, almost Dada-like. They are widely exhibited in galleries and museums in Delhi, Mumbai, Chandigarh, Singapore, Hiroshima, Dusseldorf, Stockholm, Bradford, London, Boston and San Francisco.

In 2003, Arpana exhibited her paintings devoted entirely to Guru Nanak, and in 2005 she collaborated with Maya Dayal to illustrate *Nanak: The Guru*, which is meant for children, but is no less meaningful for adults.[10] Here, Arpana evocatively renders a post-modern perspective to the Janamsakhi narratives. The two recurring motifs are the Guru's rosary and his footprints. The rosary is a universal symbol of spirituality; for men and women across cultures and centuries, the touch of the circular beads creates a synergy with their mental currents. The footprint is the marker of Guru Nanak—the traveller to places far and wide, the spiritual seeker, the discoverer of a new way of being in the world, the path-setter. We learn about the Guru, our emotions expand, we open up to the larger community and society.

Her illustrations of the children's book begin with the birth of Nanak. Against a midnight-blue backdrop lies an endearing baby on his back. His body is of a golden hue, his feet curl upwards, and both his hands reach up to a luminous full moon. The utterly normal human baby is intimately in touch with infinity! As spirituality flows out of his tiny toes and hands and open mouth, we marvel at baby Nanak; we marvel at the miracle of birth itself. We think of Mata Tripta, we hear the scriptural exaltation, '*Dhan janedi mai*—blessed are the mothers' (GGS: 138).

The final illustration is that of the Guru's departure. It replays the Puratan Janamsakhi account, in which the community is left solely with a shroud and flowers. Arpana's grey patternist brushstrokes sweep across a horizontal white shawl, its tassels not quite reaching the end. At the centre are yellow and orange flowers popping out of their green stems. These are not any fading or drooping bunch, they are hearty blossoms spreading in all directions—up and down, left and right, with no beginning or end. Recasting the Janamsakhi account that community members were free to take flowers and follow their own rites of passage, the Mala-Arpana volume ends with the popular quotation '*Baba nanak shah fakir, hindu ka guru, musalman ka pir*'. Thus, in the public memory, Baba Nanak is an all-in-one guide for his society: the greatest (shah) for sages (fakir), a guru for Hindus, and a pir for Muslims. Somehow, in her illustration, in the way Arpana arranges and places the spread of flowers on the shawl, we can trace the figure of Guru Nanak seated cross-legged on the funeral pyre he asked to be prepared in the B-40 Janamsakhi. The modern artist visually translates the pre-modern Punjabi Janamsakhi text:

Ja adhi rat hoi akhiai kasturi aggar anek sodhe ka mahikar ethe hoe rahia hai /ate jharnat anahad dhuni vajantr anek bhanti ke vajia ka hoe rahia / baba parmesur chaukari mar utha baitha . . .

[They say when it was midnight, many fragrances of musk and incense infused the air. The unstruck melody played by countless musical instruments flooded the air. The supreme Baba got up sitting cross-legged . . .]

B-40, p. 155

Rather than loss, the lingering impact is the perennial vibrancy of the First Sikh in this wondrous world of ours. The marigolds on the white sheet evoke exquisite beauty, fragrance, sensuousness and the soundless music experienced by the First Sikh, and the multisensorial spirituality he wished his society to re-experience. Baba Nanak lives on for all those who walk his way. Isn't it a continuous journey that the two footprints in motion on the facing page lead our eyes towards? The volume concludes with the image of a tiny marigold that says it all.

And between these two bookends is a sequence of incidents illustrating Guru Nanak's love for and communion with his environment as he grows from childhood on. Arpana interlaces the episodes in a variety of exquisite scenes and changing seasons, consistently unfurling the pluralistic threads of Guru Nanak's biography. The marigolds that appear at the end on the shroud are in fact prefigured earlier—we saw them not spread out but threaded in symmetric garlands—metonymic markers of the joyous wedding celebration of Guru Nanak and Bebe Sulakhni. The artist strikingly conveys the First Sikh's metaphysical worldview: the overlap of the transcendent and the sensuous, the finite and the infinite, life and death.

Arpana, whose grandparents were forced to migrate in 1947 and who lived through the 1984 riots, is a devoted philanthropist, one acutely aware of the absence of a biophilial and pluralistic consciousness. She effectively conveys the violence, sexism and bigotry around us. Entitled *1947*, Arpana's painting of her grandfather carrying the Guru Granth Sahib wrapped in green materials on his head, and a bundle of white cloud-like memories on his hunched back, registers the displacement and carnage during the partition of the Punjab. Likewise, Arpana's *1984* is a traumatic reminder of the historic massacre at the Golden Temple by the Indian government, and the killings of innocent Sikhs that followed the assassination of Prime Minister Indira Gandhi by her Sikh bodyguards. For Sikh spectators, the severed head in this painting entitled *1984* is also a reminder of their Ninth Guru's sacrifice for the freedom of religion in 1675, and of the Five Beloved Sikhs who were ready to offer their head to the Tenth Guru during his creation of the Khalsa in 1699. Religious pluralism is an important theme for this internationally renowned artist. For the fiftieth anniversary of India's independence, she created *Where Many Streams Meet*. Figures from Sikhism, Jainism, Buddhism, Hinduism and Islam converge on Arpana's canvas to evoke India's rich legacy. Music from the harmoniums and *tanpura* fills the air. A royal blue river flows through the brown soil.

Guru Nanak may have left this world, but as Arpana illustrates, lovely flowers on his shroud continue to blossom and spread their fragrance. A tragic contrast is her 1995 work for the Hiroshima Museum of Modern Art. Arpana was commissioned to commemorate the fiftieth anniversary of the nuclear holocaust. In the last panel of her triptych, *Where Have All the Flowers Gone*, Arpana paints a dark female figure crouched under a black cloud. Against a bright yellow backdrop, the matching darkness spells out her emotional and physical charring from the atomic bombings. The receding yellow intimates the first panel of the triptych with its flowers emerging from a river. In a horrifying way, a stem extends into the next panel, and becomes the strap of a gun of one of the many soldiers framed in the middle panel. Empathetically arid, our global society desperately needs blooming flowers.

Arpita Singh

Born in 1937, Arpita has been a prolific painter and winner of numerous awards. Her illustrations for the *Hymns of Guru Nanak*[11] convey Guru Nanak's spiritual longing expressed in a wide range of musical melodies. Instead of his biography, Arpita highlights Guru Nanak's aesthetics. Through her vibrant colours and tender forms, she evokes the specific emotion (raga literally means colour), distinguishing the respective compositions. Here she sets Punjabi folk tradition in Persian miniature layouts, and they appear in her modernist style reminiscent of the biblical illustrations of Chagall.

Her paintings accompanying Guru Nanak's hymns from Sri Raga colour the mind with a gentle mystery—characteristic of this evening melody, which is the first in the GGS ('sri' means supreme). Likewise, Arpita illustrates the cooling impact of Guru Nanak's composition 'Barah Mah' (Twelve Months), set in the melody called Tukhari, from the Sanskrit tushar (means winter frost) to be sung in the morning. Arpita articulates the psyche of Guru Nanak's protagonist as she goes through the different seasons of the year. In the spring she sits lonely on her terrace, her loneliness augmented by the bountiful nature around her. Shades of greens and pinks, and her own bright yellow scarf and magenta shirt manifest her angst. During the monsoon (following the scorching summer) when everybody buzzes with joy, the lonely woman is frightened by thunder and lightning, and so with large anxious eyes we see her holding on to a pillar. Dark purples, blues and greens with a patch of dazzling white dominate the landscape. Finally, at the end of the lunar year, which is the month of Phalgun (February–March), the woman discovers her lover. During the tender coolness of the season, the duality and its ensuing anguish dissolve. She is soothed. The smile on her face and the flowers in her hand perfectly render the First Sikh's message, '*Ghar var paia nari*—the woman found her Beloved in her inner self' (GGS: 1109).[12]

Arpita's visual translations appropriately depict the female figure at the centre of Guru Nanak's spirituality. In an illustration for Sri Raga we see two women dressed in striking green, gold, red and white outfits embracing each other.[13] They validate female bonds and human relationships vital to the Guru's worldview. In her illustration for Raga Vadhans, Arpita depicts a woman in a pink scarf sitting on the ground in her courtyard, braiding her hair in front of a mirror.[14] The pillow and the neat bedspread, a basket of pink flowers, a tray with two cups— signify the presence of her absent lover. She must dress herself in ways that will bring union with the beloved. Arpita's scenario replays Guru Nanak's affirmation of the feminine as a category of being with essential values and strength; she is the one who has the quest for her divine Lover, and her adornment serves as a vital metaphor for spiritual refinement. If we look into *her* mirror, we too can see who we are and what we might hope to become.

Phoolan Rani

For the First Sikh's Fifth Birth Centennial in 1969, reputed female artist Phoolan Rani wrote the life of the Guru and illustrated it in a series of forty remarkable paintings for which she has received many honours. Phulan Rani's female eyes catch the presence of women in the First

Guru's life: not only the female relatives of the Guru (mother Tripta, wife Sulakhni and sister Nanaki), but also women from his village and town—women who saw Nanak go to school, and women who attended his various rites of passage. In the one that captures the sister and brother walking together in the serenity of nature, the older sister has her arm lovingly around her little brother who in turn is holding on to her left arm as it gently rests on his shoulder.[15] Both are wearing loose and rather similar outfits. Both are in a contemplative mood; while he looks close down at the ground, she gazes far into the horizon. As her chin bends over him almost as a protection for his head with its halo, they form a beautiful whole. Nanaki and Nanak, the sister and brother, female and male, are physically and psychologically integrated. In this picture of oneness and harmony, Nanaki gently leads her little brother forward into a new world.

When we see Bibi Nanaki at the forefront we realize her influence on her younger brother's social and religious consciousness, which was then carried on by his nine successor Gurus. The founder Sikh Guru spent a lot of his formative years with sister Nanaki, and even went to live with her in her new home after she was married. The Guru's condemnation of the beliefs in purdah (segregation and veiling), sati (upper-class women obligated to die in the funeral pyre of their husbands) and pollution (associated with menstruation and childbirth) would have been affected by his close relationship with his sister. Parallel to Mary Magdalene in the Christian context, Bibi Nanaki was the one to recognize Guru Nanak. *Her* love, guidance, and togetherness at the core of the Sikh tradition is gracefully captured by Phulan Rani.

Devinder Singh

Internationally known for his realistic and abstract art, Devinder Singh paints events deeply etched in the Sikh consciousness. His paintings are displayed in Sikh sacred spaces and in museums across India and abroad. He is the beloved illustrator for the Sikh comics of *Amar Chitra Katha*. Devinder Singh has won numerous awards and honours. His paintings for the Sikh Foundation Calendar 2012 are particularly significant for depicting the contributions of Sikh women. The style of these paintings is a unique fusion of traditional popular art with modern cubism. Pastel colours dominate his artist's palette. But the yellows and blues offset by the dark brown and grey hues render a dramatic quality to the historic scenes. The 2012 Sikh Foundation calendar makes the past come vividly alive. Dr Narinder Singh Kapany, the president of the Sikh Foundation, has to be lauded for his superb choice of the theme, and for his dedication to bringing the Guru's message into homes, offices and campuses. On Devinder Singh's canvas we see three-dimensional figures from Bibi Nanaki to Maharani Jindan dynamically engaged in various aspects of the tradition founded by the First Sikh. As our eyes see them, heads rise and chests broaden; a Sikh sense of selfhood expands with confidence and authenticity.

The set of paintings opens with Bibi Nanaki, the First Sikh's sister, handing the rabab to Bhai Mardana. We can interpret this gesture as an invitation to Bhai Mardana to accompany the hymns of divine epiphany with his music. Reminiscent of Phoolan Rani's rendition, this exquisite painting in pastel yellows discloses not only the bond between the sister and brother, but also between Sikh and Muslim, visual and aural, word and music, divine revelation and aesthetic experience.

The other women are post-Nanak, but each of them embodies a foundational Sikh attribute generated by Guru Nanak. We see the Second Guru's wife, Mata Khivi, directing langar service. Dressed in a yellow outfit, she is vigorously stirring a steaming pot over a flaming wood-fire. The blazing wood matches her yellow dupatta and reflects her spiritual radiance. The backdrop is composed of a group of men and women preparing *parshadas* (flat bread) on the left of the canvas, and another partaking langar on the right. Mata Khivi at the centre is completely absorbed in feeding the community. The scriptural verse by Balvand comes out alive: '*Balvand khivi nek jan jis bahuti chao patrali/ langar daulat vandiai ras amrit kheer ghiali*—Balvand says, noble Khivi offers a thick leafy shade/She hands out a rich meal with delicious ambrosial rice-pudding full of ghee' (GGS: 967).

Bibi Bhani, the daughter of the Third Guru (Amar Das), wife of the Fourth Guru (Ram Das), and mother of the Fifth Guru (Arjan) stands between her elderly father having his meal seated on a cot, and her baby son playing beside her. This very ordinary scene underscores an

extraordinary principle of Guru Nanak's metaphysics: the coalescence of
the sacred and the secular. The transcendent Divine is not disconnected
from the world but is an intrinsic part of daily life. A major factor in
the Gurus' vehement rejection of asceticism and renunciation would
be the constructive relationships they had with their own families,
as captured in this father–daughter, mother–son scene. Brushstrokes
of tender love sweeping through these three protagonists resonate
throughout Sikh scripture. No wonder the GGS celebrates, 'Amidst
mother, father, brother, son, and wife, has the Divine yoked us' (GGS:
77). In these divinely bound relationships, every human relationship is
vitally significant.

Mata Gujari, the wife of the Ninth Guru (Tegh Bahadur) and
mother of the Tenth Guru (Gobind Singh), is shown sitting with her
young grandsons. While she appears to be speaking, the two boys are
avidly listening to her. The variegated nocturnal blue landscape gives
a chilly feeling, evoking the historical cold fort where she was held
captive with her two grandsons. But rather than a weak, imprisoned
figure we encounter in the painting a real force who exudes confidence,
intellectual vigour and a warm spiritual halo. Her hands in motion
bespeak of her stirring the imagination and spirit of her audience.
The boys subsequently withstood their cruel death because of Mata
Gujari's courageous personality and heroic narratives. Clearly, across
generations, Sikh mothers and grandmothers have been crucial in the
perpetuation of supreme heroism and moral fervour. Once again, Guru
Nanak's exaltation 'Dhan janedi mai—blessed are the mothers' (GGS:
138) fills the air.

When we see Mata Sahib Kaur as an active co-partner in Guru
Gobind Singh's momentous Khalsa institution, we cannot but think
of the marvellous trajectory set forth by the First Sikh. Mataji (Sikh
memory also recalls Mata Jitoji in this event) stands in the painting,
offering patase (sugar-puffs) to the Guru, who is seated with a bowl
in front of him. Powerful diagonals artistically flow out to connect
Mataji with the Guru—her eyes with his, her white scarf with his
white sash, the patase in her hand with the bowl near him. A perfect
picture of togetherness, they are preparing the nourishing im+mortal
fluid, the amrit (a = not + mrt = death), which was initially sipped by

Guru Nanak during his divine encounter. In a very meaningful way, the Tenth Sikh Guru with his partner returns to this primal moment of Sikhism and opens it up into the future through his inauguration of the Khalsa. The 'beginning' of Sikhism, embodied in the private, individual and mystical experience of the First Guru culminates in a public, social and institutional of the amrit initiation at Anandpur on Baisakhi day in 1699. The vigour of Nanak's amrit is extended into perpetuity: the meta-historic drink becomes an essential part of the psyche and practice of the Sikh community and of their Sikh sacred history; it is an enduring and integral part of daily life. The Guru's wife is an active agent in the phenomenon of the birth of the Khalsa, and Sikhs continue to regard themselves as 'the progeny of both father and mother'. A woman participates vitally in Sikhism's most profound rite of passage. No stigma is attached to her body, and no cultural taboos are associated with her performance. In contrast with many religious traditions in which women are barred, she is essential to the sacred moment in Sikhism. It is with her input that the historic drink reaches its perfection. The inner fruition is tasted, blending physical sugar with the metaphysical experience of joy and unity.

Devinder Singh's set also displays female paradigms fighting battles to change the course of history. Included are Mai Bhago and Sada Kaur. When Mai Bhago saw how some Sikhs of her area had fled Anandpur in the face of the privations brought on by a prolonged siege, she chided them with pusillanimity. She led them back to fight for Guru Gobind Singh. Devinder Singh's painting records her fighting valiantly in the battle that ensued at Khidrana in 1705. Almost a century later, Sada Kaur proved to be instrumental to her nineteen-year-old son-in-law, the future Maharaja Ranjit Singh. A passionate patriot with unparalleled administrative skills, Sada Kaur was the architect who united the Punjab into a Sikh State for the young Ranjit Singh. She possessed great courage on the battlefield as well, but the best part of her triumph lay in victory without bloodshed. The painting depicts her capture of the fort of Lahore in 1799, which led to the establishment of the Sikh Empire.

These palpable images of Mai Bhago and Sada Kaur fighting valiantly send internal messages to their spectators; they reproduce reflexes that fight against the injustices confronting us today. They motivate Sikh men and women to change oppressive customs and discriminatory attitudes, and to live the egalitarian and liberating path envisioned by their founding Guru. These courageous women from Sikh history make Guru Nanak's spiritual realm (Japji, Stanza 37) a palpable reality—that of *sito-sita*, the realm of mighty warriors and heroes.

The artist depicts Maharani Jindan as the symbol of Sikh sovereignty. Regent to her five-year-old son, Dalip, who was crowned as the maharaja of the Sikh kingdom in 1843, she is not observing purdah or any suffocating customs of widowhood prevalent in her society. To the contrary, Maharani Jindan is squarely facing her male Khalsa army. Behind her is an entourage of women, with one holding a royal umbrella in attendance. With her right hand stretched up in a fist, and the index finger of her left pointing sternly, she is the embodiment of a robust commander galvanizing her troops. The painting explains why the British Raj was in awe of her, calling her the only courageous 'man' in the area. With her sharp intelligence and acute statesmanship, Jindan was able to restore a balance between the Khalsa army and the civil administration. After the annexation of the Punjab in 1849, the British administrators were so threatened by her leadership qualities that they expelled her from the province and interned her at Benares under strict surveillance. Even after her dramatic escape to Nepal, they kept a vigilant eye on her, and when her son carried her final remains from England to disperse them in the Punjab, he was refused. Her last years had been spent in Kensington as a frail woman with poor eyesight and without much jewellery or attendants. In Devender Singh's visual commemoration, the feisty Jindan continues to electrify not only her mid-nineteenth-century subjects but also her modern spectators. Such visual hermeneutics give us a sense of history and usher us into wide emotional and spiritual horizons opened up by the First Sikh.

His Global Legacy

Countless poets reach back to Guru Nanak to praise him for championing unity and harmony. These men and women happen to be not only Sikhs, but also Muslims and Hindus, which manifests the multi-religious legacy of the First Sikh. In this section, we will mainly sample two

Punjabi poets, Firoz Din Sharaf (1898–1955) and Shiv Kumar Batalvi (1937–73). Their poetic mnemonics are a very valuable testimony to the pluralistic impact of the First Sikh. His vision of the singular Divine, his inclusivism, his poetic artistry, his rapturous spirituality grounded in earthly realities struck a chord with Sikhs and non-Sikhs alike. When the Indian subcontinent was bleeding from the wounds of religious bigotry, poets on both sides of the border remembered Guru Nanak's humanism. Poets have no religion, we know, but when we hear the First Sikh evoked touchingly by Muslims and Hindus from a religiously torn soil, we recognize the enormous power of his legacy. In turn, their poetic memories create arabesques of mutuality between the divided Hindu, Muslims and Sikhs that the First Sikh deeply desired.

Firoz Din Sharaf

Muslim poet Firoz Din Sharaf made remarkable contributions to the Punjabi literary world. With has great admiration for Guru Nanak, he depicts him vividly in his poetic compositions. Sharaf was born in pre-partitioned Punjab. The period was rife with religious conflict, his own Muslim community was staunchly promoting Urdu, and yet Sharaf was courageously advancing Punjabi language and the Sikh Gurus. Greatly respected by people across borders, he served as the cabinet minister of the Punjab in the newly created Pakistan.[16]

In Sharaf's lyrics, Sikh history and philosophy come out alive. In 'Defeated' (*Hare*) he sketches several popular events from Guru Nanak's life: the tree stands still to provide shade to the sleeping Nanak, the granary he worked in remained perpetually full in spite of the Guru giving away generously to the needy, with his outstretched palm he stops a huge rock hurled at him, and when his shroud is lifted flowers are found instead of his body so both Hindus and Muslims could carry them away for cremating or burying according to their respective customs. But by admitting his own 'defeat' to fully express Guru Nanak's grandeur, Sharaf keeps the reader's imagination reeling. He consummately reproduces the crucial feature of Guru Nanak's pluralistic personality: '*Hindu kahin sada, Muslim kahin sada*—Hindus say he belongs to us; Muslims say he belongs to us . . .' In an elemental flow, Sharaf returns to the First Sikh's universal message and reinforces its pluralism for his contemporaries. Sensitive to language, the poet praises the Guru for his hermeneutic expertise: 'You explain the terms from the Veda and the Quran better than all the Pandits and the Maulvis.' Latent here is his critique of those elite theologians and scholars who were fomenting communalist ideologies amongst the Muslim, Hindu and Sikh masses.

Sharaf also has some lovely poems on the First Sikh's companions, the Muslim Bhai Mardana and the Hindu Bhai Bala. In the case of Bhai Mardana, Sharaf uses the ubiquitous Sufi symbol of a mystic lover. A moth attracted to the candle's flame, Sharaf makes a delightful pun on Mardana's name. 'Discerning the divine light of Nanak, Mardana came flying over and became intoxicated with the name . . . In his love, he died over and over (*mar mar ke*) and so became Mardana.'

> At the flash of the divine light
> The moth came flying over;
> Drinking the name of Nanak
> He was inebriated.
> People thought he was drunk
> But he was gone far beyond;
> Sharaf, he died in the name of love
> And so Mardana he was born[17]

For the Hindu Bhai Bala:

> As the divine light appeared
> Thick darkness receded
> Seeing the Guru's intoxicated eyes
> He was inebriated.
> On the rosary of his mind
> He turns the beads day and night.
> Sharaf, for his devotion to the Guru
> Bala is known across the world[18]

His companions here are specifically taken by his 'intoxicated eyes' (*nain nasheele*). In love with the divine One, the First Sikh has lost his individuality; his self is annihilated (*fana*) and taken over completely by the Beloved (*baqa*), and in turn his divine ecstasy becomes contagious for the Muslim Mardana and the Hindu Bala. The Guru's externally 'drunk' eyes show it all. With his Sufi aesthetics centred on the concepts of fana and baqa, Sharaf presents a mesmerizing portrait. In Bhai Bala's instance, Sharaf evokes Guru Nanak's quintessential devotional practice—inner contemplation over all external acts. The disciple follows his Guru: he holds no rosary in his hand; he but turns beads on the rosary of his mind! Most exquisitely, Sharaf reveals Guru Nanak's enduring impact.

Shiv Kumar Batalvi

Likewise, a youngster born in a Hindu family, named after the Hindu god of death and dance, Shiva Nataraja, Shiv Kumar Batalvi would recall the Sikh Guru to offer therapeutic possibilities for the charred Punjabi psyche. Shiv was barely nine years old when he and his family were forced to cross the Indo-Pak Border. The murder of his motherland witnessed by him as a youngster later took the form of anguished lyrics that seek solace in the comforting and nurturing First Sikh.

It is interesting that Shiv's poem on the Guru does not mention him by name. The poem is titled 'Kartarpur Vich' (In Kartarpur). Thus, the identity marker is Kartarpur, the town Guru Nanak founded by the banks of the Ravi. For Shiv it is adorned with 'a glittering necklace'. The message and person of Nanak attracts people. They come to Kartarpur and live together like a family. While offering a glimpse of this first community, Shiv reproduces the keynote message of First Sikh as his finale: '*Uh rabb hai ikk oan kar*—That Divine is the One Being!'

In Kartarpur
Travelling far and wide
He came home
He settled in Kartarpur

Beside the river Ravi
Glittering as it flowed
A silver necklace

An ascetic's outfit he wore no more
He seated himself in this world
He who could do miracles,
Worked with his hands
His lips recite the Japji
His eyes reflect bliss
Hearing his praise
       People came from far and wide
And a family they became

The world lighted up
Filth and falsity disappeared
The four corners burst forth
uh rabb hai ikk oankar
That Divine is the One Being!

In another composition, 'Baba Te Mardana', Shiv offers snapshots of the
life of the First Guru as he travels with his Muslim companion Mardana,
and discourses with people of different religious backgrounds—Pir,
Brahmin, Sheikh. With a pluralistic milieu as the backdrop, Shiv
zooms in on the profound closeness between the First Sikh and the
Muslim Mardana, a closeness that would serve as a balm for Sikh–
Muslim lacerations from the horrific events of Partition. This is how
his poem begins:

Off they go, Baba and Mardana
Travelling near and far
Here they are in Varanasi Kashi
Meeting the learned
Under his arm is the Muslim prayer mat
And Gita in the hand.

What a magical holy outfit
Pir, Brahmans and Sheikhs alike
Sit beside to discourse.
There is no Hindu, there is no Muslim
He proclaims his magical decree
Instead of making offerings with the Ganges
He waters his fields
Scared are they to face him
Who live and die in selfish ego.
He calls the Divine neither Allah
Nor Ram or Shiva, but
The timeless, the formless
The fearless, belongs to no sect . . .

Shiv depicts the Sikh Guru carrying a Muslim prayer-mat under his arm (*kachh mussala*) and the Bhagavad Gita in his hand (*hath vich gita*)—a figure beyond all religious circumscriptions. The B-40 Janamsakhi motifs of the seli and the tilak come to be the mussala and the Gita in Shiv's poem. During that horribly contentious Hindu–Muslim divide this indeed would appear as the most magical ensemble. Shiv underscores the pronouncement by the icon of religious harmony: 'There is neither Hindu nor Muslim—*na koi hindu na koi muslim*.' For the twentieth-century poet these words are 'a magical decree' (*ajab adesh*). Bracketing out misconceptions harboured by the recently divided Punjabis, Shiv zooms in on Guru Nanak's insight into the essential connectivity of individuals underlying diverse faiths and systems of belief.

Such praise by these two poets resounds in many more. The famous Bhai Vir Singh (1872–1957) devoted his entire life to the study of the First Sikh and his legacy. Poet, novelist, editor, exegete, historian, lexicographer and journalist, he was the most prominent person in the Singh Sabha, the Sikh renaissance movement that aspired to revive Punjabi culture on the core principles of the Sikh Gurus. Like Shiv, he too marvels, 'Baba Nanak! This is your wonder, you kindled our innermost spirit—*Baba nanak! eh tera kamal, ruhan tumb jagaian*' (in his poem on Guru Nanak).[19] With the same elation, Vidhata Singh Teer (1901–72) poetically bursts out, 'You take the form of the divine One

Nanak, your heart is set in the formless One—*tera roop hai rabb da roop Nanak, tera dil hai sada nrinkar andar*' (in his poem 'Beloved Nanak'). Dhani Ram 'Chatrik' (1876–1954) who made major contributions to Punjabi typography, language and literature remembers Guru Nanak joining the sacred space of the Hindus and Muslims: '*Mandir masjit sanjhe kite*—he connected the mandir with the masjid' (poem 'Baba Nanak'). Dr Javed Zaki (d. 2005), poet and professor of Sociology at Michigan State University, pictures Guru Nanak as 'the cherished star of the Punjab' (*punjab da surjan tara*), 'protector of the five rivers' (*punj nadian da vali*), and he entreats the First Sikh to 'usher light into the dark hearts of his contemporaries' (*andar nuri karcha*), to 'drench their charred spirit in ambrosia' (*ruh nun amrit karcha*), and thus 'end raucous conflicts' (*mukk javan sabh raule gaule*). Lal Chand Yamla Jatt's (1914–91) popular song, strummed on his single-stringed tumbi, continues to feed the soil and spirit of the divided Punjab: '*Satgur nanak teri lila niariai neejhan la la vehndi dunia sariai*—how magical your play our true Guru Nanak! This whole world longs to behold you.'

We find a unique trope in a poem by the national poet of Pakistan, Sir Muhammad Iqbal (1877–1938). Regarded as the greatest Urdu poet of the twentieth century, Iqbal praises the First Sikh as the Perfect Person (*mard-e-kamal*) for illuminating the Punjab with his vision of unicity (*tawhid*):

Butkada phir bad muddat ke magar roshan hua
noor-e-ibrahim se azar ka ghar roshan hua
phir uthi akhir ada tawhid ki Punjab se
hind ko ek mard-e-kamil ne jagaya khawab se

[Ages later the house of idols was lit up again—
Azar's house was lit up by the luminous Abraham
Once more from the Punjab unicity was finally decreed
A perfect person awoke India from its sleep]

In his glorious tribute to the First Sikh, Iqbal compares him with the luminous Abraham, the son of Azar and the spiritual ancestor to the Jewish, Christian and Islamic religions. Just as Abraham brought the light of monotheism to his idolatrous world, Guru Nanak enlightened India with a unicity of the divine One (tawhid). Iqbal gives a nuanced rationale for the popular public memory: '*Baba Nanak shah fakir, hindu ka guru, musalman ka pir.*' This perfect person kindles the consciousness of his people lost in darkness. We hear in Iqbal echoes of poet Nazeer Akbarabadi (ca.1740–1830) as he exquisitely extols the First Sikh in his poem entitled 'Guru Nanak Shah':

> *Iss bakshash ke iss azmat ke hain baba nanak shah guru*
> *sabh sees nava ardas karo, aur hardam bolo wah guru!*

[So blessed, so glorious shah guru Baba Nanak
All bow your heads, make humble requests and
Say forever, wondrous Guru!]

Indeed, poets across centuries and across religions champion Guru Nanak's universality. The First Sikh does not belong exclusively to the Sikhs; his person and voice transcends all man-made boundaries, all their ideological systems and categories.

We see non-Sikhs in the West also being inspired by him. On a Friday evening during a memorable weekend in 2016 in Fresno, California, forty or so non-Sikh men and women sat reverently at the local Gurdwara Sahib in the presence of the GGS with their bare feet and heads covered to hear the First Sikh's holy songs and take part in the ceremony of putting the scriptural Guru to rest for the night (sukhasan). These included Muslim, Roman Catholic, Unitarian Universalist, Hindu, Latter Day Saints, Congregationalists/United Church of Christ, Christian Scientists, Mennonites, Methodists, Episcopalians and Presbyterians. At the conclusion everybody had the langar meal together. The 'togetherness' was extremely special, for the bond of community expanded from just the Sikhs living in Fresno to the wide-ranging communities on the American West coast. The spiritual energy in the Sikh gurdwara acquired a whole new dimension.

That Sunday in Fresno, Rev. Tim Kutzman orchestrated a beautiful and moving Sikh service at the Unitarian Universalist Church. It was based entirely on Guru Nanak's biography, Guru Nanak's verse,

Guru Nanak's message and Guru Nanak's melodies. It began with the reading of his prelude to the Japji—'There is One Being Truth by Name', and the gathering then burst into a harmonious chant. Passages from the morning hymn, the Japji, resonated in the stylistically modern Church. Rev. Kutzman then spoke on Guru Nanak, the founder of the faith. He shared the narrative of Guru Nanak coming out of the river after disappearing for three days and proclaiming, 'There is no Hindu, there is no Muslim.' The Sikh founder's message that humanity should go beyond institutionalized categories and become more fully human was insightfully conveyed by Rev. Kutzman. The singing of hymns was followed by melodious vocalists and instrumentalists directed by Lorenzo Bassman. From the beginning to the end of the service, these were the basics of the Sikh faith that I had been hearing and singing and reciting since childhood. However, in the ambiance of the Unitarian Universalist Church, the hymns spoken and sung in different accents with different instruments and different juxtapositions and translations, became a whole new rich experience. Come to think of it, the very first time I heard Guru Nanak's hymns in public worship on American soil was at a Sindhi gurdwara gathering in Boston in 1974. I am grateful to the Sindhi community, just as I am to director Jim Grant of the Social Justice Ministry, Diocese of Fresno, who invited me to be the interfaith scholar for their annual programme in April 2016. It was exciting to witness the First Sikh being welcomed by people of multiple faiths.

Over the years, more and more Sikhs and non-Sikhs are coming together to celebrate the First Sikh. Just a few examples: at the University of California in Davis, academics and the early Yuba Sikh community jointly organized an exciting venue, Indians and Americans commemorated his birthday together at the Indian consulate in New York City, the Pothohar community hosted an elaborate evening at the Mayfair Theatre in the heart of London, at Colby College, valedictorian Will Polkinghorn recited Guru Nanak's hymn at his baccalaureate service.

Such moments of 'collective effervescence' are enormously meaningful. The feeling here is not a simple tolerance of people of other faiths, or adding aspects from different faiths into a syncretic blend; to the contrary, it is real respect for and a rejoicing in the difference and distinctive richness of our shared humanity. In the twenty-first century how easily we connect over email, Twitter, Skype, Facebook and Instagram—but do we connect emotionally and spiritually? The First Sikh offers us a strong and enduring infrastructure with fellow humans. We remember him, we imagine him, and we praise him for breaking barriers; innovatively and gently he guides us to envision the single Reality—timeless, formless, fearless, who cannot and must not be confined to any sect or religion. Men and women of all ages, stages of life, sexual orientations and religious backgrounds are inspired by his 'magical' personality and 'magical' words. They are magical for sure, precisely because they are so real, applicable, and empowering. The 'Nanak effect' surges across multiferous channels and moves us to embrace fellow beings. Seeing 'our' self in the 'other' is what Guru Nanak's visual, poetic, philosophical and musical renditions bring about. His repertoire of 974 hymns is an extraordinary gift for humanity. Guru Nanak does not belong exclusively to the Sikhs; his person and voice transcend all man-made boundaries, all their ideological systems and categories. There is no conclusion here. The momentum of his legacy is taking on a dynamic trajectory. The First Sikh's 550th birth anniversary is but the beginning of exciting new encounters.

Notes

Introduction: Getting in Touch: Sources and Aspirations

1. S.H. Nasr, *Knowledge and the Sacred* (New York: Crossroad, 1981), p. 12.
2. George Dumezil, *The Plight of a Sorcerer*, eds. Jaan Puhvel and David Weeks (Berkeley & LA: University of California, 1986), pp. viii–ix, 42.
3. Guninder Kaur, *The Guru Granth Sahib: Its Physics and Metaphysics* (New Delhi: Sterling Publishers), 1981; reprinted, New Delhi: Manohar Publications, 1995.
4. Harbans Singh, *Guru Nanak and Origins of the Sikh Faith* (Bombay: Asia Publishing House, 1969), pp. 215–16.
5. Christopher Shackle, 'Survey of Literature in the Sikh Tradition' in *The Oxford Handbook of Sikh Studies*, eds. Pashaura Singh and Louis E. Fenech (Oxford & NYC: Oxford University Press, 2014), p. 111.
6. Attar Singh, 'Punjabi: Mainly a Guru Nanak Year' in *Indian Literature* 13.4 (December 1970): 69–76.
7. Shackle, 'Survey of Literature in the Sikh Tradition', p. 112.
8. D.S. Maini, 'Guru Nanak's Poetry—Sublime Humanism' in the Sikh Foundation International, 3 November 2014.
9. Francesca Orsini, 'Clouds, Cuckoos and an Empty Bed: Emotions in Hindi–Urdu Barahmasas' in *Monsoon Feelings: A History of Emotions in the Rain*, eds. Imke Rajamani, Margrit Pernau and Katherine Butler Schofield (New Delhi: Niyogi Books, 2018), pp. 99–100.
10. For a fuller discussion see Nikky-Guninder Kaur Singh, 'The Sikh Bridal Symbol: An Epiphany of Interconnections' in *Journal of Feminist Studies in Religion* 8.2 (Fall, 1992): 41–64.

11. G.H. von Wright, ed., in collaboration with Heikki Nyman, *Ludwig Wittgenstein, Culture and Value*, trans. Peter Winch (Chicago: University of Chicago Press, 1980), p. 24e.

12. For Bhai Gurdas's ballads, I have used the volume edited by Bhai Vir Singh, *Varan Bhai Gurdas* (Amritsar: Khalsa Samachar, 1977).

13. Singh, *Guru Nanak and Origins of the Sikh Faith*, pp. 20–21.

Chapter 1: The First Sikh: Continuing Reality

1. All translations from the Guru Granth Sahib are mine. Clifford Geertz, 'Religion as a Cultural System' in *The Interpretation of Cultures: Selected Essays* (New York: Basic Books, 1973), pp. 87–125.

2. According to the SGPC site.

3. Marie Joy Curtiss, 'Gurmat Sangit' in Harbans Singh, ed., *Encyclopedia of Sikhism* (Patiala: Punjabi University, 1996).

4. E. Trumpp, trans., *The Adi Granth or the Holy Scriptures of the Sikhs* (London: W.H. Allen, 1877); R.C. Zaehner, *The Concise Encyclopaedia of Living Faiths* (Boston: Beacon Press, 1959); S.M. Ikram, *Muslim Civilization in India* (New York: Columbia University Press, 1964); J.N. Farquhar, *Modern Religious Movements in India,* reprint ed. (New Delhi: Munshiram Manoharlal Publishers, 1977); William de Bary, ed., *Sources of Indian Tradition* (New York: Columbia University Press, 1958).

5. W.H. McLeod, *Guru Nanak and the Sikh Religion* (Oxford: Clarendon Press, 1968), p. 157. For more details see my work, 'The Myth of the Founder: The Janamsakhis and Sikh Tradition' in *History of Religions* (University of Chicago, 1992), pp. 329–43. Dr J.S. Grewal offers a comprehensive critique of McLeod's premise in J.S. Grewal, 'W.H. McLeod and Sikh Studies', www.global.ucsb.edu/punjab/sites/secure.lsit. ucsb.../JPS_17_nos_1-2_Grewal.pdf

6. W.C. Smith, *The Meaning and End of Religion* (New York: Macmillan, 1962), pp. 66–67.

7. McLeod, *Guru Nanak and the Sikh Religion*, pp. 150–52.

8. Nripinder Singh, 'Guru Nanak, Prophecy and the Study of Religion', in *Studies in Sikhism and Comparative Religion* (New Delhi: Guru Nanak Foundation, April 1989), p. 23.

9. Harbans Singh, *Berkeley Lectures on Sikhism* (Delhi: Guru Nanak Foundation, 1983), pp. 7–8.

10. W.H. McLeod, 'The Influence of Islam upon the Thought of Guru Nanak' in *History of Religions* 7.4 (May 1968): 302.

11. Charles Hartshorne and Paul Weiss, eds., *Collected Papers of Charles Sanders Peirce* (Cambridge: Harvard University Press, 1931, third printing 1974), pp. 302–03.

12. *Puratan Janamsakhi Guru Nanak Devji* (Amritsar: Khalsa Samachar, 1948), Sakhi entitled 'Bein Pravesh', pp. 16–19.

13. Nripinder Singh, *The Sikh Moral Tradition* (New Delhi: Manohar Publications, 1990), pp. 20–23.

14. See B.N. Goswamy and Caron Smith, *I See No Stranger: Early Sikh Art and Devotion* (New York: Rubin Museum of Art, 2006); also see B.N. Goswamy, *Piety and Splendour: Sikh Heritage in Art* (New Delhi: National Museum, 2000).

15. For more details on the Harsahai volume, see Pashaura Singh, *The Guru Granth: Canon, Meaning and Authority* (New Delhi: Oxford University Press, 2000), pp. 32–34; Gurinder Singh Mann, *The Making of Sikh Scripture* (New York: Oxford University Press, 2001), pp. 37–40.

16. See Gurinder Singh Mann, *Goindval Pothis: The Earliest Extant Source of the Sikh Canon* (Cambridge: Harvard University Press, 1997).

17. Bob van der Linden, 'Pre-Twentieth-Century Sikh Sacred Music: The Mughals, Courtly Patronage and Canonisation' in *South Asia: Journal of South Asian Studies* 38.2 (2015): 1.

18. See further, Pashaura Singh, 2000; Gurinder Mann, 2001; and S.S. Kohli, *A Critical Study of the Adi Granth* (New Delhi: Punjabi Writers Cooperative, 1961).

19. Alexander Rogers, trans., and Henry Beveridge, ed., *Memories of Jahangir* (London: Royal Asiatic Society. Beveridge 1897–1939), Volume 3, 1114–19, Chapter 135 entitled 'Expedition for the Taking of Ahmadnagar'.

20. W.H. McLeod, *Historical Dictionary of Sikhism* (Lanham, Toronto, Oxford: The Scarecrow Press, 2005), p, 5.

21. A contemporary Sikh document, *Bhatt Vahi Talauda Parganah Jind*, describes the event in detail. See further, Harbans Singh, *Sri Guru Granth Sahib: Guru Eternal for the Sikhs* (Patiala: Academy of Sikh Religion and Culture, 1988), p. 19. For the transference of guruship to the GGS, see my 'Guru Granth: The Quintessential Sikh Metaphor' in *Postscripts: The Journal of Sacred Texts & Contemporary Worlds* 4.2 (London: Equinox) (2008): 157–76.

22. Quoted in the original in Harbans Singh, *The Heritage of the Sikhs* (New Delhi: Manohar, 1985), pp. 108–09.

23. Harbans Singh, *Sri Guru Granth Sahib: The Guru Eternal for the Sikhs* (Academy of Sikh Religion and Culture, 1988), p. 19.

24. Gurdwara (literally, 'door to the guru') is the Sikh space for worship. Its focal point is the GGS. Most gurdwaras have areas for a communal meal (langar), and some even have libraries and residential areas for pilgrims.

25. The entire GGS is read in forty-eight hours. The reading goes on continuously day and night, by a sequence of readers who take turns.

26. McLeod, *Historical Dictionary of Sikhism*, p. 2.

27. W.C. Smith, *On Understanding Islam: Selected Studies* (Netherlands: Moulton Publishers, 1981), p. 181.

28. Harbans Singh, ed., *Perspectives on Guru Nanak: Seminar Papers* (Patiala: Punjabi University, 1969 conference held at the Punjabi University), p. 27.

29. *Guru Nanak and Origins of the Sikh Faith*, p. 214.

30. Grewal in 'W.H. McLeod and Sikh Studies', www.global.ucsb.edu/punjab/sites/secure.lsit.ucsb.../JPS_17_nos_1-2_Grewal.pdf

31. W.C. Smith, *On Understanding Islam*, p. 180.

32. Wittgenstein, No. 43.

33. Hans-Georg Gadamer, *Truth and Method* (New York: Crossroads, 1989), p. 462.

34. Wendy Doniger, *Textual Sources for the Study of Hinduism* (Manchester: Manchester University Press, 1988), pp. 2–3.

35. Annette Wilke and Oliver Moebus, *Sound and Communication: An Aesthetic Cultural History of Sanskrit Hinduism* (Berlin/New York: De Gruyter, 2011), p. 838.

36. One wishes Wilke and Moebus had applied their superb sonic expertise to the Sikh holy book.

37. Wilke and Moebus, *Sound and Communication*, p. 836.

38. Embracing the infinite One in mind is Guru Nanak's essential prescription; it is frequently repeated in the Japji, and all through the GGS.

39. *Ma + I* = Laxmi and Sarasvati. I am very glad to see that G.S. Talib acknowledges the three goddesses, Parvati, Laxmi and Sarasvati, in his translation, *Japuji: The Immortal Prayer-Chant*, (New Delhi: Munshiram Manoharlal, 1976), p. 42.

40. Prithwish Neogy, ed., *Rabindranath Tagore on Art and Aesthetics* (Calcutta: Orient Longmans, 1966), p. 23.

Chapter 2: Janamsakhis: Remembering the First Sikh

1. The B-40 Janamsakhi surfaced in Lahore in the nineteenth century and was acquired by the India Office Library in 1907. Factual details on the

Janamsakhis here come from Hew McLeod, *Popular Sikh Art* (Delhi: Oxford University Press), pp. 5–6.

2. Though the sketches are extremely minimalist, each episode is numbered and identified with a brief inscription in Persian and Gurmukhi characters. In B.N. Goswamy and Caron Smith, *I See No Stranger: Early Sikh Art and Devotion* (NY: Rubin Museum of Art, 2006), pp. 36–37.

3. See Mircea Eliade, *Myth and Reality* (NY: Harper and Row, 1963).

4. James Jarrett, *The Quest for Beauty* (Englewood Cliffs: Prentice Hall, 1957), p. 74.

5. W.H. McLeod, *Early Sikh Tradition: A Study of the Janam-sakhis* (Oxford: Clarendon Press, 1980).

6. W.H. McLeod, The *B-40 Janam-sakhi* (Amritsar: Guru Nanak Dev University, 1981).

7. McLeod, *Early Sikh Tradition*, pp. 82–105.

8. For a detailed study, see my 'Corporeal Metaphysics: Guru Nanak in Early Sikh Art' in *History of Religions* 53.1 (August 2013): 28–65.

9. I am very grateful to Sardar Sikandar Singh Bagarian for showing me the manuscript at his home in Chandigarh, 17 July 2011.

10. Surjit Hans, ed., *B-40 Janamsakhi Guru Baba Nanak Paintings* (Amritsar: Guru Nanak Dev University, 1987), p. 8.

11. Otto Rank, *The Myth of the Birth of the Hero* (New York: Vintage, 1959).

12. *Janam Sakhi Sri Guru Nanak Dev Ji* (Amritsar, 1974), p. 52.

13. For a fuller typological analysis, see my 'Mythic Inheritance and the Drink of the Khalsa' in Nikky-Guninder Kaur Singh, *The Birth of the Khalsa: A Feminist Re-Memory of Sikh Identity* (New York: SUNY Press, 2005), pp. 69–96.

14. Victor Turner, *The Forest of Symbols: Aspects of Ndembu Ritual* (Ithaca: Cornell University Press, 1967), p. 96.

15. 'Bein Parvesh' in *Puratan Janamsakhi Guru Nanak Devji* (Amritsar: Khalsa Samachar, 1946), pp. 16–19.

16. Even though McLeod denies Guru Nanak's divine inspiration in 'The Influence of Islam upon the Thought of Guru Nanak', in *History of Religions* 7.4 (May 1968): 302.

17. Margaret Miles, 'Image', in Mark C. Taylor, *Critical Terms for Religious Studies* (Chicago, University of Chicago Press), pp. 170–71.

18. Richard Davis, ed., *Images, Miracles, and Authority in Asian Religious Traditions* (Boulder: Westview Press, 1998), p. 4.

19. This episode appears in the B-40 Janamsakhi, dated 1733.

20. Hans-Georg Gadamer, *Truth and Method* (New York: Crossroads, 1989), p. 429.

21. McLeod in his notes, *The B-40 Janam-sakhi*, p. 227.

22. Paul Ricoeur, *Interpretation Theory: Discourse and the Surplus of Meaning* (Fort Worth: Texas Christian University Press, 1976), p. 68.

23. These three distinct categories—'ontological', 'orientational' and 'structural'—are made by Lakoff and Johnson in their influential study, *Metaphors We Live By* (Chicago and London: University of Chicago Press, 1980), pp. 25–32, 14–21, 61–68. For a detailed discussion see my 'Guru Granth: The Quintessential Sikh Metaphor' in *Postscripts: The Journal of Sacred Texts & Contemporary Worlds* 4.2 (2008): 157–76.

24. Harbans Singh, *Guru Nanak and Origins of the Sikh Faith* (Patiala: Punjabi University, 1969), pp. 116–17.

25. Details are from Kristina Myrvold, *Inside the Guru's Gate: Ritual Uses of Texts among the Sikhs in Varanasi* (Lund University, 2007), pp. 34, 98–101.

26. Earlier in his text, Bhai Gurdas mentions that Guru Nanak on his travels carried a manuscript tucked under his arm (Var I: 32), so it is likely that the jasmine flower that he brings out from under his arm symbolizes his poetic utterances.

27. Gadamer, *Truth and Method*, p. 92.

28. *North Indian Notes and Queries: Monthly Periodical* Vol. III August 1893, 'Popular Religion'; *Journal of the Society of Arts* 50 (22 November 1901).

29. Patrick Olivelle, *Ascetics and Brahmins: Studies in Ideologies and Institutions* (UK & USA: Anthem Press, 2011), pp. 101–25.

30. Opaque watercolour at the Government Museum and Art Gallery in Chandigarh. See Goswamy and Smith, *I See No Stranger*, p. 69.

31. Goswamy and Smith, *I See No Stranger*, p. 93. It is now at the Asian Art Museum in San Francisco.

32. W.H. Mcleod, 'The Influence of Islam upon the Thought of Guru Nanak' in *History of Religions* 7.4 (May 1968): 312.

33. 'Precious objects were often called *lal* "ruby"', notes Annemarie Schimmel in 'Color Symbolism in Persian Literature', *Encyclopedia Iranica*, http://www.iranicaonline.org/articles/color-pers-rang

34. McLeod translates, 'In everything that he could see he perceived God—in everything that existed, both visible and concealed . . .' *B-40 Janam-sakhi*, p. 212. I feel his translation glosses over the textual emphasis on jama and burqa, and thereby on what is behind them in the Sikh original text—the bodies of Muslim men and women.

35. www.sarbat.net/nanak-b40janamsakhi.htm

36. Goswamy, *Piety and Splendour*, pp. 38–39.

37. Goswamy, *Piety and Splendour*, p. 38.

38. See Goswamy, *Piety and Splendour*, pp. 38–39.

Chapter 3: The Mystic Philosopher

1.   George Pattison, *God and Being: An Enquiry* (Oxford University Press, 2011), p. 6.
2.   Pattison, *God and Being*, p. 173.
3.   Trilochan Singh, et al., *Selections from the Sacred Writings of the Sikhs* (London: George Allen & Unwin, 1960). For a fuller discussion see my article 'Translating Sikh Scripture into English' in *Sikh Formations* (Routledge, United Kingdom) 3.1 (June 2007): 1–17.
4.   For further discussion, see Arvind-Pal S. Mandair, *Religion and the Specter of the West: Sikhism, India, Postcoloniality, and the Politics of Translation* (New York: Columbia University Press, 2009), pp. 175–239.
5.   Hans-Georg Gadamer, *Truth and Method* (New York: Crossroad, 1989), p. 17.
6.   For instance, Sri Granth.org (widely used electronic resource).
7.   This is how Guru Nanak defines the blind: *'Andha soi ji andhu kamavai tisu ridai lochan nahi'* (GGS: 1289).
8.   W.H. McLeod, *Guru Nanak and the Sikh Religion* (Oxford: Clarendon, 1968), pp. 222–23.
9.   M.A. Macauliffe, *The Sikh Religion: Its Gurus, Sacred Writings and Authors* in six volumes (Oxford: Oxford University Press), p. 216.
10. Elizabeth Grosz, *Volatile Bodies: Toward a Corporeal Feminism* (Bloomington: Indiana University Press, 1994), p. 5.
11. John Dewey, 'Art as Experience' in *Philosophies of Art & Beauty*, eds. Albert Hofstadter and Richard Kuhns (University of Chicago, 1964), p. 592.
12. Wassily Kandinsky, *Concerning the Spiritual in Art* (New York: Dover, 1977), p. 54.
13. Lyof N. Tolstoi, *What is Art?* trans. A. Maude (New York: Thomas Y. Crowell, 1899), p. 43,
14. Citations here are all taken from Adrienne Rich's essay, 'Permeable Membrane' in *Virginia Quarterly Review* 82.2 (2006): 208–10.
15. McLeod, *Guru Nanak and the Sikh Religion*, p. 223.
16. Kartar Singh, *Nitnem Stik* (Amritsar, 1977), p. 10.
17. Nikky-Guninder Kaur Singh, *The Name of My Beloved: Verses of the Sikh Gurus* (New Delhi: Penguin Classics, 2001).
18. Introduced by McLeod, *Guru Nanak and the Sikh Religion*, pp. 222–23. See also, Macauliffe, *The Sikh Religion*, p. 216. Teja Singh,

The Japji (Lahore, 1930), p. 14, 40. Khushwant Singh, *Jupji: The Sikh Prayer* (London), p. 22.

19. Here, 'karam' still retains the Sanskrit meaning of karma but with an emphasis upon fulfillment, the reaping of the rewards of previous action. According to McLeod, if Saram Khand is to be regarded as the Realm of Effort and Karam Khand as the Realm of Action, there is scarcely any difference between the third and the fourth stages.

20. Simone de Beauvoir, *The Second Sex* (New York: Vintage, 1974), p. 179.

21. See my paper, 'From Flesh to Stone: The Divine Metamorphosis in Satyajit Ray's *Devi*' in *Journal of South Asian Literature* (Michigan State University) 28: 227–50.

22. Trilochan Singh, et al., *Selections from the Sacred Writings of the Sikhs* (London: George Allen & Unwin, 1960).

23. G.S. Talib, *Japuji: The Immortal Prayer-Chant*, p. 135.

24. The term 'Sita' is taken by some exegetes in the sense of *seetal* (cold). For example, Gyani Harbans Singh, *Japu-nirnaya* (Chandigarh, 1963: the publisher is not specified, but the volume has a preface by Gyani Lal Singh, director, Punjab Languages Department); p. 230. Even in his commentary, *Japuji: The Immortal Prayer-Chant*, G.S. Talib includes the possibility of its meaning 'cold'. He writes: '*Sito Sita* in the line may be either Sita by herself— that is, few others like Sita attain to that realm. Or sito may be an epithet, meaning cool (*shital*), of great poise, one who has subdued all passion' (p. 135). For a balanced discussion of this verse, see Avtar Singh, *Ethics of the Sikhs* (Patiala: Punjabi University, 1970), pp. 236–38.

25. Ernest Trumpp, *The Adi Granth or The Holy Scriptures of the Sikhs* (London: George Allen & Unwin, 1877; reprint Delhi: Munshiram Manoharlal Publishers, 1978), p. 13.

26. Kartar Singh, *Japuji Sahib Te Hor Bania Da Steek* (Amritsar: SGPC, 1996), p. 72.

27. Reference to the circles of birth and death.

28. Patrick Reid, *Readings in Western Religious Thought: The Middle Ages through the Reformation* (Paulist Press, 1995), p. 178.

29. Mary Potter Engel, Carol P. Christ, M. Shawn Copeland, Wonhee Anne Joh, Julie B. Miller, Nancy Pineda-Madrid and Masako Kuroki, 'Roundtable Discussion: Mysticism and Feminist Spirituality' in *Journal of Feminist Studies in Religion* 24.2 (Fall 2008): 164–67.

30. See my chapter, 'Sikh Mysticism and Sensuous Reproductions' in *Ineffability: An Exercise in Comparative Philosophy of Religion*, eds. T. Knepper and L. Kalmanson (Springer International), pp. 113–34.

31. Evelyn Underhill, *Mysticism* (NY: E.P. Dutton, 1961, first published 1911), p. 81.

32. Afterword, 'Why Did Henry David Thoreau Take the Bhagavad-Gita to Walden Pond' in Barbara Stoller Miller, *The Bhagavad-Gita* (Bantam), p. 160.

33. Annemarie Schimmel, *Mystical Dimensions of Islam* (Chapel Hill: University of North Carolina), pp. 124–25.

34. For instance, Macauliffe, in *The Sikh Religion* 1, p. 217.

35. Richard Shusterman, *Thinking Through the Body: Essays in Somaesthetics* (Cambridge: Cambridge University Press, 2013), pp. 20–21.

36. Wikipedia article 'Tool Use by Animals': Otters even carry a rock to open hard shells. An otter may pound its prey with both paws against the rock, which it places on its chest.

37. Wikipedia cites N.J. Mulcahy, J. Call, R.I.B. Dunbar, 'Gorillas (*Gorilla gorilla*) and Orangutans (*Pongo pygmaeus*) Encode Relevant Problem Features in a Tool-using Task', *Journal of Comparative Psychology* 119 (2005): 23–32.

38. Bellows used for metallurgical purposes in Guru Nanak's milieu are today used for cameras as well as harmoniums, the musical instrument used in Sikh worship to accompany the singing of scriptural hymns.

39. Opposite of Rudolph Otto's conception of god as the 'Wholly Other'.

40. Patricia M. Matthews, 'Kant's Sublime: A Form of Pure Aesthetic Reflective Judgment' in *The Journal of Aesthetics and Art Criticism* 54.2, (Spring 1996): 165–80.

41. Evelyn Underhill, *Mysticism* (New York: E.P. Dutton, 1961, first published 1911), pp. 71–72.

42. John Cooper, ed., *Plato: Complete Works* (Hackett, 1997), p. 941.

Chapter 4: The Revolutionary Thinker

1. Salman Rushdie, 'Censorship', *New Yorker*, 11 May 2012.

2. Charles G. Whiting, 'The Case for 'Engaged' Literature', *Yale French Studies*, No. 1, Existentialism (Yale University Press,1948), pp. 84–89.

3. Harbans Singh, *Berkeley Lectures on Sikhism* (New Delhi: Guru Nanak Foundation, 1983), p. 9.

4. Cow dung used for plastering a kitchen floor to purify it.

5. 'Outsiders' (*mleccha* in the original text) who did not belong to the Brahmanical varna (class) order. In this context it refers to Mughal rulers and their officers.

6. Alluding to the establishment of the new Mughal regime.

7. Ira M. Lapidus, *A History of Islamic Society* (Cambridge: Cambridge University Press, 1988), p. 448.

8. J.S. Grewal, *From Guru Nanak to Maharaja Ranjit Singh: Essays in Sikh History* (Amritsar: Guru Nanak University, 1972), p. 25.

9. Apostolic Journey to Korea, Meeting with the Bishops of Asia, 17 August 2014.

10. From the root *brh*—to grow, expand, flourish.

11. Lila Abu-Lughod, 'Do Muslim Women Really Need Saving? Anthropological Reflections on Cultural Relativism and Its Others', *American Anthropologist* 104.3: 789. Also see my 'Baburvani and the Call for Gender Justice', *Sikh Formations: Religion, Culture, Theory* (December 2016).

12. See Henry J. Walker, *Valerius Maximus: Memorable Deeds and Sayings* (Hackett, 2004). In Book 2, Chapter 6, Story 14:

> But why should I praise men [warriors] for being so very brave and practical? Consider the women of India. It is their ancestral custom that several women should be married to one man, and when he dies they have a competition to decide which of them he loved the most. The winner jumps for joy, and she is led off by her happy-faced friends and relatives. She flings herself on top of her husband's funeral pyre, and she is burned alive on it beside her husband's body, as if she were the happiest of women. The wives who lost the competition stay on in this life in sadness and grief.

13. Harbans Singh, *Guru Nanak and Origins of the Sikh Faith*, p. 206.

14. In his hymn, Guru Nanak does use the term 'Hindustan' for India which was commonly used by Arab and Persian writers who referred to the Indian subcontinent as Sindh-wa-Hind (from the River Sidhu).

15. George Lakoff and Mark Johnson, *Metaphors We Live By* (Chicago and London: University of Chicago Press, 1980), p. 45.

16. Wendy Doniger, trans., *The Laws of Manu* (Penguin, 1991), 5: 85.

17. Ibid., 4: 208.

18. See H. Tonomura's article, 'Birth-giving and Avoidance Taboo', *Japan Review* 19 (2007): 3–45.

19. BBC, 'The Village in Ghana Where Childbirth is Banned', 17 March 2019, https://www.bbc.com/news/av/world-africa-47570753/the-village-in-ghana-where-childbirth-is-banned

20. H. Cixous and C. Clement, *The Newly Born Woman*, trans., B. Wing (Minneapolis: University of Minnesota Press, 1986), p. 93.

21. Luce Irigaray, *Sexes and Genealogies*, trans. G. Gill (New York: Columbia University Press, 1993), p. 18.

22. Rosemary Ruether, *Sexism and God-Talk: Toward a Feminist Theology* (Boston: Beacon Press, 1983), p. 79.

23. Gayatri Spivak, 'The Politics of Translation', *Outside in the Teaching Machine* (Routledge, 1993), p. 185.

24. Nawal El Saadawi, 'Women Are Pushed to Be Just Bodies—Veiled under Religion or Veiled by Makeup', 6 June 2018, https://www.refinery29.com

25. G.S. Talib, *Sri Guru Granth Sahib: In English Translation* (Patiala: Punjabi University, 1987), Volume 3, p. 2098: 'In each being's heart pervasive . . .' See also, Gopal Singh, *Sri Guru Granth Sahib: English Version* (Delhi: Gurdas Kapur; reprinted in 1978: Chandigarh, World Sikh University Press), Volume 4, p. 979: 'And he pervaded the hearts of all . . .'

26. *Sabdarath Sri Guru Granth Sahib* (Amritsar: Shromani Gurdwara Prabandhak Committee, fourth edition, 1964), Volume 3, p. 1026.

27. See gurbani.org, which for the most part is very thorough and accessible. Nevertheless, uses belly for womb on p. 1026.

28. W.H. McLeod, ed. and trans., *The Chaupa Singh Rahit-nama* (Dunedin, NZ: University of Otago Press, 1987), pp. 556, 567.

29. Illustration 63 in *Marg,* Volume XXX Number 3, June 1977.

30. W.G. Archer, *The Paintings of the Sikhs* (London: Victoria and Albert, 1966), p. 30.

31. In her *Recollections* Lady Login notes how uncomfortably her Sikh guest sat with 'crinoline spread around like a cheese'. On that hot stuffy day in June 1861, Jindan had come to pay Lady Login a visit in her Kensington home. In *Lady Login's Recollections: Court Life and Camp Life 1820-1904* (New York: EP Dutton and Company, 1916), p. 213. For more on this subject, see my chapter, 'My Dinner in Calgary: Sikh Diaspora in the Making' in Michael Hawley, ed., *Sikh Diaspora: Theory, Agency, and Experience* (Brill, 2013), pp. 89–101.

32. Valerie Kaur, *Huffington Post*, 22 March 2012.

33. Jagbir Jhutti-Johal, *Sikhism Today* (New York: Continuum, 2011), pp. 47–48.

34. Opinderjit Kaur Takhar, *Sikh Identity: An Exploration of Groups among Sikhs* (Burlington, VT: Ashgate, 2005), pp. 49–50.

35. For more details see my 'Translating Sikh Scripture into English', *Sikh Formations* 3.1 (June 2007): 1–17.

36. Huffington Post, 'Women in the U.S. Are Still Second-Class Citizens: Not Interested? You Should Be', 5 August 2014.

37. Philip Cohen, 'SEXES: America Is Still a Patriarchy', *Atlantic*, 19 November 2012.

38. Samantha Paige Rosen, Huffington Post, 5 August 2014.

39. Diana Eck, *A New Religious America* (San Francisco: HarperCollins, 2001), Chapter 6 is entitled 'Afraid of Ourselves'.

Chapter 5: The Environmentalist

1. CNN, 'All About: Religion and the Environment', 28 January 2008.

2. Lynn White's 1937 thesis cited by Gregory E. Hitzhusen and Mary Evelyn Tucker in 'The Potential of Religion for Earth Stewardship' in *Frontiers in Ecology and the Environment* 11.7 (September 2013): 368–76.

3. Reminiscent of the epilogue of the Japji, the opening hymn of the GGS.

4. G.S. Talib, *Japuji: The Immortal Prayer-Chant*, p. 141.

5. Sallie McFague, *Models of God* (Fortress Press, 1987), p. 106.

6. Citations from David G. Hallman, *Ecotheology: Voices from South and North* (Eugene OR: Wipf and Stock Publishers), p. 119.

7. The original Panjabi term for 'side', *pur*, refers to the two sides of a hand mill.

8. Martin Luther King, Jr., "The Quest for Peace and Justice," Nobel Prize Lecture, 11 December 1964.

9. R. Hitchings and V. Jones, 'Living with Plants and the Exploration of Botanical Encounter within Human Geographic Research Practice', *Ethics, Place & Environment* 7. 1 and 2 (2004): 3–18.

10. Alice Peck, ed.. *Bread, Body, Spirit: Finding the Sacred in Food* (Woodstock, VT: SkyLight Paths, 2008), pp. 9–10.

11. Maywa Montenegro and Terry Glavin, 'In Defense of Difference', *Seed Magazine*, 2008.

12. E.O. Wilson, 'Biophilia and the Conservation Ethic', in *The Biophilia Hypothesis*, eds. S.R. Kellert and E.O. Wilson (Washington D.C.: Island Press, 1993), p. 31.

13. Grace Jantzen, *Becoming Divine: Towards a Feminist Philosophy of Religion* (Bloomington: Indiana University Press, 1999), p. 132.

14. See my chapter, 'Female Feticide in the Punjab' in Vanessa Sasson, ed., *Imagining the Fetus* (American Academy of Religion: Oxford University, 2009), pp. 120–36.

15. Luce Irigaray, *Sexes and Genealogies*, trans. Gillian Gill (NY: Columbia University Press, 1993), p. 16.

16. Susan Griffin, *The Eros of Everyday Life: Essays on Ecology, Gender and Society* (New York: Doubleday, 1995), p. 9.

17. Rosemary Ruether, *Sexism and God-Talk: Toward a Feminist Theology* (Boston: Beacon Press, 1983), p. 92.

Conclusion: The Enduring Legacy of the First Sikh

1. Especially Chapters 2 and 4 of my book, *Birth of the Khalsa: A Feminist Re-Memory of Sikh Identity*.
2. Hans-Georg Gadamer, *Truth and Method* (New York: Crossroad, 1989), p. 78.
3. BBC, 'Why Homeless Britons are Turning to the Sikh Community for Food', 22 February 2015.
4. Gopalkrishna Gandhi, 'Light in a Dark Time: Sikhs in New Zealand Exemplify Courageous Compassion', *Telegraph*, 24 March 2019.
5. For a fuller discussion see my 'Sacred Fabric and Sacred Stitches' for *History of Religions* (University of Chicago) 43.4 (2004): 284–302.
6. Susan Stronge, ed., *The Arts of the Sikh Kingdoms* (London: Victoria and Albert, 1999).
7. B.N. Goswamy, *Piety and Splendour: Sikh Heritage in Art* (New Delhi: National Museum, 2000).
8. Paul Michael Taylor and Sonia Dhami, eds, *Sikh Art from the Kapany Collection*, Sikh Foundation and Smithsonian's Asian Cultural History Program, 2017.
9. Displayed at the National Gallery of Modern Art in New Delhi.
10. Arpana Caur and Mala Kaur Dayal, *Nanak: The Guru* (New Delhi: Rupa, 2005).
11. Khushwant Singh and Aprita Kaur, *Hymns of Guru Nanak* (Orient Longman, 1991).
12. Arpita's painting in *Hymns of Guru Nanak*, p. 109.
13. *Hymns of Guru Nanak*, p. 27.
14. *Hymns of Guru Nanak*, p. 81.
15. Painting by Phulan Rani, in *Life of Guru Nanak Through Pictures* (Amritsar: Modern Sahit Academy, 1969), p. 17.
16. For Sharaf's biography and works, see Nikky-Guninder Kaur Singh, *Of Desire Sacred and Secular* (IB Tauris, 2012), pp. 151–57.
17. My translation, *Of Sacred and Secular Desire*, p. 200.
18. Ibid.
19. For more on Bhai Vir Singh's poetry see my *Cosmic Symphony: The Early and Later Poems of Bhai Vir Singh* (New Delhi: Sahitya Akademi, 2008; republished 2010).

Hymns of the Sikh Gurus

TRANSLATED BY NIKKY-GUNINDER KAUR SINGH

'A significant contribution to the understanding of the essentials of the Sikhs' sacred scriptures'—Khushwant Singh

The vision of Guru Nanak, the fifteenth-century founder of the Sikh faith, celebrated the oneness of the Divine that both dwells within and transcends the endless diversity of life. Guru Nanak's boundless vision inspired the rich and inclusive philosophy of Sikhism, which is reflected in this exquisite and highly acclaimed translation of hymns from the religion's most sacred texts: the Guru Granth Sahib, the principal sacred text of the Sikh religion, which consists of compositions by Guru Nanak, his successors and Hindu and Islamic saints; and the Dasam Granth, a collection of devotional verses of the tenth Sikh Guru.

Poetry from these highly revered texts is heard daily and at rites of passage and celebration in Sikh homes and gurudwaras, carrying forward the Sikh belief in the oneness and equality of all humanity.